# Practical Data Science with Hadoop® and Spark

# Practical Data Science with Hadoop® and Spark

Designing and Building Effective Analytics at Scale

Ofer Mendelevitch
Casey Stella
Douglas Eadline

✦✦Addison-Wesley

Boston • Columbus • Indianapolis • New York • San Francisco • Amsterdam • Cape Town
Dubai • London • Madrid • Milan • Munich • Paris • Montreal • Toronto • Delhi • Mexico City
São Paulo • Sydney • Hong Kong • Seoul • Singapore • Taipei • Tokyo

For information about buying this title in bulk quantities, or for special sales opportunities (which may include electronic versions; custom cover designs; and content particular to your business, training goals, marketing focus, or branding interests), please contact our corporate sales department at corpsales@pearsoned.com or (800) 382-3419.

For government sales inquiries, please contact governmentsales@pearsoned.com.

For questions about sales outside the U.S., please contact intlcs@pearson.com.

Visit us on the Web: informit.com/aw

Library of Congress Control Number: 2016955465

ISBN-13: 978-0-13-402414-1
ISBN-10: 0-13-402414-1

1  16

# Contents

# Foreword

Hadoop and data science have been sought after skillsets respectively over the last five years. However, few publications have attempted to bring the two together, teaching data science within the Hadoop context. For practitioners looking for an introduction to data science combined with solving those problems at scale using Hadoop and related tools, this book will prove to be an excellent resource.

The topic of data science is introduced with topics covered including data ingest, munging, feature extraction, machine learning, predictive modeling, anomaly detection, and natural language processing. The platform of choice for the examples and implementation of these topics is Hadoop, Spark, and the other parts of the Hadoop ecosystem. Its coverage is broad, with specific examples keeping the book grounded in an engineer's need to solve real-world problems. For those already familiar with data science, but looking to expand their skillsets to very large datasets and Hadoop, this book is a great introduction.

Throughout the text it focuses on concrete examples and providing insight into business value with each approach. Chapter 5, "Data Munging with Hadoop," provides particularly useful real-world examples on using Hadoop to prepare large datasets for common machine learning and data science tasks. Chapter 10 on anomaly detection is particularly useful for large datasets where monitoring and alerting are important. Chapter 11 on natural language processing will be of interest to those attempting to make chatbots.

Ofer Mendelevitch is the VP of Data Science at Lendup.com and was previously the Director of Data Science at Hortonworks. Few others are as qualified to be the lead author on a book combining data science and Hadoop. Joining Ofer is his former colleague, Casey Stella, a Principal Data Scientist at Hortonworks. Rounding out these experts in data science and Hadoop is Doug Eadline, frequent contributor to the Addison-Wesley Data & Analytics Series with the titles *Hadoop Fundamentals Live Lessons*, *Apache Hadoop 2 Quick-Start Guide*, and *Apache Hadoop YARN*. Collectively, this team of authors brings over a decade of Hadoop experience. I can imagine few others that have as much knowledge on the subject of data science and Hadoop.

I'm excited to have this addition to the Data & Analytics Series. Creating data science solutions at scale in production systems is an in-demand skillset. This book will help you come up to speed quickly to deploy and run production data science solutions at scale.

—*Paul Dix*
*Series Editor*

# Preface

Data science and machine learning are at the core of many innovative technologies and products and are expected to continue to disrupt many industries and business models across the globe for the foreseeable future. Until recently though, most of this innovation was constrained by the limited availability of data.

With the introduction of Apache Hadoop, all of that has changed. Hadoop provides a platform for storing, managing, and processing large datasets inexpensively and at scale, making data science analysis of large datasets practical and feasible. In this new world of large-scale advanced analytics, data science is a core competency that enables organizations to remain competitive and innovate beyond their traditional business models. During our time at Hortonworks, we have had a chance to see how various organizations tackle this new set of opportunities and help them on their journey to implementing data science at scale with Hadoop and Spark. In this book we would like to share some of this learning and experiences.

Another issue we also wish to emphasize is the evolution of Apache Hadoop from its early incarnation as a monolithic MapReduce engine (Hadoop version 1) to a versatile data analytics platform that runs on YARN and supports not only MapReduce but also Tez and Spark as processing engines (Hadoop version 2). The current version of Hadoop provides a robust and efficient platform for many data science applications and opens up a universe of opportunities to new business use cases that were previously unthinkable.

## Focus of the Book

This book focuses on real-world practical aspects of data science with Hadoop and Spark. Since the scope of data science is very broad, and every topic therein is deep and complex, it is quite difficult to cover the topic thoroughly. We approached this problem by attempting a good balance between the theoretical coverage of each use case and the example-driven treatment of practical implementation.

This book is not designed to dig deep into many of the mathematical details of each machine learning or statistical approach but rather provide a high-level description of the main concepts along with guidelines for its practical use in the context of the business problem. We provide some references that offer more in-depth treatment of the mathematical details of these techniques in the text and have compiled a list of relevant resources in Appendix C, "Additional Background on Data Science and Apache Hadoop and Spark."

When learning about Hadoop, access to a Hadoop cluster environment can become an issue. Finding an effective way to "play" with Hadoop and Spark can be challenging for some individuals. At a minimum, we recommend the Hortonworks virtual machine sandbox for those that would like an easy way to get started with Hadoop. The sandbox is a full single-node Hadoop installation running inside a virtual machine. The virtual machine can be run under Windows, Mac OS, and Linux. Please see http://hortonworks .com/products/sandbox for more information on how to download and install the sandbox. For further help with Hadoop we recommend *Hadoop 2 Quick-Start Guide: Learn the Essentials of Big Data Computation in the Apache Hadoop 2 Ecosystem* (and supporting videos), all mentioned in Appendix C.

## Who Should Read This Book

This book is intended for those readers who are interested to learn more about what data science is and some of the practical considerations of its application to large-scale datasets. It provides a strong technical foundation for readers who want to learn more about how to implement various use cases, the tools that are best suited for the job, and some of the architectures that are common in these situations. It also provides a business-driven viewpoint on when application of data science to large datasets is useful to help stakeholders understand what value can be derived for their organization and where to invest their resources in applying large-scale machine learning.

There is also a level of experience assumed for this book. For those not versed in data science, some basic competencies are important to have to understand the different methods, including statistical concepts (for example, mean and standard deviation), and a bit of background in programming (mostly Python and a bit of Java or Scala) to understand the examples throughout the book.

For those with a data science background, you should generally be comfortable with the material, although there may be some practical issues such as understanding the numerous Apache projects. In addition, all examples are text-based, and some familiarity with the Linux command line is required. It should be noted that we did not use (or test) a Windows environment for the examples. However, there is no reason to assume they will not work in that and other environments (Hortonworks supports Windows).

In terms of a specific Hadoop environment, all the examples and code were run under Hortonworks HDP Linux Hadoop distribution (either laptop or cluster). Your environment may differ in terms of distribution (Cloudera, MapR, Apache Source) or operating systems (Windows). However, all the tools (or equivalents) are available in both environments.

## How to Use This Book

We anticipate several different audiences for the book:

- data scientists
- developers/data engineers
- business stakeholders

While these readers come at the Hadoop analytics from different backgrounds, their goal is certainly the same—running data analytics with Hadoop and Spark at scale. To this end, we have designed the chapters to meet the needs of all readers, and as such readers may find that they can skip areas where they may have a good practical understanding. Finally, we also want to invite novice readers to use this book as a first step in their understanding of data science at scale. We believe there is value in "walking" through the examples, even if you are not sure what is actually happening, and then going back and buttressing your understanding with the background material.

Part I, "Data Science with Hadoop—An Overview," spans the first three chapters.

Chapter 1, "Introduction to Data Science," provides an overview of data science and its history and evolution over the years. It lays out the journey people often take to become a data scientist. For those not versed in data science, this chapter will help you understand why it has evolved into a powerful discipline and provide some insight into how a data scientist designs and refines projects. There is also some discussion about what makes a data scientist and how to best plan your career in that direction.

Chapter 2, "Use Cases for Data Science," provides a good overview of how business use cases are impacted by the volume, variety, and velocity of modern data streams. It also covers some real-world data science use cases in order to help you gain an understanding of its benefits in various industries and applications.

Chapter 3, "Hadoop and Data Science," provides a quick overview of Hadoop, its evolution over the years, and the various tools in the Hadoop ecosystem. For first-time Hadoop users this chapter can be a bit overwhelming. There are many new concepts introduced including the Hadoop file system (HDFS), MapReduce, the Hadoop resource manager (YARN), and Spark. While the number of sub-projects (and weird names) that make up the Hadoop ecosystem may seem daunting, not every project is used at the same time, and the applications in the later chapters usually focus on only a few tools at a time.

Part II, "Preparing and Visualizing Data with Hadoop," includes the next three chapters.

Chapter 4, "Getting Data into Hadoop," focuses on data ingestion, discussing various tools and techniques to import datasets from external sources into Hadoop. It is useful for many subsequent chapters. We begin with describing the Hadoop data lake concept and then move into the various ways data can be used by the Hadoop platform. The ingestion targets two of the more popular Hadoop tools—Hive and Spark. This chapter focuses on code and hands-on solutions—if you are new to Hadoop, its best to also consult Appendix B, "HDFS Quick Start," to get you up to speed on the HDFS file system.

Chapter 5, "Data Munging with Hadoop," focuses on data munging with Hadoop or how to identify and handle data quality issues, as well as pre-process data and prepare it for modeling. We introduce the concepts of data completeness, validity, consistency, timeliness, and accuracy. Examples of feature generation using a real data set are provided. This chapter is useful for all types of subsequent analysis and, like Chapter 4, is a precursor to many of the techniques mentioned in later chapters.

An important tool in the process of data munging is visualization. Chapter 6, "Exploring and Visualizing Data," discusses what it means to do visualization with big data. As background, this chapter is useful for reinforcing some of the basic concepts behind data visualization. The charts presented in the chapter were generated using R. Source code for all the plots is available so readers can try these charts with their own data.

Part III, "Applying Data Modeling with Hadoop," encompasses the final six chapters.

Chapter 7, "Machine Learning with Hadoop," provides an overview of machine learning at a high level, covering the main tasks in machine learning such as classification and regression, clustering, and anomaly detection. For each task type, we explore the problem and the main approaches to solutions.

Chapter 8, "Predictive Modeling," covers the basic algorithms and various Hadoop tools for predictive modeling. The chapter includes an end-to-end example of building a predictive model for sentiment analysis of Twitter text using Hive and Spark.

Chapter 9, "Clustering," dives into cluster analysis, a very common technique in data science. It provides an overview of various clustering techniques and similarity functions, which are at the core of clustering. It then demonstrates a real-world example of using topic modeling on a large corpus of documents using Hadoop and Spark.

Chapter 10, "Anomaly Detection with Hadoop," covers anomaly detection, describing various types of approaches and algorithms as well as how to perform large-scale anomaly detection on various datasets. It then demonstrates how to build an anomaly detection system with Spark for the KDD99 dataset.

Chapter 11, "Natural Language Processing," covers applications of data science to the specific area of human language, using a set of techniques commonly called natural language processing (NLP). It discusses various approaches to NLP, open-source tools that are effective at various NLP tasks, and how to apply NLP to large-scale corpuses using Hadoop, Pig, and Spark. An end-to-end example shows an advanced approach to sentiment analysis that uses NLP at scale with Spark.

Chapter 12, "Data Science with Hadoop—The Next Frontier," discusses the future of data science with Hadoop, covering advanced data discovery techniques and deep learning.

Consult Appendix A, "Book Webpage and Code Download," for the book web page and code repository (the web page provides a question and answer forum). Appendix B, as mentioned previously, provides a quick overview of HDFS for new users and the aforementioned Appendix C provides further references and background on Hadoop, Spark, HDFS, machine learning, and many other topics.

## Book Conventions

Code and file references are displayed in a monospaced font. Code input lines that wrap because they are too long to fit on one line in this book are denoted with this symbol ➥ at the start of the next line. Long output lines are wrapped at page boundaries without the symbol.

## Accompanying Code

Again, please see Appendix A, "Book Web Page and Code Download," for the location of all code used in this book.

---

Register your copy of *Practical Data Science with Hadoop® and Spark* at informit.com for convenient access to downloads, updates, and corrections as they become available. To start the registration process, go to informit.com/register and log in or create an account. Enter the product ISBN (9780134024141) and click Submit. Once the process is complete, you will find any available bonus content under "Registered Products."

# Acknowledgments

Some of the figures and examples were inspired and copied from Yahoo! (yahoo.com), the Apache Software Foundation (http://www.apache.org), and Hortonworks (http://hortonworks.com). Any copied items either had permission from the author or were available under an open sharing license.

Many people have worked behind the scenes to make this book possible. Thank you to the reviewers who took the time to carefully read the rough drafts: Fabricio Cannini, Brian D. Davison, Mark Fenner, Sylvain Jaume, Joshua Mora, Wendell Smith, and John Wilson.

## Ofer Mendelevitch

I want to thank Jeff Needham and Ron Lee who encouraged me to start this book, many others at Hortonworks who helped with constructive feedback and advice, John Wilson who provided great constructive feedback and industry perspective, and of course Debra Williams Cauley for her vision and support in making this book a reality. Last but not least, this book would not have come to life without the loving support of my beautiful wife, Noa, who encouraged and supported me every step of the way, and my boys, Daniel and Jordan, who make all this hard work so worthwhile.

## Casey Stella

I want to thank my patient and loving wife, Leah, and children, William and Sylvia, without whom I would not have the time to dedicate to such a time-consuming and rewarding venture. I want to thank my mother and grandmother, who instilled a love of learning that has guided me to this day. I want to thank the taxpayers of the State of Louisiana for providing a college education and access to libraries, public radio, and television; without which I would have neither the capability, the content, nor the courage to speak. Finally, I want to thank Debra Williams Cauley at Addison-Wesley who used the carrot far more than the stick.

## Douglas Eadline

To Debra Williams Cauley at Addison-Wesley, your kind efforts and office at the GCT Oyster Bar made the book-writing process almost easy (again!). Thanks to my support crew, Emily, Carla, and Taylor—yet another book you know nothing about. Of course, I cannot forget my office mate, Marlee, and those two boys. And, finally, another big thank you to my wonderful wife, Maddy, for her constant support.

# About the Authors

**Ofer Mendelevitch** is Vice President of Data Science at Lendup, where he is responsible for Lendup's machine learning and advanced analytics group. Prior to joining Lendup, Ofer was Director of Data Science at Hortonworks, where he was responsible for helping Hortonwork's customers apply Data Science with Hadoop and Spark to big data across various industries including healthcare, finance, retail, and others. Before Hortonworks, Ofer served as Entrepreneur in Residence at XSeed Capital, Vice President of Engineering at Nor1, and Director of Engineering at Yahoo!.

**Casey Stella** is a Principal Data Scientist at Hortonworks, which provides an open source Hadoop distribution. Casey's primary responsibility is leading the analytics/data science team for the Apache Metron (Incubating) Project, an open source cybersecurity project. Prior to Hortonworks, Casey was an architect at Explorys, which was a medical informatics startup spun out of the Cleveland Clinic. In the more distant past, Casey served as a developer at Oracle, Research Geophysicist at ION Geophysical, and as a poor graduate student in Mathematics at Texas A&M.

**Douglas Eadline, PhD,** began his career as an analytical chemist with an interest in computer methods. Starting with the first Beowulf how-to document, Doug has written hundreds of articles, white papers, and instructional documents covering many aspects of HPC and Hadoop computing. Prior to starting and editing the popular ClusterMonkey.net website in 2005, he served as editor in chief for *ClusterWorld Magazine* and was senior HPC editor for *Linux Magazine*. He has practical hands-on experience in many aspects of HPC and Apache Hadoop, including hardware and software design, benchmarking, storage, GPU, cloud computing, and parallel computing. Currently, he is a writer and consultant to the HPC/analytics industry and leader of the Limulus Personal Cluster Project (http://limulus.basement-supercomputing.com). He is author of the *Hadoop Fundamentals LiveLessons* and *Apache Hadoop YARN Fundamentals LiveLessons* videos from Pearson, and is co-author of *Apache Hadoop YARN: Moving beyond MapReduce and Batch Processing with Apache Hadoop 2* and author of *Hadoop 2 Quick Start Guide: Learn the Essentials of Big Data Computing in the Apache Hadoop 2 Ecosystem*, also from Addison-Wesley, and *High Performance Computing for Dummies*.

# Data Science with Hadoop—An Overview

# 1

# Introduction to Data Science

*I keep saying that the sexy job in the next 10 years will be statisticians,*
*and I'm not kidding.*

Hal Varian
Chief Economist at Google

## In This Chapter:

- What data science is and the history of its evolution
- The journey to becoming a data scientist
- Building a data science team
- The data science project life cycle
- Managing data science projects

Data science has recently become a common topic of conversation at almost every data-driven organization. Along with the term "big data," the rise of the term "data science" has been so rapid that it's frankly confusing.

What exactly is data science and why has it suddenly become so important?

In this chapter we provide an introduction to data science from a practitioner's point of view, explaining some of the terminology around it, and looking at the role a data scientist plays in this era of big data.

## What Is Data Science?

If you search for the term "data science" on Google or Bing, you will find quite a few definitions or explanations of what it is supposed to be. There does not seem to be clear consensus around one definition, and there is even less agreement about when this term originated.

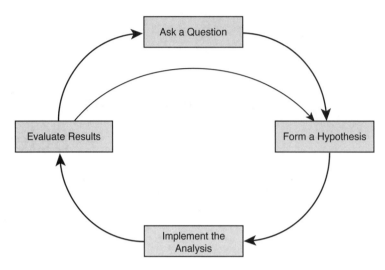

Figure 1.1    Iterative process of data science discovery.

We will not repeat these definitions here, nor will we try to choose one that we think is most correct or accurate. Instead, we provide our own definition, one that comes from a practitioner's point of view:

> **Data science** is the exploration of data via the scientific method to discover meaning or insight and the construction of software systems that utilize such meaning and insight in a business context.

This definition emphasizes two key aspects of data science.

First, it's about exploring data using the scientific method. In other words, it entails a process of discovery that in many ways is similar to how other scientific discoveries are made: an iterative process of ask-hypothesize-implement/test-evaluate.

This iterative process is shown in Figure 1.1.

The iterative nature of data science is very important since, as we will see later, it dramatically impacts how we plan, estimate, and execute data science projects.

Secondly, and not less important, data science is also about the implementation of software systems that can make the output of the technique or algorithm available and immediately usable in the right business context of the day-to-day operations.

## Example: Search Advertising

Online search engines such as Google or Microsoft Bing make money by providing advertising opportunities on the search results page, a field often referred to as **search advertising**. For example, if you search for "digital cameras," the response often will include both links to information and separately marked advertising links, some with local store locations. A generic example is provided in Figure 1.2.

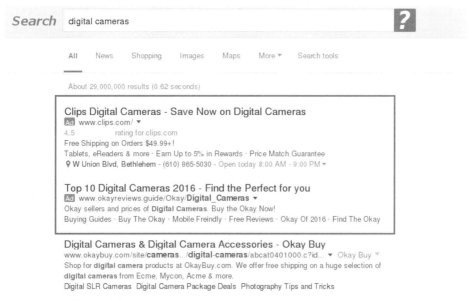

Figure 1.2   Search ads shown on an Internet search results page.

The revenues generated by online advertising providers depend on the capability of the advertising system to provide relevant ads to search queries, which in turn depend on the capability to predict click-through rate (CTR) for each possible <ad, query> pair.

Companies such as Google and Microsoft employ data science teams that work tirelessly to improve their CTR prediction algorithms, which subsequently results in more relevant ads and higher revenues from those ads.

To achieve this, they work iteratively—form a hypothesis about a new approach to predicting CTR, implement this algorithm, and evaluate this approach using an A/B test on a "random bucket" of search traffic in production. If the algorithm proves to perform better than the current (incumbent) algorithm, then it becomes the new algorithm applied by default to all search traffic.

As the search wars continue, and the search advertising marketplace continues to be a dynamic and competitive environment for advertisers, data science techniques that are at the core of online ad business remain a highly leveraged competitive advantage.

# A Bit of Data Science History

The rise of data science as a highly sought–after discipline coincides with a few key technological and scientific achievements that happened in the last few decades.

First, research in statistics and machine learning has produced mature and practical techniques that allow machines to learn patterns from data in an efficient manner. Furthermore, many open source libraries provide fast and robust implementations of the latest machine learning algorithms.

Second, as computer technology matured—with faster CPUs, cheaper and faster RAM, faster networking equipment, and larger and faster storage devices—our ability to collect, store, and process large sets of data became easier and cheaper than ever before. With that, the cost/benefit trade-off of mining large datasets for insight using advanced algorithms from statistics and machine learning became a concrete reality.

## Statistics and Machine Learning

Statistical methods date back as early as the 5th century BC, but the early work in statistics as a formal mathematical discipline is linked to the late 19th and early 20th century works by Sir Francis Galton, Karl Pearson, and Sir Ronald Fisher, who invented some of the most well-known statistical methods such as regression, likelihood, analysis of variance, and correlation.

In the second half of the 20th century, statistics became tightly linked to data analysis. In a famous 1962 manuscript titled "The Future of Data Analysis,"[1] John W. Tukey, an American mathematician and statistician (best known for his invention of the FFT algorithm, the box plot, and Tukey's HSD test), wrote: "All in all, I have come to feel that my central interest is in data analysis…." To some, this marks a significant milestone in applied statistics.

In the next few decades, statisticians continued to show increased interest and perform research in applied computational statistics. However, this work was, at that time, quite disjointed and separate from research in machine learning in the computer science community.

In the late 1950s, as computers advanced into their infancy, computer scientists started working on developing artificial intelligence systems based on the neural model of the brain—neural networks. The pioneering work of Frank Rosenblatt on the perceptron, followed by Widrow and Hoff, resulted in much excitement about this new field of research.

With the early success of neural networks, over the next few decades new techniques designed to automatically learn patterns from data were invented such as nearest-neighbors, decision trees, k-means clustering, and support vector machines.

As computer systems became faster and more affordable, the application of machine learning techniques to larger and larger datasets became viable, resulting in more robust algorithms and better implementations.

In 1989, Gregory Piatetsky-Shapiro started a set of workshops on knowledge discovery in databases, known as KDD. The KDD workshops quickly gained in popularity and became the ACM-SIGKDD conference, which hosts the KDD Cup data mining competition every year.

At some point, statisticians and machine learning practitioners realized that they live in two separate silos, developing techniques that ultimately target the same goal or function.

---

1. http://www.stanford.edu/~gavish/documents/Tukey_the_future_of_data_analysis.pdf

In 2001, Leo Breiman from UC Berkeley wrote "Statistical Modeling: The Two Cultures,"[2] in which he describes one of the fundamental differences in how statisticians and machine learning practitioners view the world. Breiman writes, "There are two cultures in the use of statistical modeling to reach conclusions from data. One assumes that the data are generated by a given stochastic data model. The other uses algorithmic models and treats the data mechanism as unknown." The focus of the statistics community on the data generation model resulted in this community missing out on a large number of very interesting problems, both in theory and in practice.

This marked another important changing point, resulting in researchers from both the statistics and machine learning communities working together, to the benefit of both.

During the last decade, machine learning and statistical techniques continued to evolve, with a new emphasis on distributed learning techniques, online learning, and semi-supervised learning. More recently, a set of techniques known as "deep-learning" were introduced, whereby the algorithm can learn not only a proper model for the data but also how to transform the raw data into a set of features for optimal learning.

## Innovation from Internet Giants

While the academic community was very excited about machine learning and applied statistics becoming a reality, large internet companies such as Yahoo!, Google, Amazon, Netflix, Facebook, and PayPal started realizing that they had huge swaths of data and that if they applied machine learning techniques to the data they could gain significant benefit to their business.

This led to some famous and very successful applications of machine learning and statistical techniques to drive business growth, identify new business opportunities, and deliver innovative products to their user base:

- Google, Yahoo! (and now Bing) apply advanced algorithms to large datasets to improve search engine results, search suggestions, and spelling.

- Similarly, search giants analyze page view and click information to predict CTR and deliver relevant online ads to search users.

- LinkedIn and Facebook analyze the social graph of relationships between users to deliver features such as "People You May Know (PYMK)."

- Netflix, eBay, and Amazon make extensive use of data to provide a better experience for their users with automated product or movie recommendations.

- PayPal is applying large-scale graph algorithms to detect payment fraud.

---

2. Breiman, Leo. Statistical Modeling: The Two Cultures (with comments and a rejoinder by the author). Statist. Sci. 16 (2001), no. 3, 199--231. doi:10.1214/ss/1009213726. http://projecteuclid .org/euclid.ss/1009213726.

These companies were the early visionaries. They recognized the potential of using large existing raw datasets in new, innovative ways. They also quickly realized the many challenges they faced if they wanted to implement this at Internet scale, which led to a wave of innovation with new tools and technologies, such as Google File System, MapReduce, Hadoop, Pig, Hive, Cassandra, Spark, Storm, HBase, and many others.

## Data Science in the Modern Enterprise

With the innovation from Internet giants, a number of key technologies became available both within commercial tools and in open source products.

First and foremost is the capability to collect and store vast amounts of data inexpensively, driven by cheap, fast storage, cluster computing technologies, and open source software such as Hadoop. Data became a valuable asset, and many enterprises are now able to store all of their data in raw form, without the traditional filtering and retention policies that were required to control cost. The capability to store such vast amounts of data enables data science enterprise applications that were previously not possible.

Second, the commoditization of machine learning and statistical data mining algorithms available within open source packages such as R, Python scikit-learn, and Spark MLlib enables many enterprises to apply such advanced algorithms to datasets with an ease and flexibility that was practically impossible before. This change reduced the overall effort, time, and cost required to achieve business results from data assets.

# Becoming a Data Scientist

So how do you become a data scientist?

It's a fun and rewarding journey, and, like many others in life, requires some investment to get there.

We meet successful data scientists that come from a variety of different backgrounds including (but not limited to) statisticians, computer scientists, data engineers, software developers, and even chemists or physicists.

Generally speaking, to be a successful data scientist, you need to combine two types of computer science skillsets that are often distinct: data engineering and applied science.

## The Data Engineer

Think of a **data engineer** as an experienced software engineer who is highly skilled in building high-quality production-grade software systems with a specialization in building fast (and often distributed) data pipelines.

This individual will likely have significant expertise in one or more major programming languages (such as Java, Python, Scala, Ruby, or C++) and associated toolsets for software development such as build tools (Maven, Ant), unit testing frameworks, and various other libraries.

A data engineer will possess expertise in building systems that collect, store, and process data such as relational databases, NoSQL datastores, as well as the Hadoop stack, including HDFS, MapReduce, HBase, Pig, Hive, and Storm.

## The Applied Scientist

Think of an **applied scientist** as someone who comes from a research background, usually with a degree in computer science, applied math, or statistics.

This individual deeply understands the math behind algorithms such as $k$-means clustering, random forest, or Alternating Least Squares, how to tune and optimize such algorithms and the trade-offs associated with various choices when applying these algorithms to real-world data.

In contrast to a **research scientist**, who tends to focus on academic research and publishing papers, an applied scientist is primarily interested in solving a real-world problem by applying the right algorithm to data in the right way. This distinction can sometimes become blurry, however.

Applied scientists therefore tend to be hands-on with statistical tools and some scripting languages such as R, Python, or SAS, with a focus on quick prototyping and rapid testing of new hypotheses.

### Ofer's Data Science Work at Yahoo! Search Advertising

I joined Yahoo! in 2005 just as Yahoo! Search Advertising was undergoing a tremendous change, tasking its engineering leadership with project "Panama."

Panama was a large-scale engineering project with the goal of creating a new, innovative Search Advertising platform and replacing most (if not all) of the old components that came with Yahoo!'s Overture acquisition.

Panama had many different sub-teams creating all kinds of new systems, from front-end ad-serving, to fast in-memory databases, to a brand new advertiser-friendly user interface. I joined a group whose mission was to re-invigorate the algorithmic underpinnings of Yahoo! Search Advertising.

Although we called it "applied science" at the time, as the term "data science" was not invented yet, our work was really a poster-child example of data science applied to the prediction of ad click-through rates. We followed the iterative cycle of hypothesize, implement/test, evaluate, and over very many iterations and the span of a few years we were able to significantly improve CTR prediction accuracy and, subsequently, the revenues of Yahoo! Search Advertising.

One of the major challenges in those days was how to compute click-through rate given the large raw datasets of page views and clicks. Fortunately, Yahoo! invested in building Hadoop in those days, and we were one of the first teams using Hadoop inside of Yahoo!. We migrated our initial CTR prediction code onto Hadoop with MapReduce and thereafter enjoyed shorter cycles of hypothesize-implement-evaluate, ultimately leading to better CTR prediction capabilities and increased revenues.

## Transitioning to a Data Scientist Role

To be successful as a data scientist you need to have a balanced skillset from both data engineering and applied science, as shown in Figure 1.3.

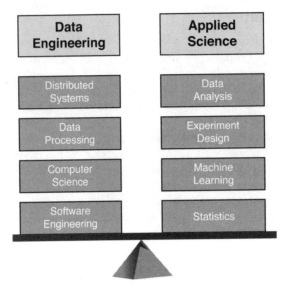

Figure 1.3   The skillset of the data scientist.

If you've been a data engineer, it's likely you have already heard a lot about some machine learning techniques and statistical methods, and you understand their purpose and mechanism. To be successful as a data scientist, you will have to obtain a much deeper understanding of and hands-on experience with the techniques in statistics and machine learning that are used for accomplishing tasks such as classification, regression, clustering, and anomaly detection.

If you've been an applied scientist, with a good understanding of machine learning and statistics, then your transition into a data scientist will likely require stronger programming skills and becoming a better software developer with some basic software architecture skills.

Many successful data scientists also transition from various other roles such as business analyst, software developer, and even research roles in physics, chemistry, or biology. For example, business analysts tend to have a strong analytical background combined with a clear understanding of the business context and some programming experience—primarily in SQL. The role of a data scientist is rather different, and a successful transition will require stronger software development chops as well as more depth in machine learning and statistics.

One successful strategy for building up the combined skills is to pair up a data engineer with an applied scientist in a manner similar to the pair programming approach from extreme programming (XP). With this approach, the data engineer and applied scientist work continuously together on the same problem and thus learn from each other and accelerate their transition to becoming a data scientist.

### Casey's Data Science Journey

When I was in graduate school in the Math department at Texas A&M, my advisor was after me to take my electives outside of my major. Because my background was in computer science, I decided to load up on computer science electives. One semester, the only remotely interesting electives available were a survey course in peer-to-peer networking and a graduate course in machine learning. After completely neglecting my Math for a semester to focus on big data and data science, I decided that this might be for me.

After graduate school and a couple of entry-level positions, I made my way into the oil industry doing scientific programming and helping them build a MapReduce platform in Erlang and C++ to do signal processing on seismic data. It was my first foray into blending my interests in big data and advanced analytics or data science and I was totally hooked. I moved windingly through a series of other data science jobs in different domains, including voice over IP and medical informatics, where I did a lot of natural language processing.

Finally, I landed at Hortonworks, doing consulting in data science for customers using Hadoop. I wanted to get the lay of the land to understand how people were really using this big data platform with a specific interest in how they might leverage data science as a driver for the advanced analytic capabilities of the platform. I spent years helping customers get their data science use cases implemented, going from start to production. It was a fantastic journey that taught me a lot about the constraints of the real world and how to exist within it and still push the boundaries of data science.

Recently I have moved within Hortonworks to building advanced analytics infrastructure and cyber security models for the Apache Metron (incubating) project. It's a new domain and has new challenges, but all of the important lessons learned from graduate school, the oil industry, and the years in consulting have been invaluable in helping direct what to build, how to build it, and how to use it to great effect on a great project.

## Soft Skills of a Data Scientist

Working as a data scientist can be very rewarding, interesting, and a lot of fun. In addition to expertise in specific technical skills such as machine learning, programming, and related tools, there are a few key attributes that make a data scientist successful:

- *Curiosity*—As a data scientist you are always looking for patterns or anomalies in data, and a natural sense of curiosity helps. There are no book answers, and your curiosity leads you through the journey from the first time you set your eyes on the data until the final deliverable.

- *A love of learning*—The number of techniques, tools, and algorithms seems at times to be infinite. To be successful at data science requires continuous learning.

- *Persistence*—It never works the first time in data science. That's why persistence, the ability to keep hammering at the data, trying again, and not giving up is key to success.

- *Story-telling*—As a data scientist, you often have to present to management, or to other business stakeholders, results that are rather complex. Being able to present the data and analysis in a clear and easy to understand manner is of paramount importance.

### There and Back Again—Doug's Path to Data Science

As a trained analytical chemist, the concept of data science is very familiar to me. Finding meaningful data in experimental noise is often part of the scientific process. Statistics and other mathematical techniques played a big part of my original research on high frequency measurements of dielectric materials. Interestingly, my path has taken me from academia in the mid 1980's (3 years as an assistant chemistry professor) to High Performance Technical Computing (HPTC) and back several times.

My experience ranges from signal analysis and modeling, to Fortran code conversion, to parallel optimization, to genome parsing, to HPTC and Hadoop cluster design and benchmarking, to interpreting the results of protein folding computer models.

In terms of Figure 1.3, I started out on the right-hand side as an academic/applied scientist then slid over to the data engineering side as I worked within HPTC. Currently, I find myself moving back to the applied scientist side. My experience has not been an "either-or" situation, however. Many big problems require skills from both areas and the flexibility to use both sets of skills. What I have found is that my background as an applied scientist has made me a better practitioner of large-scale computing (HPTC and Hadoop Analytics) and vice-versa. In my experience, good decisions require the ability to provide "good" numbers and "goodness" depends on understanding the pedigree of these numbers.

## Building a Data Science Team

Like many other software disciplines, data science projects are rarely executed by a single individual but rather by a team. Hiring a data science team is not easy due to a number of reasons:

- The gap between demand and supply for data science talent is very high. A recent Deloitte report entitled "Analytics Trends 2016: The Next Evolution" states, "Despite the surge in data science–related programs (more than 100 in the US alone), universities and colleges cannot produce data scientists fast enough to meet the business demands." Continuing, the report also notes, "International Data Corporation (IDC) predicts a need for 181,000 people with deep analytical skills in the US by 2018 and a requirement for five times that number of positions with data management and interpretation capabilities."

- The hiring marketplace for data scientists is extremely competitive, with companies such as Google, Yahoo!, Facebook, Twitter, Uber, Netflix, and many others all looking for such talent, driving compensation up.

- Many engineering managers are not familiar with the data science role and don't have experience with interviewing and identifying good data science candidates.

When building a data science team, a common strategy for overcoming the talent gap is the following: instead of hiring data scientists with the combined skillsets of data engineers and applied scientists, build a team comprised of data engineers and applied scientists, and focus on providing a working environment and process that will drive productivity for the overall team.

This approach solves your hiring dilemma, but more importantly, it provides an environment for the data engineers to learn from the applied scientists and vice versa. Over time, this collaboration results in your team members becoming full-fledged data scientists.

Another consideration is whether to hire new team members or transition existing employees in the organization into a data engineering role, applied science role, or a data science role in the newly formed team.

The advantage of transitioning existing employees is that they usually are a known quantity, and they have already acquired significant business and domain expertise. For example, a data engineer in an insurance company already understands how insurance works, knows the terminology, and has established a social network within the organization that can help her avoid various challenges a new employee might not even see.

Potential downsides of existing employees are they may not have the required skills or knowledge on the technical side, and they may be too invested in the old ways of doing things and resist the change.

In our experience, working with many data science teams around the world, a hybrid approach often works best—build a team from both internal and external candidates.

# The Data Science Project Life Cycle

Most data science projects start with a question you would like answered or a hypothesis you would like to test related to a certain business problem. Take, for example, the following questions:

- What is the likelihood of a user continuing to play my game?
- What are some interesting customer segments for my business?
- What will the click-through rate of an ad be if I present it to a customer on a web page?

As shown in Figure 1.1, the data scientist translates this question into a hypothesis and iteratively explores whether this question can be answered by applying various machine learning and statistical techniques to the data sources that are available to her.

A more detailed view of this process is presented in Figure 1.4 where the typical iterative steps involved in most data science projects are given.

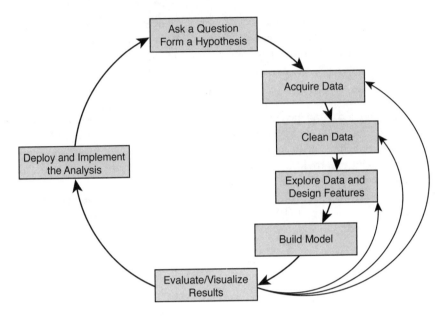

Figure 1.4   Expanded version of Figure 1.1 further
illustrating the iterative nature of data science.

## Ask the Right Question

At the beginning of a project, it is essential to understand the business problem and translate it into a form that is easy to understand and communicate, has a well-defined success criterion, is actionable within the business, and can be solved with the tools and techniques of data science.

To clarify what this means, consider the following example: An auto insurance company would like to use sensor data to improve their risk models.[3] They create a program whereby drivers can install a device that records data about the driving activity of the vehicle, including GPS coordinates, acceleration, braking, and more. With this data, they would like to classify drivers into three categories—low risk, medium risk, and high risk—and price their policies accordingly.

Before starting on this project, the data scientist might define this problem as follows:

1. Build a classifier of drivers into the three categories of risk: low, medium, and high.

2. Input data: sensor data.

3. Success criterion: expecting model accuracy of 75% or higher.

---

3. This is sometimes called UBI—usage-based-insurance.

Setting success criteria is often difficult, since the information content of the data is an unknown quantity, and it is therefore easier to just say, "We'll just work on it and do our best." The risk is of an unbounded project, without any "exit criteria."

The success criteria are often directly influenced by how the model will be used by the business and what makes sense from a business point of view. Furthermore, these must be translated into actionable criteria from a data science perspective. This may require negotiation and education with business stakeholders to translate a high-level intuitive business goal into measurable, well-understood criteria with defined error bounds. These negotiations can be difficult but very important as they force the matter that not all data science solutions can have an error bound of zero.

## Data Acquisition

Once the question is well understood, the next step is acquiring the data needed for this project. The availability of the data in a data science project is absolutely imperative to the success of the project. In fact, data availability and triage should be a primary consideration when considering feasibility of any data science project.

Data acquisition is often more difficult than it seems. In many enterprise IT organizations, acquiring the data means you have to find where the data currently reside, convince the curators of its current data-store to give you access to the data, and then find a place to host the data for analysis. In some circumstances, the data do not yet exist, and a new mechanism to capture and store the data is required.

In a large company, it is not always easy to know if a certain dataset exists and, if so, where it may be stored. Further, given the typically siloed nature of organizations, quite often the curators of such data are reluctant to provide you with these data, since it requires some extra work on their part. In addition, you have to go and ask your manager or CIO for some number of servers where you can store the data for your analysis.

All of this extra friction is a hurdle that makes data acquisition far from trivial. One of the often unrecognized values of the Hadoop **data-lake** concept is that it creates a company-supported data-store where ultimately all data reside. Thus, data acquisition is reduced to a very minimal effort—essentially, as long as you have access to the Hadoop cluster, you have access to the data.

In Chapter 4, "Getting Data into Hadoop," we discuss in more detail the various tools and techniques that enable easy and consistent ingestion of data into a Hadoop cluster, including Flume, Sqoop, and Falcon.

## Data Cleaning: Taking Care of Data Quality

The next challenge is that of data quality. It is very common that the data required for the project are comprised of multiple different datasets, each arriving from a different legacy data-store, with a different schema and distinct format conventions. The first thing we need to do is merge these datasets into a single, consistent, high-quality dataset.

Let's look at an example: Consider a healthcare organization, comprised of various hospitals, clinics, and pharmacies. The organization may have various systems to represent patient information, including demographics data, labs data, claims data, and pharmacy data. Since doctors, nurses, and pharmacists enter the data, there is no guarantee that the data are consistent and without human error. In fact, it is quite common that various datum values such as lab results, blood pressure, or BMI (body mass index) have invalid clinical values due to simple data entry errors. Clearly, any doctor or nurse that would later read this information may easily detect that a data item is invalid, but when used in the context of data science, we have to make sure that we apply some rules to prevent bad data from negatively impacting our models.

The issue of data quality is (unfortunately) quite pervasive, and bad data exist almost universally in modern enterprises. Data scientists and data engineers spend a significant amount of time exploring data quality and applying various techniques to clean up and normalize their input datasets.

Hadoop provides a great platform to clean data since you can keep both the raw data and multiple versions of the cleaned data on the same platform at relatively low cost, and data cleaning can happen at scale across the entire cluster.

In Chapter 5, "Data Munging with Hadoop," we discuss data quality in greater detail and provide a framework to identify, categorize, and resolve many problems that arise in data quality analysis.

## Explore the Data and Design Model Features

After data are acquired, and data quality issues are resolved, the data scientist is finally ready to do real modeling: build a predictive model, perform clustering analysis, or build a recommender system.

To do this, she needs to select which variables or features of the data are most suitable for the task. Sometimes these features will already exist in the dataset; other times, a feature is created (engineered) by combining multiple existing features.

Let's look at an example. Imagine you are a cell phone provider, building a customer churn model. Your existing dataset may include variables like customer ID, the date the customer joined your service, the mobile device they currently use, average minutes per month, payment plan, and zip code. Your dataset also provides a complete log of all calls in the last 6 months.

Many of these variables may be used as a feature of the model, but it is very typical to consider complex features, derived from one of the raw variables or some complex computation with these variables. For example, you might consider a variable like "number of calls out of state in the last month" as a feature (derived from the call logs) or "most common cell tower."

The trick is to figure out which features are most useful or predictive for the specific type of model you are tasked with building. Determining the answer to this is part art and part science and is probably one of the most difficult and important tasks in data science.

In performing this task, also known as **feature engineering**, the data scientist commonly uses various techniques from statistics, information theory, visualization, and text analytics. We provide some more in-depth coverage of feature engineering in Chapter 5.

## Building and Tuning the Model

Building a machine learning model involves choosing the modeling technique to use and applying the learning technique to the dataset. At a high level, there are two types of modeling techniques: supervised learning and unsupervised learning.

With supervised learning, a training set is provided that includes a set of instances, each instance is comprised of features and a *target* variable. Using this set of examples, the machine learning algorithm *learns* how to map a set of features to a value for the target variable. Within supervised learning, we distinguish between classification and regression. With classification, the target variable is a categorical variable with a set of discrete values, such as the driver risk level in the previous example from insurance. Whereas in regression, it is a variable with continuous values, such as expected price.

Unsupervised learning is a bucket of techniques where a training set is not available, and the purpose of the modeling exercise is to identify patterns in the data without any such labeled training set. Common tasks that fall into this category are clustering, anomaly detection, and frequent item-set analysis.

Collaborative filtering, a technique for creating product recommendations, falls somewhere between supervised and unsupervised learning. It does not take as input the standard supervised learning training set but instead a dataset of historical recommendations of products by users. It then provides a set of recommendations for a user.

The mathematical detail for each machine learning technique can be quite daunting and may require advanced knowledge of statistics, probability, and applied mathematics, which is beyond the scope of this book. However, it is often possible to use many of the machine learning techniques without complete mastery of the underlying mathematics. In Chapter 7, "Machine Learning with Hadoop," we provide a more detailed description about these techniques and their application.

Once the model is built, we evaluate its performance using standard metrics such as accuracy or precision/recall to determine whether it meets the success criteria negotiated and informed by the business stakeholder.

If the model does not provide the expected outcome, then we typically find ourselves getting back to one of the earlier steps: acquiring new or different data, pre-processing or cleaning up the data in a different way, using different features, choosing a different model, or all of the above.

## Deploy to Production

Once the model is built, evaluated, and meets the acceptance criteria, we are ready to deploy it into our production systems.

It's challenging to give a hard-and-fast rule for how to deploy to production, as this process varies based on the type of production environment that's available for an organization.

Typically, you have to consider all aspects of the modeling process, including data acquisition, data pre-processing, and modeling. Often strict response time service level agreements (SLAs) have to be met, which dictate architecture or algorithm implementation choice.

# Managing a Data Science Project

Data science teams are relatively new. It is only natural to assume that managing a data science project can be accomplished with the same general techniques and best practices that have been proven successful in other software development projects.

But that is not the case. Data science projects that involve applying machine learning techniques to data are usually strikingly different than your typical software development project and require a different approach and mindset.

- Data quality is unknown at the start of the project. As we will see later in the book, data quality is a key aspect of data science. Providing quality data requires significant effort, usually of unknown scope and level.

- With data science projects, measurement and evaluation is of utmost importance. Without being able to accurately measure how your algorithm is doing, you are running blind. Developing the supporting infrastructure for instrumenting your algorithm, collecting data, and measuring results is as important as the algorithm itself. This takes time and effort that's outside of the obvious project goal itself.

- Even with the infrastructure in place to measure your algorithm's performance, it is often difficult to determine the expected level of accuracy for statistical techniques and machine learning. This creates a problem with defining clear "exit criteria" for a modeling effort: When is the model good or finished? Instead, it is important to realize that modeling is iterative and empower data scientists with an environment and tools to make them as productive as possible so that iteration times are shortened.

To our knowledge there is no field-tested methodology to manage data science projects (such as Scrum or eXtreme Programming for software engineering). We believe that such a methodology (or a few methodologies) will emerge in the coming years.

# Summary

In this chapter

- We defined data science as the art and science of discovering insight from data and building software systems to apply this insight in a business context.

- We reviewed the history of data science in academia and industry, how it started in both the statistics and machine learning communities and was made practical through innovation from big Internet companies like Yahoo! and Google.

- We discussed the role of a data scientist as one with the combined skillset of a data engineer and an applied scientist and the challenges with building a data science team.

- We looked at the data science life cycle, from asking the right question, through data quality control, pre-processing modeling, evaluation, and deployment to production.

# Use Cases for Data Science

*Hiding within those mounds of data is knowledge that could change the life of a patient,*
*or can change the world.*

Atul Butte, Stanford

**In This Chapter:**

- We discuss how big data drives change in data-driven organizations
- We review common business use cases for data science

In Chapter 1, "Introduction to Data Science," we covered a lot of the basic terminology around data science and its history. As Hadoop adoption accelerates and organizations build their so-called data lake[1]—a central location for all of their datasets—many businesses are discovering new and innovative ways to use these large datasets, reaping business benefits that were not possible before.

In this chapter we explore the main drivers for this transformation and examine in more detail some of the most common business use cases for data science. If you're familiar with the use cases already, you can jump directly to Chapter 3, "Hadoop and Data Science."

## Big Data—A Driver of Change

The modern IT infrastructure is undergoing tremendous change; more data than ever, in various formats, is now available to organizations. Previously, most organizations were limited (mainly due to cost) in the amount of data they could store and process in a cost-effective manner. Thus, a common best practice was to limit data sizes to the minimum necessary.

With the era of big data upon us, the competitive advantage provided by a big data strategy is widely recognized by IT leaders.

---

1. The term "data lake," first coined by James Dixon of Pentaho, is often used to describe a large storage repository for data coupled with a processing engine for such data at scale. Hadoop is the prime example of a technology stack enabling the data lake. See Chapter 4, "Getting Data into Hadoop," for more about Hadoop data lakes.

Let's look more carefully at three important characteristics underlying the big data transformation (volume, variety, and velocity), and how they impact the modern IT revolution.

## Volume: More Data Is Now Available

The first (and perhaps simplest) driver of change is the availability of a lot more data.

Since the commercialization of databases in the 1960s, businesses have been collecting, storing, and processing data. For example, healthcare insurance organizations stored data about patients and insurance claims. Retailers stored information about purchase history. Banks stored data about deposits, withdrawals, and investments.

This data typically consisted of post-transaction information. There was a lot more data available—the pre-transaction data, such as clickstream data—but IT decisions were primarily driven by the (previously high) cost of storing this data, and thus most of this data was typically discarded.

In the past decade we've seen this dramatically change. With a significant reduction in the cost of large-scale storage clusters enabled by Hadoop and the advances in machine learning algorithms that can extract significant business value from this data, businesses are rethinking what data they keep and for how long. In many cases, they keep *all* the data *in raw form*.

With the explosion of connected devices and sensor data, the sheer amount of data available every year is growing exponentially. For example, IDC predicts that from now until 2020, the digital universe will double every two years, reaching an estimated 40,000 exabytes (or 40 trillion gigabytes).

Storing so much data is a challenge for any business, since existing data stores and data warehouse solutions can't scale at a reasonable cost. Recognizing the tremendous value of such data, businesses are creating modern data lakes to accommodate this new inflow of data and enable them to utilize this data effectively and at a reasonable cost.

## Variety: More Data Types

Not only is more data available, but new types of data are now available. These new data types open up opportunities for analysis and prediction that were not possible before. Let's look at a few examples:

- **Sensor data** is quickly becoming ubiquitous, as more and more devices around us are equipped with capabilities to store and collect various new types of data that were not available before. For example, cell phones provide GPS information, the NEST thermostat provides temperature information, and cars collect and provide driving status information.
- **Log files** are not new. They've been around for a while as a standard way to log various types of information about the activity on a certain server such as a web server. Typically, the log files will be kept for a few days or weeks and then recycled, since their primary role was to help diagnose problems with the server. However, server logs often include invaluable information about user page views and click behavior and are now often kept in raw form for many years to enable advanced clickstream analytics.

- **Text data** is commonly available in various business environments. Whether in PDF format, JSON, XML, or simple text, it may contain doctor's notes in the healthcare setting, case details in a call center, or case-notes for an equipment services company. Applying advanced natural language techniques to this textual information in order to understand it is now possible at scale. This approach is finding more and more use cases within modern data-driven businesses.
- **Audio and video** data is often stored for audit/compliance reasons. More recently, businesses realize they can use audio and video data in new and innovative ways. For example, they are using audio data to analyze customer satisfaction in call-centers or video data for defect detection.

## Velocity: Fast Data Ingest

Another driver of change is the rate of data acquisition.

Consider, for example, cell phone network providers such as AT&T, Verizon, T-Mobile, or Sprint. These companies store every event recorded by every cell tower across their national or global network. The speed of ingestion for such events can be overwhelming and often stretches the limits of their existing technical infrastructure.

# Business Use Cases

Equipped with a better understanding of the three basic aspects of big data—volume, variety, and velocity—and how they impact the way we use data, let's examine some common use cases of data science with big data.

## Product Recommendation

Recommender systems have become rather common for online retailers and many other businesses with an online retail presence. We are familiar with various flavors of product recommendation techniques used by companies such as Amazon, Netflix, Facebook, LinkedIn, and, more recently, Google/YouTube.

Amazon shows product recommendations in many places on their website. For example, when you view a watch on the Amazon website, similar items are recommended for you, providing you with additional options before you make a purchase.

Netflix has provided movie recommendations since its early days. It is believed that as much as 75% of Netflix' streaming video can be attributed to movie recommendations— clearly a critical product feature and huge driver of their business success.

Google's YouTube is an extremely popular user-generated video platform. Early on in its evolution, search was the main mechanism by which a user could find videos. Later on, Google added the "Recommended videos" feature that provides additional "similar" videos that may be of interest to you. In many cases, the recommended list changes after watching just one new video.

LinkedIn, the most popular professional networking platform on the planet, implemented the "people you may know" (PYMK) feature very early in its product evolution.

This feature simply recommends to a user other users that they may know and therefore may want to connect with on LinkedIn.

This feature made a significant contribution to LinkedIn's network growth, as it encouraged members to connect to more and more people over time, increasing the value of the network to each member. Similar to LinkedIn, Facebook and Twitter implement such functionality within their social networks.

Although the Internet giants were the first ones to implement recommender systems, the benefits of such data products are now adopted by the whole retail industry. Personalized product recommendations have the following benefits:

- **Increasing sales**—Recommender systems provide an easy way for consumers to find items that they like or need. This drive ups the number of items sold and subsequently increases revenue.

- **Selling more diverse items**—A recommender system often helps users find items that they may not necessarily know how to find, and this drives sales of items that are difficult to find.

- **Increasing user satisfaction and loyalty**—A well-designed recommender system often improves the overall user experience. As users find interesting and relevant items, they are happier with the website and come again, driving repeat business.

## Customer Churn Analysis

It is well known that keeping an existing customer is often much cheaper than finding a new one. Whether you are a bank, a retailer, a gaming company, an Internet service provider, a cell phone provider, an airline, or an insurance company, there is a strong desire in almost any business to actively pursue programs for customer retention and prevent customer churn (also known as "attrition").

Churn models differ by industry, due to the different business models and specific customer engagement and lifetime value models. Customer churn analysis uses machine learning to predict the likelihood of each customer "leaving." Businesses then use this data to drive and guide customer-retention programs (such as discounts or other incentive programs) to encourage these at-risk customers to stay.

For example, in the gaming industry, more than 70% of free-to-play gamers quit within the first 30 days. Being able to predict who those players will be and enact a personalized campaign to engage and retain them in the game is highly beneficial to the game developer.

## Customer Segmentation

Customer segmentation is a common technique used to identify segments of customers that behave similarly with regard to their interaction with the business.

A grocery store may be interested in segmenting its customers by the type of food products they purchase. For example, one segment of customers might be "people who favor meat," while another might be "people who favor gourmet products."

Table 2.1  **Segmenting grocery shoppers.**

| Discovered Customer Prototypes | Basic Shoppers | Favor Meat | Favor Produce | Favor Gourmet | Variety Shoppers |
|---|---|---|---|---|---|
| % of Customers | 39% | 15% | 8% | 3% | 35% |
| Fresh Meat | 3% | 59% | 9% | 1% | 14% |
| Packaged Foods | 75% | 15% | 21% | 12% | 39% |
| Dairy | 2% | 5% | 4% | 0% | 8% |
| Seafood | 6% | 5% | 6% | 3% | 12% |
| Gourmet | 1% | 3% | 2% | 73% | 6% |
| Fresh Produce | 10% | 9% | 49% | 6% | 19% |
| Bakery | 3% | 5% | 7% | 4% | 2% |

Similarly, airlines and hotels are interested in segmenting customers into business travelers versus non-business travelers. Airlines are also interested in "domestic passengers" versus "international passengers."

An immediate benefit of such segmentation is the ability to increase marketing efficiency. For example, airlines may customize email campaigns based on effective segmentation to achieve much higher response rates. Similarly, a grocery store could try attracting meat lovers through special discounts on meat products (see Table 2.1).

Clustering techniques such as $k$-means clustering are common techniques for accomplishing customer segmentation.

With big data, organizations are now able to apply new data inputs to their customer segmentation algorithms (such as data coming from social networks), apply the clustering algorithms on larger datasets, improving overall accuracy, and execute these algorithms faster and more often.

## Sales Leads Prioritization

Many sales professionals enjoy a pipeline of sales leads that result from good, effective marketing (see Figure 2.1).

A key question is "On which sales lead should I focus my effort"?

There are many ways by which a business can prioritize the sales efforts, but one of the most natural parameters is "likelihood to close within N days."

Applying data science, businesses can model each lead with various features (such as geographic location, customer type, website engagement, previous sales, etc.), and build a predictive model to determine the likelihood of each lead to close within the desired time period.

Based on such models, sales operations improve in efficiency and overall revenues increase.

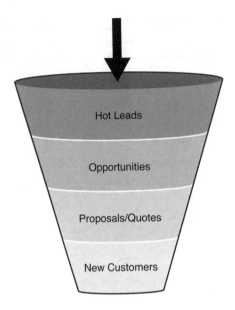

Figure 2.1    Sales pipeline.

## Sentiment Analysis

With the increased adoption of crowd-sourced feedback from customers in online forums and the growth of social networks such as Facebook and Twitter, there is a lot of information available about customer sentiment.

Sentiment analysis is an application of text analytics and natural language processing techniques, with the goal of understanding customer sentiment about a certain topic (e.g., a product or service).

For example, a company may launch a certain product or service and would like to know how its customers react to it—do they like the product or not? Furthermore, sentiment may change over time, so it is beneficial to track sentiment over time (see Figure 2.2) to understand the temporal aspect of customer sentiment.

Traditionally, you would conduct focus groups or other forms of market research. But with sentiment analysis, you can look at customer Tweets, Facebook posts, or TripAdvisor reviews and analyze customer responses to understand the overall sentiment about the product or service at a much lower cost and often with improved accuracy.

This technique is not limited to social networks such as Twitter and Facebook. It can be effectively applied to call center transcripts to understand customer satisfaction from call center operations, to stock review sites for investment decisions, and many other similar applications.

## Number of Tweets by Time and Sentiment

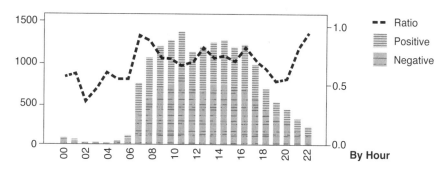

Figure 2.2    Sentiment from Tweets by hour of the day.

## Fraud Detection

Fraud or payment abuse is a serious problem for many businesses as well as government organizations. Every time money changes hands based on some criteria or set of rules, there is potential for fraud and abuse for monetary gain by malicious actors.

Clearly fraud detection is a critical capability for companies involved in payments such as banks, PayPal, or Square. But fraud detection is also highly effective in improving the bottom line for insurance companies, retailers, and many others.

In healthcare alone, it is estimated that claim fraud and abuse accounts for $300B in annual cost in the US alone. For retailers, the cost of credit-card fraud is estimated at billions every year, as show in Table 2.2.[2]

Fraud detection capabilities are often well-guarded secrets due to their sensitive nature. In most cases, these systems utilize a combination of rules, supervised learning, and unsupervised learning. Transactions that are flagged by the system are sent for manual review and follow-on action.

Table 2.2    **Cost of credit card fraud to retailers.**

| Year | 2010 | 2011 | 2012 | 2013 | 2014 |
|---|---|---|---|---|---|
| Cost of Fraud ($ Billions) | 20 | 26 | 23 | 23 | 32 |
| Fraud as Percent of Revenue | 0.52% | 0.64% | 0.54% | 0.51% | 0.68% |

2. Source: http://www.businessinsider.com/how-payment-companies-are-trying-to-close-themassive-hole-in-credit-card-security-2015-3

## Predictive Maintenance

Equipment doesn't operate forever and will ultimately fail at some point; it always fails sometime in the future. Unfortunately, such failure may have dire consequences given the binary nature of the failure. There are many examples of this, in various industries. Let's look at a few:

- When a component in a cell tower fails, the cell tower may stop operating and many cell phone users in the nearby vicinity may not be able to use their mobile services until the component is fixed and the tower is fully functional again.
- When an A/C compressor fails in an office building, the employees working there may suffer from poor working conditions for a day or two until a technician is able to fix the problem.
- If an engine in a helicopter or airplane fails, there could be dire consequences indeed. Fortunately, this is not a common safety issue as testing of these engines is rather thorough before lift-off. Nevertheless, if a failure is found on the ground, the vessel may need lengthy repair, which may result in flight delay or cancellation.
- If a freezer in a fast-food restaurant fails, the restaurant will need to replace it. However, that may take a few days. What will it do in the meantime with all the frozen food kept in that freezer?

The idea behind predictive maintenance is that the failure patterns of various types of equipment are predictable. If we can predict when a piece of hardware will fail accurately, and replace that component before it fails, we can achieve much higher levels of operational efficiency.

With many devices now including sensor data and other components that send diagnosis reports, predictive maintenance using big data becomes increasingly more accurate and effective.

## Market Basket Analysis

A common use case for retailers is known as market basket analysis (also known as affinity analysis or association mining).

In this type of analysis, we are trying to understand the purchasing behavior of the user. More specifically, with market basket analysis, retailers hope to gain insights into which products tend to be purchased together. For example, a shampoo and a conditioner would typically be purchased together.

It's rather obvious that shampoo and conditioner tend to be related—we don't need a complex algorithm to reach that conclusion. The goal of market basket analysis is, of course, to find non-obvious relationships of this type. A famous example (suspected of being an urban legend) is that of a retailer that discovered there is strong association between purchases of beer and diapers, the buyer group being "new dads."

Retailers use market basket analysis to guide a few key business decisions:

- Market basket analysis often drives store layout design, where items with strong association are placed strategically close to each other, making it more likely that the customer will purchase the related item. In the aforementioned example, the retailer may put diapers close to the beer cooler.

- Retailers can also use the results of market basket analysis for effective marketing campaigns to drive foot traffic into a physical store. For example, a retailer might advertise a significant discount on a digital camera, while keeping a high price on memory cards (an item typically purchased together with the camera), luring the customer to walk into the store for the purchase of the camera but without losing the margin on the overall sale.

- Retailers often use the output of a market basket analysis to segment their products into natural groups, to better align their category management.

## Predictive Medical Diagnosis

Making decisions about a medical diagnosis is hard, partly because there is often a lot of uncertainty and not enough data. Furthermore, the implications of an incorrect decision can be dire. For example, if a doctor misdiagnoses a patient with cancer, the patient will undergo the very unpleasant (and potentially harmful) chemotherapy treatment protocol. Even worse, if a doctor mistakenly fails to diagnose a patient as having cancer, it might cost that patient his or her life, since an appropriate treatment protocol is not prescribed.

"Medical education is fundamentally conservative, indoctrinating new generations into the failed ways of the old", says Richard Horton, chief editor of *The Lancet*. In many cases, diagnosis is a tedious analytic task that is limited to a 10-15-minute office visit in a busy day.

Arming medical professionals with computer-assisted, data-based medical diagnosis tools is a tremendous opportunity to improve healthcare. Let's explore a few specific applications:

- Machine learning algorithms can detect unknown patterns of diagnosis and, if validated clinically, can add to the existing repository of medical knowledge.

- Electronic patient records use the ICD10 standard to record existing diagnoses for patients. Sometimes the electronic record is missing a few key diagnoses, and automated diagnosis of disease can be used for identifying these coding gaps.

- Various care quality measures such as HEDIS (Healthcare Effectiveness Data and Information Set) can be improved by, for example, screening based on automated diagnosis results.

The value of these use cases is well recognized, and as evidence of this the National Institute of Health (NIH) recently announced the Precision Medicine Initiative (PMI) Cohort Program that will be a data-driven research program bringing together human biology, behavior, genetics, environment, data science, and computation to develop more effective ways to prolong health and treat disease. The initial cohort (participant) base is expected to be one million people.

All of these use cases provide a significant opportunity for healthcare organizations to both improve the overall well-being of patients as well as create significant business benefits and revenue potential.

## Predicting Patient Re-admission

Using predictive models for hospital re-admission is another example where accurate predictive models can help healthcare organizations, especially for patients under the Medicare program in the United States.

In 2012, Centers for Medicare and Medicaid Services (CMS) started implementing a new regulation that dictates reduced payments to hospitals with excess re-admissions (within the first 30 days after discharge). This creates a direct incentive for healthcare providers and insurance companies to reduce re-admissions.

Being able to predict whether a patient will be re-admitted before they are discharged from the hospital has a direct monetary impact. Such predictive models can be used to trigger further treatments to reduce the likelihood of re-admission, which is, of course, beneficial to the patient.

This incentive is so strong, in fact, that in 2012 the Heritage Provider Network launched a Kaggle.com competition to build a model for predicting re-admission using historical data, with a prize of $3M to the winning team.

## Detecting Anomalous Record Access

Many organizations have sensitive customer records. For example, healthcare providers such as clinics and hospitals store private patient information and are required by law to protect this information from illegal access. A doctor or a nurse, for example, should only have access to health information about the patient they are treating that is necessary for them to perform their duties.

It is unfortunately the case that data breaches occur. For example, a Hollywood star may be hospitalized and a rogue employee in the hospital may try to inspect her health records and sell the information to a journalist for a quick buck.

The common solution to this is via very strict access control mechanisms and role-based access controls. However, the typical static role-based access control mechanisms are often not sufficient, since employees often change roles, change departments, and even share IDs and passwords. IT is not always able to track these changes effectively.

Many such organizations apply anomaly detection algorithms to detect employees who access data in a way that is not "typical" or "normal" for their role or as compared to historical patterns for that employee. For example, if a doctor from the internal medicine department accesses records of patients from oncology, that may be flagged as a potential anomaly for further investigation.

## Insurance Risk Analysis

Insurance is a risk-based industry. Products such as property, auto, or life insurance are always priced based on risk assessment and the application of the risk pooling principle.

Insurance companies have been using predictive risk modeling for some time, modeling risk based on key indicators such as age, gender, geographic location, and historical data about the consumer. For example, it is well known that younger drivers tend to be more accident-prone than experienced drivers. Thus, auto insurance companies will typically charge a higher premium for drivers under the age of 25.

Since accurate risk analysis is so critical to the profitability of an insurance company, every attempt is made to improve this and gain a competitive edge. For example, auto insurance companies are looking at sensor data coming from automobiles (GPS data, etc.) as a new source of data to be used to improve accuracy of risk prediction. By tracking driving behavior, the insurance company can more accurately assess the risk of accident for that driver.

## Predicting Oil and Gas Well Production Levels

The basic asset of any oil and gas company is the well, from whence oil and natural gas are produced. Oil and gas companies such as Schlumberger, Haliburton, Noble Energy, and Chesapeake therefore invest heavily in research and development to maximize oil production levels, resulting in direct impact on the top line of the business.

There are many variables that may impact the production levels of a given well. With sensor data, geophysics data about the well, and other data sources, models can be constructed to predict well production.

With this predictive model, the oil and gas company can understand what impacts production levels and address issues negatively impacting this level ahead of time, resulting in streamlined production and increased revenues.

# Summary

In this chapter

- We reviewed how volume, variety, and velocity of data impacts organizations data efforts and the opportunities it provides.
- We looked at a series of real-world business use cases where data science provides tangible business benefit, including product recommendations, customer churn analysis, fraud detection, sales lead prioritization, customer segmentation, and others.

# 3

# Hadoop and Data Science

*What happened is the data scientists not only got interesting research results—
what we had anticipated—but they also prototyped new applications and demonstrated that those
applications could substantially improve Yahoo's search relevance or Yahoo's advertising revenue.*

Eric Baldeschwieler
VP of Hadoop Software Development, Yahoo!

## In This Chapter:

- What Is Hadoop?
- Hadoop's Evolution
- Hadoop Tools for Data Science
- Pig and Hive for Data Science
- Spark for Data Science
- Why Data Scientists Love Hadoop

Data science needs tools, just as any other discipline, and Hadoop has become one of
many powerful tools the data scientists now have at their disposal. This chapter explains
what Hadoop is, its history and evolution, the new tools that have been added to the
Hadoop landscape, and why Hadoop is so important to data scientists.

## What Is Hadoop?

Apache Hadoop is an open-source, Java-based, distributed computing platform, built out
of the necessity to scale search indices. While the original tasks that Hadoop was created
for revolved around building search indices, it was quickly apparent that Hadoop's core
abstraction was more generic and broadly applicable. After years of use and revision, it has
become a software ecosystem that forms the backbone of a data center operating system
built to do scalable data processing and analytics from the ground-up.

Failure tolerance is one of the few core principles of Hadoop that have persisted
since its inception. In order to achieve scalability, the system was designed to take node

or component failure, such as hard drive loss, in stride with the underlying system taking responsibility for retrying failed jobs. This software resiliency leads to some nice economic characteristics. In particular, less reliable, and therefore less expensive, hardware may be used within a system, which is, overall, very reliable due to the resiliency established at the software layer rather than the hardware layer. Furthermore, this leads to a lower system operator to node ratio as repairs may be queued and taken care of in bulk rather than requiring immediate reaction.

The core technologies have expanded greatly since the initial commit[1] in 2005. However, at its base there are only a handful of components:

- Distributed File System
- Resource Manager and Scheduler
- Distributed Data Processing Frameworks

## Distributed File System

While there are multiple distributed file systems that can be used with Hadoop, the core file system began as and remains the Hadoop Distributed File System (HDFS). Designed as an open version of Google's GFS,[2] HDFS is a distributed, scalable file system with notions of redundancy built in. The design is to build the distributed file system on top of many nodes, each containing a regular file system. It was designed to scale and hold petabytes of data. As such, a few assumptions were baked into the design of the system: sequential reads should be fast in support of full data scanning, the file system should communicate sufficiently the location of the data so that computation can be moved to the data rather than the other way around, and node failure should be tolerated in software.

Data is organized inside of HDFS as blocks, and those blocks are transparently replicated. Replication is intelligent as it uses various strategies to ensure that data is stored not only on multiple nodes but nodes that exist within multiple racks. This strategy is to ensure that a single node, or even a single rack failure, will not result in data loss.

Because the full system is aware of block locations and can optimize where tasks are run, tasks can be run near the data with high probability. This optimization yields a substantial speedup over systems that stream data to the node running the computation. Replicated blocks and data locality combine to make HDFS a system that achieves high reliability and aggregate bandwidth, which is ideal for scaling computation. Figure 3.1 presents a high-level overview of the HDFS architecture.

---

1. Commit in this instance is in the context of submitting to a software version control system such as Git.
2. Sanjay Ghemawat, Howard Gobioff, and Shun-Tak Leung. 2003. The Google file system. *SIGOPS Oper. Syst. Rev.* 37, 5 (October 2003), 29-43. DOI=http://dx.doi.org/10.1145/1165389.945450

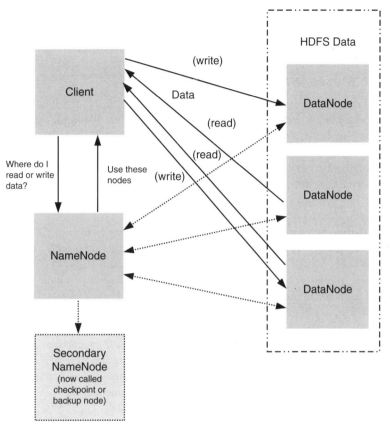

Figure 3.1   HDFS Architecture showing various system roles in a Hadoop deployment. Metadata and data are solid lines, file system and node status are dashed lines.

In Figure 3.1, you can see the general organization and how the various actors interact within the HDFS system. As you see, clients, or individual programs that wish to read from or write to the distributed file system, interact with the appropriate portion of the subsystem depending on their aim. To wit, a client who merely wants to list files, a metadata request will communicate directly with the NameNode for such a query. Whereas a client who wants to read or write data would request block locations from the NameNode—a low volume of data—and then communicate directly to the servers that house the blocks (solid lines in Figure 3.1). This architecture's hallmark is the careful direction of operations to the portion of the system best able to handle them with the least likelihood of bottlenecks (i.e., rather than passing all data through the NameNode).

In almost all Hadoop deployments, there is a secondary NameNode. While not explicitly required by a NameNode, it is highly recommended. The term "secondary NameNode" (now called checkpoint Node) is somewhat misleading. It is not an active failover node and cannot replace the primary NameNode in case of its failure. The purpose of the secondary NameNode is to perform periodic checkpoints that preserve the status of the NameNode should it fail. For more information about using HDFS see Appendix A.

## Resource Manager and Scheduler

Scheduling and resource management are at the key of any good distributed system. As such, Hadoop has a component that directs the allocation of compute resources and schedules user applications in the most efficient way. This system is called YARN—Yet Another Resource Negotiator.

Resource management entails scheduling tasks such that data locality is maximized and that resources are not starved by large jobs. YARN has a pluggable system for scheduling that can be made aware of user-limits, queue capacities, and the normal accouterment of scheduling tasks to run on a shared resource system.

YARN partitions resources into containers that at the base level are a CPU core and an amount of memory. Additional resources (extra cores, memory, GPU, storage) can be included as part of the container. YARN also monitors running containers to ensure that the memory, CPU, disk, and network quotas requested by the task are not exceeded. Unlike many other workflow schedulers, YARN provides data locality as a resource. That is, a YARN job (e.g., MapReduce) can request that specific containers run on servers that host specific data (or as close to where data reside in the cluster as possible). This level of control is important to ensure that a distributed system continues to run smoothly, resources are shared in a fair fashion, containers are private (isolated from other users), and users are able to have their tasks scheduled in a timely manner. Figure 3.2 provides a schematic look at the YARN components.

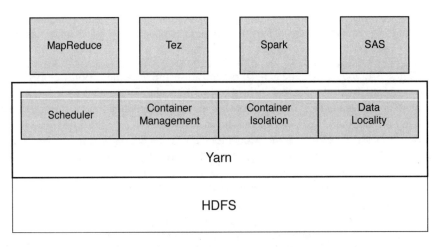

Figure 3.2   Hadoop architecture with HDFS, Yarn, and the various processing engines—MapReduce, Spark, Tez.

## Distributed Data Processing Frameworks

Being able to efficiently read and write data is the necessary bedrock upon which to build a distributed system, but generally IO alone does not make a system useful. YARN provides the abstractions needed to distribute computation across the cluster of computers and process the data held in HDFS in a scalable manner, but just how to express this computation will be our focus for the remainder of this chapter.

The first data processing model supported by Hadoop was MapReduce, a computing model championed by Google. The key insight was that many problems fit within the assumptions of MapReduce, and the model is so simple that people who are not necessarily trained in distributed systems can use it to solve their problems without the headaches of building the software infrastructure of a distributed system. This freedom enabled them to focus on their problem domain.

Parallel MapReduce is defined as the distributed processing model whereby a problem can be broken down into three phases: a map phase, a shuffle phase, and a reduce phase. MapReduce relies on the data locality characteristics of HDFS and the task/resource management of YARN to efficiently run this three-step computation. In the map phase, input data are processed in parallel across the cluster through a method that transforms raw data into keys and values. The keys are then sorted and "shuffled" into buckets by common, like keys (i.e., all values with the same key are guaranteed to go to the same reducer). The reducers then process the values for every key, often storing the results either back on HDFS or some other persistent store.

The notable characteristic of MapReduce is that each phase is either stateless or has very limited state. For instance, each input record is treated without regard for any of the input records that have gone before, because you have limited guarantees about which server runs each worker for each phase. The reduce phase, however, guarantees that you have access to all of the values that have the same key. These guarantees seem shockingly sparse but are sufficient for many tasks.

The canonical example of MapReduce is counting word occurrences in a large corpus of text. To see how this fits, let's go through each phase of the MapReduce process for this problem. First, when the text data are loaded into HDFS, data is automatically "sliced," replicated, and distributed across the HDFS servers. Next each slice is scanned in parallel to count words using a key/value pair (i.e., each occurrence of a word creates a key value pair of the form (word,1) where "word" has been found 1 time). This key/value mapping gets generated for each occurrence of "word." When the counting is complete, all identical keys are shuffled from their mapper process to a reducer process. The inputs to the reducer process are all the key/value pairs for a specific word. In the case of word counting, the reducer just sums the values associated with the word. Finally, the reducer will write out the word and the total count associated with it for inspection. The general map process is outlined in Figure 3.3 and the general reduce process is outlined in Figure 3.4.

It turns out that many problems fit within the underlying assumptions of MapReduce. It is fairly clear that so-called algebraic methods, methods which can be decomposed into partial results and have those partial results combined into a final result such as sums, averages, counts, etc., can easily be structured as a map and reduce task. What is

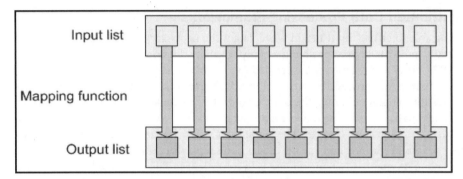

Figure 3.3   Map Phase: The Input list is sliced into independent blocks when loaded into HDFS. The mapping function is performed on each block in parallel. The Output list is a collection of key/value pairs.

less clear is that other, more complicated tasks can be structured as, possibly, a set of MapReduce jobs.

Not all tasks can easily, efficiently, or even possibly be interpreted as a series of MapReduce jobs. One particular deficiency is that highly iterative jobs do not fit well within MapReduce. These jobs may decompose into multiple MapReduce jobs, but job start-up overhead coupled with the fact that intermediate results must be written out at the end of every step combined with the programmer needing to manage the multi-step workflow for failures leads to a slow and frustrating experience. This situation occurs quite often in scientific programming or machine learning for algorithms that need many iterations to converge. Such algorithms are very common in linear algebra (e.g., the power method for finding eigenvectors) and optimization problems popular in machine learning (e.g., gradient descent).

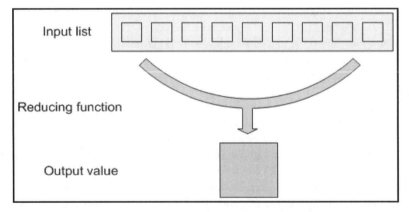

Figure 3.4   Reduce Phase: The Output list from the mapping phase becomes the Input list to the reduction phase. If multiple reducers are used, the input list is grouped by key value and shuffled from the map process to a specific reducer process. The reducer combines (reduces) the input list to an output value.

With the advent of YARN generalizing the resource allocation from the computing models, Hadoop has opened up the possibilities for computation models and data processing engines beyond just MapReduce. YARN is a relatively new addition to Hadoop, and we anticipate the support in it of many types of models, such as the traditional cluster-computing model that uses the Message Passing Interface (MPI) library. Some recent contenders that may illustrate how these communication models' new processing engines help extend and add capabilities to Hadoop are Apache Tez, Apache Spark, and Apache Flink.

Apache Tez was developed to address the fact that many problems extend beyond one MapReduce phase into multiple reduce steps and sometimes do not need data sorted between these steps. Tez was created as a more efficient layer in which to execute this kind of problem. The primary driver was the need to enable more efficient implementation of complex data flows and more efficient joining of sets of data within the native Hadoop SQL engine, Hive. In general, Tez is not an end-user tool, but more of a lower-level software API for use by other projects. The Tez model enables, among other things, data to be transferred directly from the reducer of one job to another reducer without writing out intermediate data to HDFS. Further, multi-way joins can be better represented as a directed acyclic graph[3] (DAG) of reducers rather than a linear pipeline of mappers and reducers.

Apache Spark is an in-memory data processing engine with a functional flavor and better semantics for iterative style computing that shows up frequently in data science. Spark was created at the AmpLabs at Berkeley and grew to be a top level Apache project with additional components beyond the basic processing capabilities such as Spark SQL, MLlib and stream processing. Spark's basic data construct is the RDD (resilient distributed dataset), which is a distributed sequence of objects, often stored in RAM, with an implicit mechanism to support failure. Spark may replay the operations on a subset of the data to reconstruct a portion of missing data. Spark's programming paradigm provides relational operators built into the model, such as union, distinct, filter, and join, applied lazily to RDDs.

Similar to Apache Spark, Apache Flink is also an in-memory processing engine with a heavier focus on real-time stream processing.

# Hadoop's Evolution

In the beginning, there was Apache Nutch, an open-source search engine software. Doug Cutting, the director of search at the Internet Archive, and Mike Cafarella, a graduate student at the University of Washington, developed the first parts of Hadoop to aid the Nutch project in 2005. The inspiration was taken from the 2003 Distributed File System paper, noted previously, and the 2004 MapReduce paper[4] from Google.

---

3. DAGs are basically graphs that cannot have loops.

4. Jeffrey Dean and Sanjay Ghemawat. 2004. "MapReduce: Simplified Data Processing on Large Clusters." In *Proceedings of the 6th Symposium on Operating Systems Design & Implementation*(OSDI'04), Vol. 6. USENIX Association, Berkeley, CA, USA, 10-10.

As the project matured, and Cutting came to work at Yahoo! in 2006, this particular part of Nutch became an important part of the infrastructural software at Yahoo!. It was evident that this wasn't just a part of a search engine, but a generalizable, distributed computation framework that deserved its own project. So, Nutch spun out these components into a separate open-source project named Hadoop, after a toy elephant that belonged to Cutting's child.

Even so, it was a long journey to maturity. It took years for Yahoo! to migrate its web index onto Hadoop. However, it did create a research grid for Yahoo!'s data scientists. Hadoop quickly became a vital infrastructural component for doing data science at scale at Yahoo!. This was a protective and forgiving environment that enabled an immature project to grow in maturity and features while having some of the rough edges forgiven and given time to mature.

Soon, however, Hadoop became a core piece of infrastructure at Yahoo! and developed into a general analytics workhorse for the organization. With this came maturity and features related to scheduling and guarantees made about performance to suit the business needs of a modern large-scale search engine. At this point, users began to see how Hadoop might be the core technology of many different businesses, and with that insight came the opportunity to build companies to further that aim.

In 2008 Mike Olson, Christophe Bisciglia from Google, Amr Awadallah from Yahoo!, and Jeff Hammerbacher from Facebook founded Cloudera, a company built to service the (then incipient but growing) need for Hadoop expertise in the broader world outside of Silicon Valley. Doug Cutting soon left Yahoo! and joined the group to help them evangelize and mature Hadoop.

There appeared to be a clear market for Hadoop in the wider world, and Cloudera's success did not go unnoticed by others. In 2011 Yahoo! spun out a company called Hortonworks, whose aim was precisely to bring Hadoop to the broader industry by the Yahoo! employees who had lovingly tended to Hadoop through its early years.

Startups, however, were not the only ones to get into the business of building distributions of Hadoop for the enterprise. Large industrial players such as EMC and Intel got into the game. Furthermore, the open-source vision of Hadoop was not the only business model sought as players such as MapR and Cloudera shipped proprietary components to ease some of the rough edges around Hadoop.

Since then, a renewed focus on broadening Hadoop's appeal through broadening Hadoop's functionality has been seen with its 2.0 version. The vision has moved from a MapReduce system to a data center operating system for running analytical applications at scale. Throughout all of this time we have seen increasing and pointed focus on shoring up the deficiencies in security and scheduling aimed at making the technology more palatable to the large enterprise data center.

## Hadoop Tools for Data Science

Every data scientist has a set of tools to perform their job they are comfortable with, including data acquisition, data quality analysis and cleaning, scripting, statistical computing, distributed computing, and visualization. Let's explore the tools and frameworks that are commonly used for these tasks with Hadoop.

## Apache Sqoop

Apache Sqoop is a tool designed for efficient bulk data transfer between Hadoop and structured datastores such as relational databases or NoSQL databases.

Using Sqoop version 1, you can import data from external systems on to HDFS and populate tables in Hive and HBase.[5] Sqoop uses a connector-based architecture, which supports plug-ins. Thus, it is extendable to new types of external sources. Out of the box, Sqoop comes with connectors for common database systems such as MySQL, PostgreSQL, Oracle, SQL Server, and DB2. There are some important differences between Sqoop version 1 and version 2. Consult Chapter 4, "Getting Data into Hadoop," for more information on using Sqoop.

Sqoop slices up every dataset that needs to be transferred into partitions, and a map-only job is launched for each such partition to handle transferring this data to its destination. The following example imports a list of all cities in Canada from an external MySQL geographic database using four mapper processes (-m 4). The results are placed in HDFS.

```
sqoop  --options-file world-options.txt -m 4 --target-dir \
/user/hdfs/sqoop-mysql-import/canada-city --query "SELECT ID,Name \
from  City WHERE CountryCode='CAN' AND \$CONDITIONS" --split-by ID
```

As alluded to previously, more detailed examples of Apache Sqoop can be found in Chapter 4.

## Apache Flume

Apache Flume is a distributed, reliable, and available service for efficiently collecting, aggregating, and moving large amounts of log data from servers into HDFS. It has a simple and flexible architecture consisting of "agents" that stream data from a source location to a sink location. Flume is robust and fault tolerant, with tunable reliability mechanisms and many failover and recovery mechanisms.

When using Flume, a minimum of two flume agents (each with their own source and sink location) is required—one for the source and one for the collector. There may be multiple sources, and multiple Flume agents may be pipelined. The following command starts Flume on a source host (e.g., a web server) using a web-server-source-agent.conf configuration file.

```
flume-ng agent -c conf -f web-server-source-agent.conf -n source_agent
```

The collector agent running on the Hadoop cluster will receive the source data and place it into HDFS. The configuration of the collector agent is through the web-server-target-agent.conf file. An example command is as follows:

```
flume-ng agent -c conf -f web-server-target-agent.conf -n collector
```

---

5. Apache HBase is a popular key-value store that works on Hadoop. We don't cover it in this book, but the interested reader can find more information at https://hbase.apache.org/.

Apache Oozie and Apache Falcon are data processing and management solutions for Hadoop. Each tool covers various levels of data motion, coordination of data pipelines, lifecycle management, and data discovery. Falcon enables end consumers to quickly onboard their data and its associated processing and management tasks on Hadoop clusters.

More detailed examples of Apache Flume, Oozie, and Falcon can be found in Chapter 4.

## Apache Hive

Apache Hive was created internally at Facebook to accommodate the desire for their engineers to use SQL to run analytics on Hadoop. It was subsequently open sourced and continues to be a vibrant project. Hive queries are "compiled" to a DAG of tasks in Tez[6] and executed by the Tez engine on the Hadoop cluster. While historically Hive was designed primarily for large-batch SQL queries that might take hours or days, with continued improvements by the Hive developer community, Hive became much faster and now supports interactive and real-time queries as well.

SQL has been in the toolset of the working data scientist for some time, and therefore it is not surprising that it will continue to serve in the same capacity with Hive. Understanding the shape and fundamental characteristics of the data are an important and useful function of SQL. There are multiple integrations into third-party tools via Java Database Connectivity (JDBC) or Open Database Connectivity (ODBC) as well as a robust command line interface (CLI) program to interact with Hive.

There are also some nice programmatic extension points for wrapping custom functionality within Hive. This opens up the tool-chain from the Java ecosystem to the enterprising data scientist. These are as follows:

- User-Defined Functions (UDF)
- User-Defined Aggregation Functions

User-defined functions work on some given input without any context beyond what you can pass into the function. While this sounds limiting, it's actually quite powerful. Much can be done with a single piece of data, especially if that data is complex. For instance, wrapping Natural Language Processing (NLP) functions from OpenNLP into Hive UDF's can open up some interesting data analysis opportunities.

User-defined aggregation functions are functions that operate on the entire dataset. These are operations that require building some aggregate state, the size of which does not scale with the size of the data. For instance, you might build a histogram function with fixed bucket sizes as a User-defined aggregation function. The buckets and counts function as the aggregate state, and as data are streamed across the function, the bucket counts are updated. One important aspect of user-defined aggregation functions is that they are algebraic, meaning that partial results can be merged. This capability is sensible, as the functions are applied at scale on separate nodes and merged within an underlying

---

6. As of this writing, the relatively new sub-project, Hive-on-Spark, enables Hive queries to be executed using Spark instead of Tez.

reducer. This implementation detail is not necessarily needed to create a custom aggregate function, but it helps in understanding the underlying assumptions.

There has been some work in constructing machine-learning primitives using an extension of Hive called Hivemall[7] from the Information Technology Research Institute in Japan. It boasts an assortment of algorithms including classification and regression algorithms, as well as some information retrieval primitives such as MinHash, a locality sensitive hash that enables scalable clustering based on set similarity. This illustrates the power of this type of extension.

Hive is a complex system with many features, and, as such, its full description is beyond the scope of this book. We recommend the excellent *Programming HIVE* (Capriolo, Edward, et al. 2012. Sebastopol, CA: O'Reilly & Associates) for more detail.

Let's look at a simple example of how to implement word-count with Hive that you can run from the Hive command line utility or the JDBC-based SQL utility of your choice:

```
CREATE TABLE docs (line_text STRING);
LOAD DATA INPATH '/user/demo/text_file.txt' OVERWRITE INTO TABLE docs;
CREATE TABLE word_count AS
  SELECT word, count(1) AS count FROM
    (SELECT explode(split(line, '\s')) AS word FROM docs) word
  GROUP BY word
  ORDER BY word;
```

## Apache Pig

Apache Pig was created internally at Yahoo! to accommodate the need to implement multi-step extraction, transformation, and load (ETL) inside of Hadoop.

Pig is a domain-specific language (DSL) that is designed to help with ETL tasks. It has relational primitives as well as the capability to easily split processing into multiple logical steps that are optimized into the minimal number of MapReduce or Tez jobs on execution.[8]

Whereas Hive shines for ad-hoc queries, Pig shines on slightly more complex analysis requiring many intermediate results. A good rule of thumb is when you find yourself doing many joins or many intermediate tables in Hive, Pig's syntax might be a better fit for the situation.

Pig, just as Hive, has user-defined functions to extend its functionality. For instance, functions can be created using any language on the JVM as well as streaming user-defined functions that may be implemented, at a performance cost, in any external language that may be called from within the Pig processes.

Just as Hivemall is a set of user-defined functions for Hive, there exist similar types of tooling for Pig. Apache Datafu is a set of Pig user-defined functions, the aim of which

---

7. https://github.com/myui/hivemall

8. Similar to Hive, a relatively new initiative is Pig-on-Spark, which uses Spark as the underlying execution engine.

is to provide some of the tooling required to make data science tasks easier on the Hadoop platform. Datafu is an Apache-incubated project spun out of initial work at LinkedIn. Datafu contains more robust sampling techniques than the built-in functionality within Pig. A broad variety of sampling functions are supported, such as uniform sampling of a fixed set of records rather than by percent, weighted sampling, and sampling with replacement. Descriptive statistical primitives are supported, such as computing quantiles, median, and variance. Additionally, there are user-defined functions that compute descriptive statistics using streaming algorithms, which are more efficient estimation algorithms for quantile, median, and cardinality.

A good description of Pig is far beyond the scope of this book, but we will point the reader to the excellent book, *Programming Pig* (Gates, Alan. 2011. Sebastopol, CA: O'Reilly & Associates).

Instead, let's look at a simple example of the Pig script for word count that can be run from the Pig command line shell called grunt:

```
SENTENCES = load '/user/demo/text_file.txt';
WORDS = foreach SENTENCES generate flatten(TOKENIZE((chararray)$0)) as word;
WORD_GRP = group WORDS by word;
WORD_CNT = foreach WORD_GRP generate group as word, COUNT(WORDS) as count;
store WORD_CNT into '/user/demo/wordcount.txt';
```

In this example, we first load the input file from HDFS into a relation SENTENCES comprised of input text lines. Then we use the foreach projection operator, with the TOKENIZE built-in function to split each line into words. Using the group by operator along with the COUNT built-in function, we count the number of occurrences for each word. Finally, we output the result into the wordcount.txt HDFS file.

## Apache Spark

As mentioned previously, Apache Spark is a relatively new framework for distributed, in-memory data processing. Spark's support for interactive data processing with support for Scala or Python is very effective for pre-processing of data.

Spark's main abstraction is that of a resilient distributed dataset (RDD) on which various relational algebra operators (such as select, filter, join, group by, etc.) as well as any other transformation logic (in Scala or Python) can be applied.

On top of this abstraction there is a newer, more convenient abstraction called a DataFrame to make slicing and dicing data even easier. This API is reminiscent of the convenient slicing and dicing APIs within Python's Pandas library.

Let's look at a simple example of word count with Spark (using Scala) that can be run via the Spark Scala command shell:

```
val file = sc.textFile("/user/demo/text_file.txt")
val counts = file.flatMap(line => line.split(" "))
                 .map(word => (word, 1))
                 .reduceByKey(_ + _)
counts.saveAsTextFile("/user/demo/wordcount.txt")
```

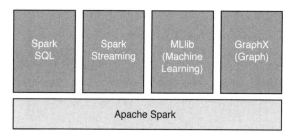

Figure 3.5   Spark architecture.

As it continues to mature, Spark is providing many more capabilities than its original RDD-based processing engine (see Figure 3.5).

Spark SQL provides an alternative to Hive for SQL on distributed datasets. Implemented on top of Spark Core, Spark SQL supports both traditional SQL queries as well as the DataFrames API that provides a more programmatic API for fast and efficient relational algebra processing of large datasets. One of the most interesting things about Spark SQL is that it enables you do to some processing in SQL and then pick up from there in Spark without ever writing out the data to disk.

Spark MLlib provides a machine-learning library that is integrated with the Spark toolset and provides an implementation of various machine-learning algorithms over distributed datasets. The library of algorithms supported continues to grow with each new release of Spark MLlib but already includes many of the most common algorithms such as linear and logistic regression, support vector machines (SVM), decision trees and random forest, $k$-means clustering, singular value decomposition (SVD), and many others.

Spark GraphX provides a library for graphs and graph-parallel computations on top of Spark, with support for common algorithms such as PageRank, label propagation, triangle count, and others.

Spark Streaming (see Figure 3.6) is a component of Spark for building scalable fault-tolerant streaming applications, similar to Apache Storm.[9] This capability takes the form of an extension to the normal Spark API and the capability to process data in slices. Whereas the normal Spark dataset abstraction is a resilient distributed dataset (RDD), the Spark streaming dataset abstraction is a discretized stream (DStream). Processing can then happen on these discretized segments of the stream.

Figure 3.6   Spark streaming.

---

9. Apache Storm is an open-source streaming platform that works on Hadoop: http://storm
   .apache.org/.

# R

R is an open-source language and environment for data manipulation, calculation, statistical analysis, and graphical display. Originally developed by AT&T Labs, R is now a mature, powerful, and very popular language for mathematical computation, statistical analysis, and machine learning.

R is often the first tool for developing new methods of interactive data analysis. It has developed rapidly and has been extended by a large collection of 6000+ packages.

With robust packages for classification, regression, clustering, Bayesian learning, and many other tasks, the R language is one of the most common tools for modeling and visualization. Capabilities include the following:

- Built-in data frame capability, extended by powerful packages such as data.table, dplyr, and others
- Built-in support for generalized linear models via lm() and glm()
- Various R packages for other machine learning algorithms, including random forest, gbm (gradient boosting machines), glmnet (lasso and elastic-net GLM), nnet (neural networks), rpart (decision trees), and cluster (cluster analysis)
- Strong visualization capabilities integrated in the base R environment or extended with packages such as ggplot
- Text mining with packages such as tm

Various R packages have been developed to enable interacting with Hadoop from within the R environment, including:

- RHadoop—A project that includes RMR (MapReduce from R), RHDFS (accessing HDFS files from R), and RHBASE
- RPlyr—"plyr" like interface for HDFS data
- RODBC—ODBC interface from R, often used to interface with Hive directly from the R console

As an example, let's see how word-count is implemented with RMR that can be run via RStudio or the R command line shell:

```
Library(rmr2)
wordcount = function(input, output=NULL) {
  wc.map = function(., lines) {
    keyval(unlist(strsplit(x = lines, split = " ")), 1)
  }
  wc.reduce = function(word, counts) {
    keyval(word, sum(counts))
  }
  mapreduce(input, output, input.format="text",
            map=wc.map, reducer=wc.reduce, combine=T)
}
```

A relatively new but highly promising entrant to the R world is the SparkR project (now formally part of Apache Spark). SparkR provides R fans some exciting (although currently limited) integration into Spark:

- The familiar Spark DataFrames API, useful for manipulating large data-frame-like datasets on Hadoop
- The capability to execute SQL queries over data held inside of Hadoop
- The beginnings of proper machine learning algorithms executable via Spark on R inside the project, including initial support for glm, naïve-Bayes, and $k$-means clustering

## Python

Python is a powerful general-purpose programming language that has recently seen an increase in usage for data science, primarily due to development of powerful Python packages for data manipulation and machine learning:

- Pandas is a powerful Python package for data manipulation and analysis using the data frame abstraction.
- NumPy is the fundamental Python library for scientific computing, which contains a powerful n-dimensional array object and tools for linear algebra, Fourier transform, and random number generation.
- SciPy is another fundamental Python library for scientific and numeric computation and optimization.
- matplotlib is a Python 2D plotting library that is often used for visualization.
- NLTK is a Python library for text mining and natural language processing.
- Spacy is a Python library for natural language processing that is designed for industrial use, with a focus on performance and stability.
- scikit-learn is a machine learning library for Python that is well-integrated with NumPy and Pandas.

Python is also the second most used language for building Hadoop applications (after Java of course):

- Python is often used for MapReduce applications with Hadoop streaming, or with Pig or Hive UDFs.
- Python is one of the core APIs for Spark (PySpark).
- There are various packages to interface with Hadoop from a Python environment, such as Pydoop.

As an example, let's see how to write word-count using PySpark that can be run via the Spark PySpark command shell:

```
file = sc.textFile("hdfs://some-file")
counts = file.flatMap(lambda line: line.split(" ")) \
```

```
        .map(lambda word: (word, 1)) \
            .reduceByKey(lambda a, b: a + b)
counts.saveAsTextFile("hdfs://wordcount-out")
```

## Java Machine Learning Packages

Although R and Python are more popular for modeling purposes in the data science community, Java is also a strong contender and has many mature libraries for both pre-processing and modeling:

- WEKA is a collection of machine learning algorithms in Java, for various data mining tasks.
- Vowpal Wabbit is a Java-based fast machine learning library, originally developed at Yahoo! and continued at Microsoft research.
- OpenNLP, CoreNLP, and Mallet are Java-based packages for statistical natural language processing and other text mining tasks.

Being a first-class citizen in the Hadoop environment, Java continues to be highly used for pre-processing tasks within MapReduce, Tez, or Spark-based applications, and for user-defined functions in Pig or Hive as well as Cascading.

# Why Hadoop Is Useful to Data Scientists

Like its namesake, much of data science is an exercise of constructing hypotheses, designing experiments, and iterating. Hadoop facilitates this type of activity with minimal resistance due to a few fundamental attributes:

- Cost-effective fault tolerant storage
- Multi-language tooling
- Schema on read
- Robust scheduling and resource management
- Multiple levels of distributed systems abstractions
- Scalable creation of models
- Scalable execution of models

## Cost Effective Storage

A happy consequence of running open-source software with resiliency built-in on commodity hardware is an extremely low cost-per-terabyte. This results in a few opportunities that were not as easy to come by in the past.

Having a system that is designed to inexpensively handle petabyte-scale data means that more data can be captured. A corollary to this is that the organizational rules around which data to capture should move from a closed model to an open model. Namely, before, in many organizations, the policy was to only capture data that are known to be useful. Now, it is possible to store and process far more data far more cheaply, so it should be the policy that data should be stored unless known to be useless.

Building transformation pipelines where intermediate forms are stored greatly assists in the analysis and troubleshooting of data. Furthermore, being able to track data through the transformation pipeline leads to better understanding of the assumptions underlying your data and makes the sometimes necessary culling of data reversible. This also means that the first transformation in any data pipeline should be the identity transformation. Put more simply, organizations should store data in raw form first within the platform. Transformations of use to more than one group of people should be stored along the way as part of the refinement of the data. This tree of transformations should maintain a store of lineage to assist the data scientist in his or her task of understanding the data.

Beyond the assistance in understanding the data that having a system of retained materialized views of the data provides, having the flexibility to retain intermediate or experimental data longer also results in a more convenient experience inside the Hadoop platform. This data is not necessarily visible or of interest beyond the individual data scientist, but having a dataset that is snapshotted and immutable greatly simplifies many tasks.

## Schema on Read

Traditionally, in systems centered around relational databases, much focus and attention is placed on perfecting the schema of the data prior to landing the data in the RDBMS (this is often called "schema on write"). Considerations include performance, usage patterns, and others and may have many stakeholders in engineering as well as data science, analytics, or other teams. Gaining consensus on these points, especially for complex data, may take time and delay the ingestion and (more importantly) the analysis of the data.

Hadoop and its ecosystem, much like other NoSQL systems, have been designed to promote a different model, namely, one of schema on read. Schema on read means that the data that is ingested may be interpreted at runtime (in the case of Hive, Pig or Spark SQL, at query time). Because the read schema is divorced from the structure on disk, we decouple interpretation of the data from storage of the data. The storage format of the data may be drastically different (e.g., JSON format or XML format), whereas the "schema on read" may unfold the structure into a tabular format on read.

This approach means that much less up-front work and negotiation must be done prior to the ingestion of the data, and that dramatically reduces the time-to-analysis of the data. Coupled with the low cost of storage, this also means that data understanding and custom transformations may be done on the data directly after ingestion from all parties at once. Once the data is better understood, use cases can be created and common materialized views may be cut. As you can see, this progresses in a much more organic way, with less up-front expense and, consequently, a much lower probability of over-architecting a unified view to fit all interested parties.

Furthermore, schema on read means that you may overlay multiple interpretations on the same raw data.

## Unstructured and Semi-Structured Data

Much of modern data warehousing rests on the principle that data that cannot be interpreted should not be stored. This tenet is due, in part, to a high cost of storage and the strong coupling of read and write schema. Unstructured and semi-structured data is often voluminous and is almost always non-trivial to interpret. This data often takes the form of free text or log data. If it must be interpretable upon ingest to fit within a given structure agreed upon by all the stakeholders, it becomes an insurmountable challenge. As such, the data is often just dropped by the wayside.

The philosophy of storing data in raw form and constructing a processing pipeline after the data is understood combined with inexpensive storage removes much of the traditional barrier to ingestion of unstructured and semi-structured data. Data may be brought into Hadoop, analyzed immediately or at a later date depending on the urgency and value, and transformed to enrich the existing datasets at the leisure of the analyst.

When this type of data was ingested traditionally, it was transformed to a structured form prior to storage. This step has the unfortunate consequence that errors in transformation require re-ingestion of the data and sometimes across all of the data processed.

With Hadoop, because the data is stored on a distributed computing environment, errors in refinement of the semi-structured or unstructured data may be corrected, and the data ingest can be rerun at linear scale. Obviously, errors are never a good thing, but being able to correct them without incurring a startling cost substantially takes the sting out.

## Multi-Language Tooling

We have talked about scripting languages on Hadoop (Hive, Pig, Spark, etc.), but one of the benefits of Hadoop is the rich integration with non-Java languages. Data science tooling varies widely by practitioner and most have a variety of languages whose use depends on the problem being solved. By and large, the prevailing philosophy is to "use the right tool for the job."

Hadoop has principal support for Java and the JVM languages because Hadoop is written largely in Java. However, there exist alternative low-level integrations with Hadoop to any runnable executable via the streaming system. This feature enables Hadoop to communicate with implementations of mappers and reducers via stdin and stdout, in typical Unix fashion.

Walking up the chain of abstractions, the scripting languages such as Hive and Pig both contain the capability to write user-defined functions in JVM languages such as Jython, JavaScript, Scala, or Clojure. Furthermore, you can write user-defined functions in non-JVM languages in the form of streaming UDFs for both Hive and Pig. With Spark, the integration with Scala, Java, or Python is built-in and well-integrated in the API.

Extension points and tighter integrations have increasingly begun to be seen as the system expands to capture the interest of people who are comfortable with a broader variety of systems. This tendency has been promoted with the advent of YARN, which allows multiple types of distributed communication frameworks. Early on you would see integrations that involved pulling data off of Hadoop and onto another proprietary system for analysis. With YARN, more systems are actually provisioning and running inside of Hadoop.

Proprietary systems such as SAS or SAP have ported their systems to run inside of Hadoop. Microsoft, through its acquisition of Revolution Analytics, is building more direct integration with open-source systems such as R to Hadoop. Fundamentally, as Hadoop's presence in the data center increases, you see more people interfacing more closely with it.

## Robust Scheduling and Resource Management

If you take seriously the much-mentioned analogy between Hadoop and an operating system for running analytical applications, one piece must be there in spades—resource management and scheduling. One of the primary roles of a modern operating system is to enable many users to execute applications simultaneously despite limited resources, such as CPU, memory, and disk. Just as in the operating system world, Hadoop must enable many applications to be run on a single Hadoop cluster with limited resources.

The resources in question are CPU and memory available across the cluster. This capability is of interest to data scientists when they consider how their algorithm is distributed across the cluster. For instance, certain algorithms have heavy memory requirements and require large chunks of data to function well, whereas other algorithms can work with limited memory and on individual data elements. Having one cluster that can accommodate both types of workloads is a boon for efficiency and means that resources across departments or groups may be pooled to have a much larger cluster with powerful bursting capabilities.

Just as important as resource management, however, is the capability to reserve computational capacity for certain types of applications. This type of cluster management and scheduling based on group or type of application enables researchers to coexist on the same cluster as high-priority, low-service level agreement jobs that must run within certain timeframes.

## Levels of Distributed Systems Abstractions

Reading what the press says about Hadoop, you would come away with the impression that Hadoop is a system for doing distributed SQL on petabytes of data. The truth, as usual, is more interesting and more complex.

There are a few levels at which you can interact with Hadoop to build analytical applications and ask questions of your data. At the bottom of this layer is interacting with a raw communication model such as MapReduce. This model tends to be useful if your application or query fits well within the bounds of the abstraction and is simple. For instance, in the case of MapReduce, useful means if the query can be asked in a direct way that decomposes into a single MapReduce job. The benefit here is generally speed, and the trade-off is complexity of interacting with a low-level component through a general purpose programming language such as Scala or Java.

At the next level of abstraction are components that will decompose your query into multiple, more fundamental units, such as MapReduce jobs or Tez flows, but which are still interacting with Hadoop at a programmatic level. The benefit here is the greater expressibility and possibly more powerful and complex primitives. For instance, Spark has some relational and set operations in its primitives. The trade-off for this is that the user must understand the consequences of using the more complex primitives as they may have unexpected performance characteristics. Also, as before, one must interact with the system through a general purpose programming language such as Scala or Java.

One level removed from this are the scripting languages aimed at specializing for a given access pattern. Examples here include Pig for ETL style operations and SQL (with Hive SQL or Spark SQL) for relational, structured queries. The benefits here are that the learning curve for picking up these types of languages are generally low, but they can be so specialized that breaking out from what they were aimed to do well can either result in horrendous complexities or be plainly impossible.

At the highest level are domain-specific applications aimed at solving one question and doing it very well. These generally create consumable visualizations or reports. The trade-off is that they are not very adaptable beyond the parameters that the developers have allowed you to modify. They are, however, often fast and full featured for their specific purpose, as they are able to specialize very directly.

## Scalable Creation of Models

The preceding capabilities are great and are (often) aimed at the shared interest of the data scientist, data application developer, and the business that must maintain the Hadoop cluster. There is, however, one aspect of Hadoop that is of interest primarily to the data scientist: the capability to create models at scale using Hadoop.

The creation of models, whether they are basic statistical models or machine learning models, involves exploring your data by aggregating, sampling, and analyzing. In this task, Hadoop can assist without a doubt.

For supervised machine learning models, examples of feature vectors and the expected outcome must be presented to the algorithm in order to build a model that can be applied to data for which the outcome is unknown. This process can be broken into two phases: data preparation/feature extraction and model training.

In the data preparation phase, the problem looks similar to an extract, transform, and load process whereby data is merged, enriched, aggregated, and transformed into the input of your model, called a feature matrix. Hadoop tools like Pig or Spark fit well for this purpose.

The training phase can involve Hadoop in a few ways depending on the machine learning algorithm used. Spark's MLlib provides a robust library of machine learning algorithms (such as generalized linear models, decision trees, random forest, etc.) that are implemented in a distributed and parallelized manner, enabling the data scientist to take advantage of the Hadoop cluster.

If the algorithm is not parallelizable or is not implemented in MLlib, then a few options are at your disposal. You can still use Hadoop to construct the samples of data on which to train your data. Also, it's possible to train multiple models on multiple samples in parallel or do hyper-parameter tuning in parallel.

Where and when Hadoop can assist in the model creation process will be covered in greater depth later in this book, but this should give you a taste of the broad approaches you will see.

## Scalable Application of Models

Model application or scoring on a large dataset is an embarrassingly parallel process and fits well within a MapReduce context or any of the higher-level abstractions such as Pig, Hive, or Spark.

In general, there are two scenarios here: applying the model in batch to a large dataset of observations and integrating the model in a real-time application flow.

For running the model in batch, the main reason for using Hadoop is speed, achieved via distributing the task over the cluster.

If the model is capable of being used from within Java, then it can easily be interacted with either by creating a user-defined function from within Pig or Hive or by being called directly from one of the programmatic interfaces such as Spark or MapReduce. If the model is not capable of being run from within the JVM, then often you will see people using Hadoop streaming, which is a way to call any executable from within a MapReduce job as its map or reduce phase. This feature is useful if a model is written in R, C/C++, or Python. There are performance penalties associated with this approach, but generally it is a drop in the bucket compared to the capability to scale the application of your model across a cluster of computers.

Also, if the model can be exported into the Predictive Model Markup Language (PMML),[10] there are special libraries and utilities designed to use models exported to PMML within Hadoop.

Streaming frameworks for Hadoop, such as Storm or Spark Streaming, provide a natural way to integrate models in a real-time application flow. For example, a trained fraud model can be used to identify potential fraudulent transactions in real time.

# Summary

In this chapter

- We reviewed the Hadoop platform, its history, and its evolution.

- We looked at some of the key data processing engines available on Hadoop such as HDFS, YARN, Hive, Pig, Spark, Sqoop, and Flume as well as popular modeling tools like R and Python.

- We discussed why data scientists love Hadoop and how cost-effective storage, schema on read, and the capability to process both structured and unstructured data makes them more efficient and productive.

---

10. PMML is a tool agnostic XML-based interchange format for predictive models. See https://en.wikipedia.org/wiki/Predictive_Model_Markup_Language for more information.

# II

# Preparing and Visualizing Data with Hadoop

# 4

# Getting Data into Hadoop

*You can have data without information,*
*but you cannot have information without data.*

Daniel Keys Moran

### In This Chapter:

- The data lake concept is presented as a new data processing paradigm.
- Basic methods for importing CSV data into HDFS and Hive tables are presented.
- Additional methods for using Spark to import data into Hive tables or directly for a Spark job are presented.
- Apache Sqoop is introduced as a tool for exporting and importing relational data into and out of HDFS.
- Apache Flume is introduced as a tool for transporting and capturing streaming data (e.g., web logs) into HDFS.
- Apache Oozie is introduced as workflow manager for Hadoop ingestion jobs.
- The Apache Falcon project is described as a framework for data governance (organization) on Hadoop clusters.

No matter what kind of data needs processing, there is often a tool for importing such data from or exporting such data into the Hadoop Distributed File System (HDFS). Once stored in HDFS the data may be processed by any number of tools available in the Hadoop ecosystem.

This chapter begins with the concept of the Hadoop data lake and then follows with a general overview of each of the main tools for data ingestion into Hadoop —Spark, Sqoop, and Flume—along with some specific usage examples. Workflow tools such as Oozie and Falcon are presented as tools that aid in managing the ingestion process.

# Hadoop as a Data Lake

Data is ubiquitous, but that does not always mean that it's easy to store and access. In fact, many existing pre-Hadoop data architectures tend to be rather strict and therefore difficult to work with and make changes to. The data lake concept changes all that.

So what is a data lake?

With the more traditional database or data warehouse approach, adding data to the database requires data to be transformed into a *pre-determined* schema before it can be loaded into the database. This step is often called "extract, transform, and load" (ETL) and often consumes a lot of time, effort, and expense before the data can be used for downstream applications. More importantly, decisions about how the data will be used must be made during the ETL step, and later changes are costly. In addition, data are often discarded in the ETL step because they do not fit into the data schema or are deemed un-needed or not valuable for downstream applications.

One of the basic features of Hadoop is a central storage space for all data in the Hadoop Distributed File Systems (HDFS), which make possible inexpensive and redundant storage of large datasets at a much lower cost than traditional systems.

This enables the Hadoop data lake approach, wherein all data are often stored in raw format, and what looks like the ETL step is performed when the data are processed by Hadoop applications. This approach, also known as schema on read, enables programmers and users to enforce a structure to suit their needs when they access data. The traditional data warehouse approach, also known as schema on write, requires more upfront design and assumptions about how the data will eventually be used.

For data science purposes, the capability to keep all the data in raw format is extremely beneficial since often it is not clear up front which data items may be valuable to a given data science goal.

With respect to big data, the data lake offers three advantages over a more traditional approach:

- All data are **available**. There is no need to make any assumptions about future data use.
- All data are **sharable**. Multiple business units or researchers can use all available data[1], some of which may not have been previously available due to data compartmentalization on disparate systems.
- All **access methods** are available. Any processing engine (MapReduce, Tez, Spark) or application (Hive, Spark-SQL, Pig) can be used to examine the data and process it as needed.

---

1. The capability to use all available data is, of course, governed, as you might expect, by the appropriate security policy with Hadoop tools such as Apache Ranger. The point here is that there is no technical hurdle to data sharing, as is often the case with traditional data architectures.

To be clear, data warehouses are valuable business tools, and Hadoop is designed to complement them, not replace them. Nonetheless, the traditional data warehouse technology was developed before the data lake began to fill with such large quantities of data. The growth of new data from disparate sources including social media, click streams, sensor data, and others is such that we are starting to quickly fill the data lake. Traditional ETL stages may not be able to keep up with the rate at which data are entering the lake. There will be overlap, and each tool will address the need for which it was designed.

The difference between a traditional data warehouse and Hadoop is depicted in Figure 4.1.

Different data sources (A, B, C) can be seen entering either an ETL process or a data lake. The ETL process places the data in a schema as it stores (writes) the data to the relational database. The data lake stores the data in raw form. When a Hadoop application

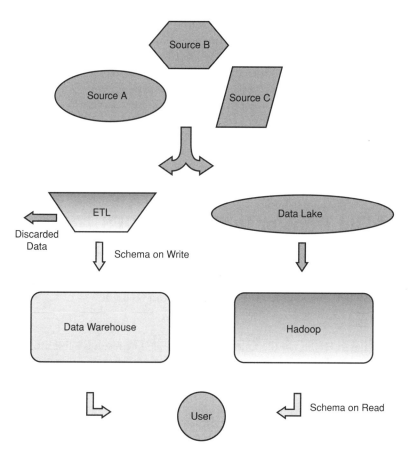

Figure 4.1   The data warehouse versus the Hadoop data lake.

uses the data, the schema is applied to data as they are read from the lake. Note that the ETL step often discards some data as part of the process. In both cases the user accesses the data they need. However, in the Hadoop case it can happen as soon as the data are available in the lake.

# The Hadoop Distributed File System (HDFS)

Virtually all Hadoop applications operate on data that are stored in HDFS. The operation of HDFS is separate from the local file system that most users are accustomed to using. That is, the user must explicitly copy to and from the HDFS file system. HDFS is not a general file system and as such cannot be used as a substitute for existing POSIX (or even POSIX-like) file systems.

In general, HDFS is a specialized streaming file system that is optimized for reading and writing of large files. When writing to HDFS, data are "sliced" and replicated across the servers in a Hadoop cluster. The slicing process creates many small sub-units (blocks) of the larger file and *transparently* writes them to the cluster nodes. The various slices can be processed in parallel (at the same time) enabling faster computation. The user does not see the file slices but interacts with whole files in HDFS like a normal file system (i.e., files can be moved, copied, deleted, etc.). When transferring files out of HDFS, the slices are assembled and written as one file on the host file system.

The slices or sub-units are also replicated across different servers so that the failure of any single server will not result in lost data. Due to its design, HDFS does not support random reads or writes to files but does support appending a file. Note that for testing purposes it is also possible to create a single instance of HDFS on a single hard drive (i.e., a laptop or desktop computer), and in this situation there is no file slicing or replication performed on the file.

# Direct File Transfer to Hadoop HDFS

The easiest way to move data into and out of HDFS is to use the native HDFS commands. These commands are wrappers that interact with the HDFS file system. Local commands, such as `cp`, `ls`, or `mv` will only work on local files. To copy a file (test) from your local file system to HDFS, the following put command can be used:

```
$ hdfs dfs -put test
```

To view files in HDFS use the following command. The result is a full listing similar to a locally executed `ls -l` command:

```
$ hdfs dfs -ls
-rw-r--r--   2 username hdfs          497 2016-05-11 14:32 test
```

To copy a file (another-test) from HDFS to your local file system, use the following get command:

```
$ hdfs dfs -get another-test
```

Other HDFS commands will be introduced in the examples. Appendix B "HDFS Quick Start," provides basic command examples including listing, copying, and removing files in HDFS.

# Importing Data from Files into Hive Tables

Apache Hive is an SQL-like tool for analyzing data in HDFS. Data scientists often want to import data into Hive from existing text-based files exported from spreadsheets or databases. These file formats often include tab-separated values (TSV), comma-separated values (CSV), raw text, JSON, and others. Having the data in Hive tables enables easy access to it for subsequent modeling steps, the most common of which is feature generation, which we discuss in Chapter 5, "Data Munging with Hadoop."

Once data are imported and present as a Hive table, it is available for processing using a variety of tools including Hive's SQL query processing, Pig, or Spark.

Hive supports two types of tables. The first type of table is an *internal table* and is fully managed by Hive. If you delete an internal table, both the definition in Hive *and* the data will be deleted. Internal tables are stored in an optimized format such as ORC and thus provide a performance benefit. The second type of table is an *external table* that is not managed by Hive. External tables use only a metadata description to access the data in its raw form. If you delete an external table, only the definition (metadata about the table) in Hive is deleted and the actual data remain intact. External tables are often used when the data resides outside of Hive (i.e., some other application is also using/creating/managing the files), or the original data need to remain in the underlying location even after the table is deleted.

Due to the large number of use cases, we do not cover all the input methods available to Hive, and instead just a basic example of CSV file import is described. Interested readers can consult the Hive project page, https://hive.apache.org, for more information.

## Import CSV Files into Hive Tables

The following example illustrates how a comma delimited text file (CSV file) can be imported into a Hive table. The input file (names.csv) has five fields (Employee ID, First Name, Title, State, and type of Laptop). The first five lines of the file are as follows:

```
10,Andrew,Manager,DE,PC
11,Arun,Manager,NJ,PC
12,Harish,Sales,NJ,MAC
13,Robert,Manager,PA,MAC
14,Laura,Engineer,PA,MAC
```

The first input step is to create a directory in HDFS to hold the file. Note that, like most Hadoop tools, Hive input is directory-based. That is, input for an operation is taken as all files in a given directory. The following command creates a names directory in the users HDFS directory.

```
$ hdfs dfs -mkdir names
```

In this example, one file is used. However, any number of files could be placed in the input directory. Next the names.csv file is moved into the HDFS names directory.

```
$ hdfs dfs -put name.csv names
```

Once the file is in HDFS, we first load the data as an external Hive table. Start a Hive shell by typing hive at the command prompt and enter the following commands. Note, to cut down on clutter, some of the non-essential Hive output (run times, progress bars, etc.) have been removed from the Hive output.

```
hive> CREATE EXTERNAL TABLE IF NOT EXISTS Names_text(
    > EmployeeID INT,FirstName STRING, Title STRING,
    > State STRING, Laptop STRING)
    > COMMENT 'Employee Names'
    > ROW FORMAT DELIMITED
    > FIELDS TERMINATED BY ','
    > STORED AS TEXTFILE
    > LOCATION '/user/username/names';
OK
```

If the command worked, an OK will be printed. The various fields and the comma delimiter are declared in the command. The final LOCATION statement in the command tells Hive where to find the input files. The import can be verified by listing the first five rows in the table:

```
hive> Select * from Names_text limit 5;
OK
10      Andrew  Manager DE      PC
11      Arun    Manager NJ      PC
12      Harish  Sales   NJ      MAC
13      Robert  Manager PA      MAC
14      Laura   Engineer PA     MAC
```

The next step is to move the external table to an internal Hive table. The internal table must be created using a similar command. However, the STORED AS format offers new options. There are four main file formats for Hive tables in addition to the basic text format. The choice of format depends on the type of data and analysis, but in most cases either ORC or Parquet are used as they provide the best compression and speed advantages for most data types.

- Text file—All data are stored as raw text using the Unicode standard.
- Sequence file—The data are stored as binary key/value pairs.
- RCFile—All data are stored in a column optimized format (instead of row optimized).
- ORC—An optimized row columnar format that can significantly improve Hive performance.
- Parquet—A columnar format that provides portability to other Hadoop tools including Hive, Drill, Impala, Crunch, and Pig.

The following command creates an internal Hive table that uses the ORC format:

```
hive> CREATE TABLE IF NOT EXISTS Names(
    > EmployeeID INT,FirstName STRING, Title STRING,
    > State STRING, Laptop STRING)
    > COMMENT 'Employee Names'
    > STORED AS ORC;
OK
```

To create a table using one of the other formats, change the STORED AS command to reflect the new format. Once the table is created, the data from the external table can be moved to the internal table using the command,

```
hive> INSERT OVERWRITE TABLE Names SELECT * FROM Names_text;
```

As with the external table, the contents can be verified using the following command:

```
hive> Select * from Names limit 5;
OK
10      Andrew  Manager DE      PC
11      Arun    Manager NJ      PC
12      Harish  Sales   NJ      MAC
13      Robert  Manager PA      MAC
14      Laura   Engineer PA     MAC
```

Hive also supports partitions. With partitions, tables can be separated into logical parts that make it more efficient to query a portion of the data. For example, the internal Hive table created previously can also be created with a partition based on the state field. The following command creates a partitioned table:

```
hive> CREATE TABLE IF NOT EXISTS Names_part(
    > EmployeeID INT,
    > FirstName STRING,
    > Title STRING,
    > Laptop STRING)
    > COMMENT 'Employee names partitioned by state'
    > PARTITIONED BY (State STRING)
    > STORED AS ORC;
OK
```

To fill the internal table from the external table for those employed from PA, the following command can be used:

```
hive> INSERT INTO TABLE Names_part PARTITION(state='PA')
    > SELECT EmployeeID, FirstName, Title, Laptop FROM Names_text WHERE
➥ state='PA';
...
OK
```

This method requires each partition key to be selected and loaded individually. When the number of potential partitions is large, this can make data entry inconvenient. To address this issue Hive now supports **dynamic-partition insert** (or multi-partition insert) that is designed to solve this problem by dynamically determining which partitions should be created and populated while scanning the input table.

## Importing Data into Hive Tables Using Spark

Apache Spark is a modern processing engine that is focused on in-memory processing. Spark's primary data abstraction is an immutable distributed collection of items called a resilient distributed dataset (RDD). RDDs can be created from Hadoop input formats (such as HDFS files) or by transforming other RDDs. Each dataset in an RDD is divided into logical partitions, which may be transparently computed on different nodes of the cluster.

The other important data abstraction is Spark's DataFrame. A DataFrame is built on top of an RDD, but data are organized into named columns similar to a relational database table and similar to a data frame in R or in Python's Pandas package.

Spark DataFrames can be created from different data sources such as the following:

- Existing RDDs
- Structured data files
- JSON datasets
- Hive tables
- External databases

Due to its flexibility and friendly developer API, Spark is often used as part of the process of ingesting data into Hadoop. With Spark, you can read data from a CSV file, external SQL or NO-SQL data store, or another data source, apply certain transformations to the data, and store it onto Hadoop in HDFS or Hive. Similar to the Hive examples, a full treatment of all Spark import scenarios is beyond the scope of this book. Consult the Apache Spark project page, http://spark.apache.org, for more information.

The following sections provide some basic usage examples of data import using PySpark (Spark via the Python API), although these steps can also be performed using the Scala or Java interfaces to Spark. Each step is explained. However, a full description of the Spark commands and API are beyond the scope of this book.

All the examples assume the PySpark shell (version 1.6) has been started using the following command:

```
$ pyspark
Welcome to
      ____              __
     / __/__  ___ _____/ /__
    _\ \/ _ \/ _ `/ __/  '_/
   /__ / .__/\_,_/_/ /_/\_\   version 1.6.2
      /_/
```

```
Using Python version 2.7.9 (default, Apr 14 2015 12:54:25)
SparkContext available as sc, HiveContext available as sqlContext.
>>>
```

## Import CSV Files into HIVE Using Spark

Comma-separated value (CSV) files and, by extension, other text files with separators can be imported into a Spark DataFrame and then stored as a HIVE table using the steps described. Note that in this example we show how to use an RDD, translate it into a DataFrame, and store it in HIVE. It is also possible to load CSV files directly into DataFrames using the spark-csv package.

1. The first step imports functions necessary for Spark DataFrame operations:

```
>>> from pyspark.sql import HiveContext
>>> from pyspark.sql.types import *
>>> from pyspark.sql import Row
```

2. Next, the raw data are imported into a Spark RDD. The input file, names.csv, is located in the users local file system and does not have to be moved into HDFS prior to use. (Assuming the local path to the data is /home/username.)

```
>>> csv_data = sc.textFile("file:///home/username/names.csv")
```

3. The RDD can be confirmed by using the type() command:

```
>>> type(csv_data)
<class 'pyspark.rdd.RDD'>
```

4. The comma-separated data are then split using Spark's map() function that creates a new RDD:

```
>>> csv_data  = csv_data.map(lambda p: p.split(","))
```

Most CSV files have a header with the column names. The following steps remove this from the RDD,

```
>>> header = csv_data.first()
>>> csv_data = csv_data.filter(lambda p:p != header)
```

5. The data in the csv_data RDD are put into a Spark SQL DataFrame using the toDF() function. First, however, the data are mapped using the map() function so that every RDD item becomes a Row object which represents a row in the new DataFrame. Note the use of the int() to cast for the employee ID as an integer. All other columns default to a string type.

```
>>> df_csv = csv_data.map(lambda p: Row(EmployeeID = int(p[0]),
➡ FirstName = p[1], Title=p[2], State=p[3], Laptop=p[4])).toDF()
```

The Row() class captures the mapping of the single values into named columns in a row and subsequently transforms the complete data into a DataFrame.

6. The structure and data of the first five rows of the `df_csv` DataFrame are viewed using the following command:

```
>>> df_csv.show(5)
+----------+---------+------+-----+--------+
|EmployeeID|FirstName|Laptop|State|   Title|
+----------+---------+------+-----+--------+
|        10|   Andrew|    PC|   DE| Manager|
|        11|     Arun|    PC|   NJ| Manager|
|        12|   Harish|   MAC|   NJ|   Sales|
|        13|   Robert|   MAC|   PA| Manager|
|        14|    Laura|   MAC|   PA|Engineer|
+----------+---------+------+-----+--------+
only showing top 5 rows
```

7. Similarly, if you'd like to inspect the DataFrame schema, use the `printSchema()` command:

```
>>> df_csv.printSchema()
root
 |-- EmployeeID: long (nullable = true)
 |-- FirstName: string (nullable = true)
 |-- Laptop: string (nullable = true)
 |-- State: string (nullable = true)
 |-- Title: string (nullable = true)
```

8. Finally, to store the DataFrame into a Hive table, use `saveAsTable()`:

```
>>> from pyspark.sql import HiveContext
>>> hc = HiveContext(sc)
>>> df_csv.write.format("orc").saveAsTable("employees")
```

Here we create a HiveContext that is used to store the DataFrame into a Hive table (in ORC format), by using the `saveAsTable()` command.

## Import a JSON File into HIVE Using Spark

Spark can import JSON files directly into a DataFrame. The following is a JSON format-ted version of the names.csv file used in the previous examples. Note that by entering the `EmployeeID` as an un-quoted integer, it will be input as an integer.

```
{"EmployeeID":10,"FirstName":"Andrew","Title":"Manager","State":"DE",
➡ "Laptop":"PC"}
{"EmployeeID":11,"FirstName":"Arun","Title":"Manager","State":"NJ",
➡ "Laptop":"PC"}
{"EmployeeID":12,"FirstName":"Harish","Title":"Sales","State":"NJ",
➡ "Laptop":"MAC"}
```

Also note that Spark expects each line to be a separate JSON object, so it will fail if you try to load a fully formatted JSON file.

1. The first step imports the needed functions and creates a `HiveContext`.

```
>>> from pyspark.sql import HiveContext
>>> hc = HiveContext(sc)
```

Similar to the CSV example, the data file is located in the users local file system.

```
>>> df_json = hc.read.json("file:///home/username/names.json")
```

2. The first five rows of the DataFrame can be viewed using the `df_json.show(5)` command:

```
>>> df_json.show(5)
+----------+---------+------+-----+--------+
|EmployeeID|FirstName|Laptop|State|   Title|
+----------+---------+------+-----+--------+
|        10|   Andrew|    PC|   DE| Manager|
|        11|     Arun|    PC|   NJ| Manager|
|        12|   Harish|   MAC|   NJ|   Sales|
|        13|   Robert|   MAC|   PA| Manager|
|        14|    Laura|   MAC|   PA|Engineer|
+----------+---------+------+-----+--------+
only showing top 5 rows
```

3. To confirm that the `EmployeeID` was indeed cast as an integer, the `df_json` `.printSchema()` command can be used to inspect the DataFrame schema:

```
>>> df_json.printSchema()

root
 |-- EmployeeID: long (nullable = true)
 |-- FirstName: string (nullable = true)
 |-- Laptop: string (nullable = true)
 |-- State: string (nullable = true)
 |-- Title: string (nullable = true)
```

4. Similar to the CSV example, storing this DataFrame back to Hive is simple:

```
>>> df_json.write.format("orc").saveAsTable("employees")
```

# Using Apache Sqoop to Acquire Relational Data

In many enterprise environments, a lot of data that is required for data science applications resides inside of database management systems such as Oracle, MySQL, PosgreSQL, or DB2. Before we can use this data in the context of a data science application, we need to ingest such data into Hadoop.

Sqoop is a tool designed to transfer data between Hadoop and relational databases. You can use Sqoop to import data from a relational database management system (RDBMS) into the Hadoop Distributed File System (HDFS) or export data from Hadoop back into an RDBMS.

Sqoop can be used with any JDBC-compliant database and has been tested on Microsoft SQL Server, PostgreSQL, MySQL, and Oracle. In the remainder of this section, a brief overview of how Sqoop works with Hadoop is provided. In addition, a basic Sqoop example walk-through is demonstrated. To fully explore Sqoop, more information can found by consulting the Sqoop project website at http://sqoop.apache.org.

## Data Import and Export with Sqoop

Figure 4.2 describes the process of importing data into HDFS using Sqoop, which includes two steps. In the first step, Sqoop examines the database to gather the necessary metadata for the data that are to be imported. The second step is a map-only[2] (no reduce step) Hadoop job that Sqoop submits to the cluster. This is the job that does the actual data transfer using the metadata captured in the previous step. Note that each node doing the import must have access to the database.

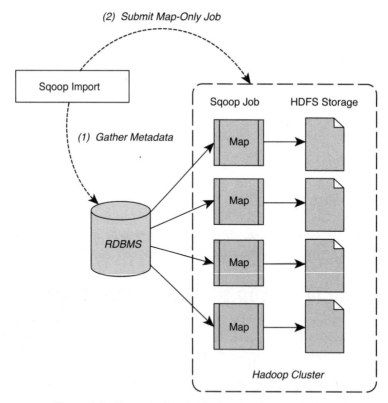

Figure 4.2    Two-step Apache Sqoop data import method.

---

2. A **map-only job** is a term used in the Hadoop ecosystem to refer to a map-reduce job that has some logic implemented in the map stage, and nothing (no-op) in the reduce job.

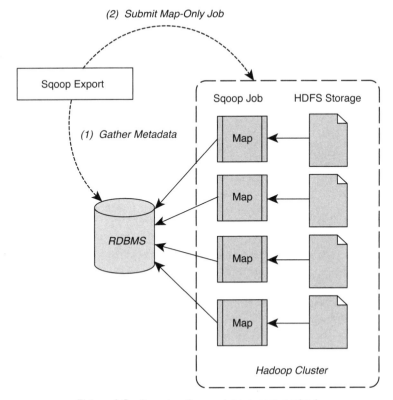

Figure 4.3   Two-step Sqoop data export method.

The imported data is saved in an HDFS directory. Sqoop will use the database name for the directory or the user can specify any alternative directory where the files should be populated. By default, these files contain comma-delimited fields, with new lines separating different records. You can easily override the format in which data is copied over by explicitly specifying the field separator and record terminator characters. Once placed in HDFS, the data are ready for further processing.

Data export from the cluster works in a similar fashion. The export is done in two steps as shown in Figure 4.3. Like the import process, the first step is to examine the database for metadata, followed by the export step that is again a map-only Hadoop job to write the data to the target database. Sqoop divides the input dataset into splits and then uses individual map tasks to push the splits to the database. Again, this process assumes the map tasks have access to the database.

## Apache Sqoop Version Changes

Two versions of Sqoop are in general use within the Hadoop ecosystem. Many users have found the features removed in version 2 to be useful and continue to use the first version. Sqoop version 2 will be used for the examples.

Table 4.1  **Apache Sqoop version comparison.**

| Feature | Sqoop Version 1 | Sqoop Version 2 |
| --- | --- | --- |
| Connectors for all major RDBMS | Supported | Not supported. Use the generic JDBC Connector. |
| Kerberos Security Integration | Supported | Not supported |
| Data transfer from RDBMS to Hive or HBase | Supported | Not supported. First import data from RDBMS into HDFS, then load data into Hive or HBase manually. |
| Data transfer from Hive or HBase to RDBMS | Not supported. First export data from Hive or HBase into HDFS, and then use Sqoop for export. | Not supported. First export data from Hive or HBase into HDFS, and then use Sqoop for export. |

Sqoop version 1 uses specialized connectors to access external database systems. These are often optimized for various RDBMS systems or those that do not support JDBC (Java Database Connectivity). Connectors are plug-in components based on Sqoop's extension framework and can be added to any existing Sqoop installation. Once a connector is installed, Sqoop can use it to efficiently transfer data between Hadoop and the external store supported by the connector. By default, Sqoop version 1 includes connectors for various popular databases such as MySQL, PostgreSQL, Oracle, SQL Server, and DB2. Sqoop version 1 also supports direct transfer to and from the RDBMS for HBase or Hive.

In order to streamline the Sqoop input methods (the issues cited were increasingly complex command lines, security, and the need to understand too many low-level issues), Sqoop version 2 no longer supports specialized connectors or direct import into HBase or Hive or direct data transfer from Hive or HBase to your RDBMS. There are more generalized ways to accomplish these tasks in version 2. All import and export is done through the JDBC interface. Table 4.1 summarizes the changes. Due to these changes, any new development should be done with attention to Sqoop version 2 capabilities.

## Using Sqoop V2: A Basic Example

To better understand how to use Sqoop in practice, we're going to demonstrate how to configure and use Sqoop version 2 via a simple example. The example can then be extended as needed to explore the other capabilities offered by Apache Sqoop. More detailed information can be found at the Sqoop website at http://sqoop.apache.org.

The following steps will be performed:

1. Download and load sample MySQL data
2. Add Sqoop user permissions for local machine and cluster
3. Import data from MySQL to HDFS
4. Export data from HDFS to MySQL

## Step 1: Download a Sample MySQL Database

For this example, we assume MySQL is installed on the Sqoop node and will use the world example database from the MySQL site (http://dev.mysql.com/doc/world-setup/en/index.html). The database has three tables:

- Country—Information about countries of the world.
- City—Information about some of the cities in those countries.
- CountryLanguage—Languages spoken in each country.

1. To get the database, use wget[3] to download and then extract the file:

```
$ wget http://downloads.mysql.com/docs/world.sql.gz
$ gunzip world.sql.gz
```

2. Next, log into MySQL (assumes you have privileges to create a database) and import that database by entering the following commands:

```
$ mysql -u root -p
mysql> CREATE DATABASE world;
mysql> USE world;
mysql> SOURCE world.sql;
mysql> SHOW TABLES;
+-----------------+
| Tables_in_world |
+-----------------+
| City            |
| Country         |
| CountryLanguage |
+-----------------+
3 rows in set (0.01 sec)
```

3. The following MySQL commands will let you see the details for each table (output omitted because of space considerations):

```
mysql> SHOW CREATE TABLE Country;
mysql> SHOW CREATE TABLE City;
mysql> SHOW CREATE TABLE CountryLanguage;
```

## Step 2: Add Sqoop User Permissions for Local Machine and Cluster

Sqoop often needs to talk to MySQL from the Hadoop cluster. Thus, there needs to be permissions added to MySQL so that these conversations can take place. Depending on your installation, you may need to add several privileges for Sqoop requests based on the location (hosts or IP addresses) from where the request originates. For example, the following permissions were assigned for the example.

---

3. wget is a command line tool for Unix/Linux environments that directly downloads files from a valid URL. If using a Windows environment, consider Winwget or a browser. If using a Macintosh environment, consider using curl -O <url> or a browser.

```
mysql> GRANT ALL PRIVILEGES ON world.* To 'sqoop'@'localhost'
➥ IDENTIFIED BY 'sqoop';
mysql> GRANT ALL PRIVILEGES ON world.* To 'sqoop'@'_HOSTAME_'
➥ IDENTIFIED BY 'sqoop';
mysql> GRANT ALL PRIVILEGES ON world.* To 'sqoop'@'_SUBNET_'
➥ IDENTIFIED BY 'sqoop';
FLUSH PRIVILEGES;
mysql> quit
```

The _HOSTNAME_ is the name of the host on which a user has logged in. The _SUBNET_ is the subnet of the cluster (for example 10.0.0.%, defines 10.0.0.0/24 network). These permissions allow any node in the cluster to execute MySQL commands as user sqoop. Also, for the purposes of this example, the Sqoop password is "sqoop."

Next, log in as user sqoop to test the MySQL permissions.

```
$ mysql -u sqoop -p
mysql> USE world;
   mysql> SHOW TABLES;
   +-----------------+
   | Tables_in_world |
   +-----------------+
   | City            |
   | Country         |
   | CountryLanguage |
   +-----------------+
   3 rows in set (0.01 sec)

   mysql> quit
```

### Step 3: Import Data Using Sqoop

As a check of Sqoop's capability to read the MySQL database, we can use Sqoop to list the databases in MySQL.

1. Enter the following commands. The results are after the warnings at the end of the output. Note the use of local _HOSTNAME_ in the JDBC statement. Extra notifications have been removed from the output (represented by ...).

   ```
   $ sqoop list-databases --connect jdbc:mysql://_HOSTNAME_/world
   ➥ --username sqoop --password sqoop
   ...
   information_schema
   test
   world
   ```

2. In a similar fashion, Sqoop can connect to MySQL and list the tables in the world database.

   ```
   $ sqoop list-tables --connect jdbc:mysql://_HOSTNAME_/world
   ➥ --username sqoop --password sqoop
   ...
   City
   Country
   CountryLanguage
   ```

3. In order to import data, we need to make a directory in HDFS:

```
$ hdfs dfs -mkdir sqoop-mysql-import
```

4. The following command will import the Country table into HDFS:

```
$ sqoop import --connect jdbc:mysql://_HOSTNAME_/world  --username
➥ sqoop --password sqoop --table Country  -m 1 --target-dir
➥ /user/username/sqoop-mysql-import/country
```

The option --table signifies the table to import, --target-dir is the directory created above, and -m 1 tells sqoop to use a single map task (which is enough in our example since it is only a small table) to import the data.

5. The import can be confirmed by examining HDFS:

```
$ hdfs dfs -ls sqoop-mysql-import/country
Found 2 items
-rw-r--r--   2 username hdfs              0 2014-08-18 16:47 sqoop-mysql-
➥import/world/_SUCCESS
-rw-r--r--   2 username hdfs          31490 2014-08-18 16:47 sqoop-mysql-
➥import/world/part-m-00000
```

6. The file can be viewed using the hdfs -cat command:

```
$ hdfs dfs -cat sqoop-mysql-import/country/part-m-00000
ABW,Aruba,North America,Caribbean,193.0,null,103000,78.4,828.0,793.0,
➥ Aruba,Nonmetropolitan Territory of The Netherlands,Beatrix,129,AW
...
ZWE,Zimbabwe,Africa,Eastern Africa,390757.0,1980,11669000,37.8,
➥ 5951.0,8670.0,Zimbabwe,Republic,Robert G. Mugabe,4068,ZW
```

To make Sqoop commands more convenient, an options file may be created and used in the command line. This file will help you avoid having to rewrite the same options. For example, a file called world-options.txt with the following contents will include the import command, --connect, --username, and --password options:

```
import
--connect
jdbc:mysql://_HOSTNAME_/world
--username
sqoop
--password
sqoop
```

The same import command from the preceding can be performed with the following shorter line:

```
$ sqoop  --options-file world-options.txt --table City  -m 1 --target-dir
➥ /user/username/sqoop-mysql-import/city
```

It is also possible to include an SQL Query in the import step. For example, if we want just cities in Canada:

```
SELECT ID,Name from City WHERE CountryCode='CAN'
```

Then we can include the `--query` option in the Sqoop import request. In the following query example, a single mapper task is designated with the `-m 1` option:

```
sqoop  --options-file world-options.txt -m 1 --target-dir
➥ /user/username/sqoop-mysql-import/canada-city --query
➥ "SELECT ID,Name from City
➥ WHERE CountryCode='CAN' AND \$CONDITIONS"
```

Inspecting the results shows only cities from Canada are imported.

```
$ hdfs dfs -cat sqoop-mysql-import/canada-city/part-m-00000
```

```
1810,Montréal
1811,Calgary
1812,Toronto
...
1856,Sudbury
1857,Kelowna
1858,Barrie
```

Since there was only one mapper process, only one copy of the query needed to be run on the database. The results are also reported in single file (`part-m-0000`). Multiple mappers can be used to process the query if the `--split-by` option is used. The split-by option is a way to parallelize the SQL query. Each parallel task runs a subset of the main query with results partitioned by bounding conditions inferred by Sqoop. Your query must include the token `$CONDITIONS`; this is a placeholder for Sqoop to put in unique condition expression based on the `--split-by` option, and Sqoop automatically populates this with the right conditions for each mapper task. Sqoop will try to create balanced sub-queries based on a range of your primary key. However, it may be necessary to split on another column if your primary key is not uniformly distributed.

The following example will help illustrate the `-split-by` option. First, remove the results of the previous query.

```
$ hdfs dfs -rm -r -skipTrash  sqoop-mysql-import/canada-city
```

Next, run the query using four mappers (`-m 4`) where we split by the ID number (`--split-by ID`).

```
sqoop  --options-file world-options.txt -m 4 --target-dir
➥ /user/username/sqoop-mysql-import/canada-city --query "SELECT ID,
➥ Name from City WHERE CountryCode='CAN' AND \$CONDITIONS" --split-by ID
```

If we look at the number of results files, we find four files corresponding to the four mappers we requested in the command. There is no need to combine these files into one entity because all Hadoop tools can manage multiple files as input.

```
$ hdfs dfs -ls  sqoop-mysql-import/canada-city
Found 5 items
-rw-r--r--   2 username hdfs        0 2014-08-18 21:31 sqoop-mysql-import/canada-
city/_SUCCESS
-rw-r--r--   2 username hdfs      175 2014-08-18 21:31 sqoop-mysql-import/canada-
city/part-m-00000
```

```
-rw-r--r--   2 username hdfs      153 2014-08-18 21:31 sqoop-mysql-import/canada-
city/part-m-00001
-rw-r--r--   2 username hdfs      186 2014-08-18 21:31 sqoop-mysql-import/canada-
city/part-m-00002
-rw-r--r--   2 username hdfs      182 2014-08-18 21:31 sqoop-mysql-import/canada-
city/part-m-00003
```

## Step 4: Export Data Using Sqoop

The first step when exporting data with Sqoop is to create tables in the target database system for the exported data. There are actually two tables needed for each exported table. The first is a table to hold the exported data (e.g., CityExport) and the second is a table to be used for staging the exported data (e.g., CityExportStaging).

1. Using the following MySQL commands, you can create the tables:

```
mysql> USE world;
mysql> CREATE TABLE `CityExport` (
         `ID` int(11) NOT NULL AUTO_INCREMENT,
         `Name` char(35) NOT NULL DEFAULT '',
         `CountryCode` char(3) NOT NULL DEFAULT '',
         `District` char(20) NOT NULL DEFAULT '',
         `Population` int(11) NOT NULL DEFAULT '0',
         PRIMARY KEY (`ID`));
mysql> CREATE TABLE `CityExportStaging` (
         `ID` int(11) NOT NULL AUTO_INCREMENT,
         `Name` char(35) NOT NULL DEFAULT '',
         `CountryCode` char(3) NOT NULL DEFAULT '',
         `District` char(20) NOT NULL DEFAULT '',
         `Population` int(11) NOT NULL DEFAULT '0',
         PRIMARY KEY (`ID`));
```

2. Next, create a cities-export-options.txt file similar to the world-options.txt file created above, using the export instead of import command. The following will export the cities data we imported above back into MySQL:

```
sqoop --options-file cities-export-options.txt --table CityExport
➥ --staging-table CityExportStaging  --clear-staging-table -m 4
➥ --export-dir /user/username/sqoop-mysql-import/city
```

3. Finally, to make sure everything worked, check the table in MySQL to see if the cities are in the table.

```
$ mysql> select * from CityExport limit 10;
+----+---------------+-------------+---------------+------------+
| ID | Name          | CountryCode | District      | Population |
+----+---------------+-------------+---------------+------------+
|  1 | Kabul         | AFG         | Kabol         |    1780000 |
|  2 | Qandahar      | AFG         | Qandahar      |     237500 |
|  3 | Herat         | AFG         | Herat         |     186800 |
|  4 | Mazar-e-Sharif| AFG         | Balkh         |     127800 |
|  5 | Amsterdam     | NLD         | Noord-Holland |     731200 |
|  6 | Rotterdam     | NLD         | Zuid-Holland  |     593321 |
```

```
|  7 | Haag          | NLD | Zuid-Holland   |  440900 |
|  8 | Utrecht       | NLD | Utrecht        |  234323 |
|  9 | Eindhoven     | NLD | Noord-Brabant  |  201843 |
| 10 | Tilburg       | NLD | Noord-Brabant  |  193238 |
+----+---------------+------------+----------------+------------+
```

10 rows in set (0.00 sec)

### Some Handy Clean-up Commands

If you are not real familiar with MySQL, the following commands may be helpful to clean up the examples.

To remove a table in MySQL:

```
mysql> Drop table `CityExportStaging`;
```

To remove the data in a table:

```
mysql> delete from CityExportStaging;
```

To clean up imported files:

```
$ hdfs dfs -rm -r  -skipTrash sqoop-mysql-import/{country,city,
➥ canada-city}
```

# Using Apache Flume to Acquire Data Streams

In addition to structured data in databases, another common source of data is log files, which usually come in the form of continuous (streaming) incremental files often from multiple source machines. In order to use this type of data for data science with Hadoop, we need a way to ingest such data into HDFS.

Apache Flume is designed to collect, transport, and store data streams into HDFS. Often data transport involves a number of Flume agents that may traverse a series of machines and locations. Flume is often used for log files, social-media-generated data, email messages, and pretty much any continuous data source.

As shown in Figure 4.4, a Flume agent is composed of three components:

- **Source**—The source component receives data and sends it to a channel. It can send the data to more than one channel. The input data can be from a real-time source (e.g. web log) or another Flume agent.

- **Channel**—A channel is a data queue that forwards the source data to the sink destination. It can be thought of as a buffer that manages input (source) and output (sink) flow rates.

- **Sink**—The sink delivers data to destinations such as HDFS, a local file, or another Flume agent.

A Flume agent can have multiple sources, channels, and sinks but must have at least one of each of the three components defined. Sources can write to multiple channels, but a sink can only take data from a single channel. Data written to a channel remain

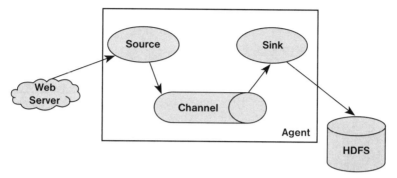

Figure 4.4    Flume Agent with Source, Channel, and Sink.

in the channel until a sink removes the data. By default, the data in a channel is kept in memory but optionally may be stored on disk to prevent data loss in the event of a network failure.

As shown in Figure 4.5, Flume agents may be placed in a pipeline. This configuration is normally used when data is collected on one machine (e.g., a web server) and sent to another machine that has access to HDFS.

In a Flume pipeline, the sink from one agent is connected to the source of another. The data transfer format normally used by Flume is called Apache Avro[4] and provides several useful features. First, Avro is a data serialization/deserialization system that uses a compact binary format. The schema is sent as part of the data exchange and is defined using JavaScript Object Notation (JSON ). Avro also uses remote procedure calls (RPC) to send data. That is, an Avro sink will contact an Avro source to send data.

Another useful Flume configuration is shown in Figure 4.6. In this configuration, Flume is used to consolidate several data sources before committing them to HDFS.

There are many possible ways to construct Flume transport networks.

The full scope of Flume functionality is beyond the scope of this book, and there are many additional features in Flume such as plug-ins and interceptors that can enhance

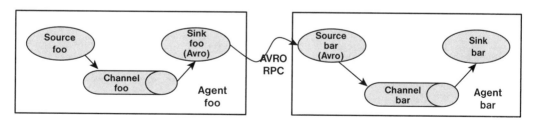

Figure 4.5    Pipeline created by connecting Flume agents.

---

4. https://avro.apache.org/

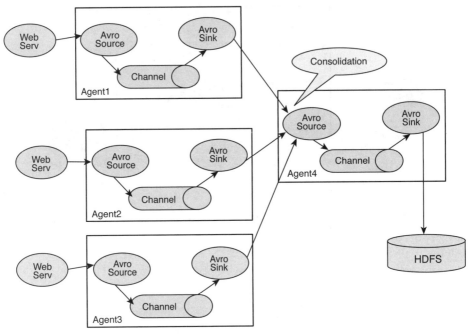

Figure 4.6    A Flume consolidation network.

Flume pipelines. For more information and example configurations, please see the
Flume Users Guide at https://flume.apache.org/FlumeUserGuide.html.

## Using Flume: A Web Log Example Overview

In this example web logs from the local machine will be placed into HDFS using Flume.
This example is easily modified to use other web logs from different machines. The full
source code and further implementation notes are available from the book web page in
Appendix A, "Book Web Page and Code Download." Two files are needed to configure
Flume. (See the sidebar "Flume Configuration Files.")

- `web-server-target-agent.conf`—The target Flume agent that writes the data
  to HDFS
- `web-server-source-agent.conf`—The source Flume agent that captures the web
  log data

The web log is also mirrored on the local file system by the agent that writes to HDFS.

1. To run the example, create the directory as root.

```
# mkdir /var/log/flume-hdfs
# chown hdfs:hadoop /var/log/flume-hdfs/
```

2. Next, as user `hdfs`, make a Flume data directory in HDFS.

```
$ hdfs dfs -mkdir /user/hdfs/flume-channel/
```

3. Now that the data directories are created, the Flume target agent can be started (as user hdfs).

```
$ flume-ng agent -c conf -f web-server-target-agent.conf -n collector
```

This agent writes the data into HDFS and should be started before the source agent. (The source reads the web logs.)

### Note

In some Hadoop distributions, Flume can be started as a service when the system boots, such as "service start flume." This configuration allows for automatic use of the Flume agent. The `/etc/flume/conf/{flume.conf,flume-env.sh.template}` files need to be configured for this purpose. For this example, the `/etc/flume/conf/flume.conf` file can be the same as the web-server-target.conf file (modified for your environment).

The source agent can be started as root, which will start to feed the web log data to the target agent. Note that the source agent can be on another machine:

```
# flume-ng agent -c conf -f web-server-source-agent.conf -n source_agent
```

To see if Flume is working, check the local log by using `tail`. Also check to make sure the flume-ng agents are not reporting any errors (filename will vary).

```
$ tail -f /var/log/flume-hdfs/1430164482581-1
```

The contents of the local log under flume-hdfs should be identical to that written into HDFS. The file can be inspected using the `hdfs -tail` command. (filename will vary). Note, while running Flume, the most recent file in HDFS may have a .tmp appended to it. The .tmp indicates that the file is still being written by Flume. The target agent can be configured to write the file (and start another .tmp file) by setting some or all of the `rollCount`, `rollSize`, `rollInterval`, `idleTimeout`, and `batchSize` options in the configuration file.

```
$ hdfs dfs -tail flume-channel/apache_access_combined/150427/FlumeData.
➥1430164801381
```

Both files should have the same data in them. For instance, the preceding example had the following in both files:

```
10.0.0.1 - - [27/Apr/2015:16:04:21 -0400] "GET /ambarinagios/nagios/nagios_alerts
.php?q1=alerts&alert_type=all HTTP/1.1" 200 30801 "-" "Java/1.7.0_65"
10.0.0.1 - - [27/Apr/2015:16:04:25 -0400] "POST /cgi-bin/rrd.py HTTP/1.1" 200 784
"-" "Java/1.7.0_65"
10.0.0.1 - - [27/Apr/2015:16:04:25 -0400] "POST /cgi-bin/rrd.py HTTP/1.1" 200 508
"-" "Java/1.7.0_65"
```

Both the target and source file can be modified to suit your system.

## Flume Configuration Files

A complete explanation of Flume configuration is beyond the scope of this chapter. The Flume website has additional information on Flume configuration at http://flume.apache .org/FlumeUserGuide.html#configuration.

The two files describe two Flume agents that have separate Source/Channel/Sink configurations. Some of the important settings used in the example above are as follows:

In `web-server-source-agent.conf`, the following lines set the source. Note that the web log is acquired by using the `tail` command to record the log file.

```
source_agent.sources = apache_server
source_agent.sources.apache_server.type = exec
source_agent.sources.apache_server.command = tail -f /etc/httpd/logs/access_log
```

Further down in the file, the sink is defined. The parameter `source_agent.sinks.avro_sink.hostname` is used to assign the Flume node that will write to HDFS. The port number is also set in the target configuration file.

```
source_agent.sinks = avro_sink
source_agent.sinks.avro_sink.type = avro
source_agent.sinks.avro_sink.channel = memoryChannel
source_agent.sinks.avro_sink.hostname =  192.168.93.24
source_agent.sinks.avro_sink.port = 4545
```

The HDFS settings are placed in the web-server-target-agent.conf file. Note the path that was used in the previous example and the data specification.

```
collector.sinks.HadoopOut.type = hdfs
collector.sinks.HadoopOut.channel = mc2
collector.sinks.HadoopOut.hdfs.path = /user/hdfs/flume-channel/%{log_type}/
%y%m%d
collector.sinks.HadoopOut.hdfs.fileType = DataStream
```

The target file also defines the port and two channels (mc1 and mc2). One of the channels writes the data to the local file system and the other writes to HDFS. The relevant lines are shown in the following:

```
collector.sources.AvroIn.port = 4545
collector.sources.AvroIn.channels = mc1 mc2

collector.sinks.LocalOut.sink.directory = /var/log/flume-hdfs
collector.sinks.LocalOut.channel = mc1
```

The HDFS file rollover counts create a new file when a threshold is exceeded. In this example, allow any file size and write a new file after 10,000 events or 600 seconds.

```
collector.sinks.HadoopOut.hdfs.rollSize = 0
collector.sinks.HadoopOut.hdfs.rollCount = 10000
collector.sinks.HadoopOut.hdfs.rollInterval = 600
```

A full discussion of Flume can be found on the website at https://flume.apache.org.

# Manage Hadoop Work and Data Flows with Apache Oozie

Apache Oozie is a workflow scheduler system designed to run and manage multiple related Apache Hadoop jobs. For instance, complete data input and analysis may require several discrete Hadoop jobs to be run as a workflow where the output of one job will be the input for a successive job. Oozie is designed to construct and manage these workflows.

Oozie is not a substitute for the YARN scheduler mentioned previously. That is, YARN manages resources for individual Hadoop jobs, and Oozie provides a way to connect and control multiple Hadoop jobs on the cluster.

Oozie workflow jobs are represented as DAGs of actions. There are three types of Oozie jobs:

- **Workflow:** A specified sequence of Hadoop jobs with outcome-based decision points and control dependency. Progress from one action to another cannot happen until the first action is complete.

- **Coordinator**: A scheduled workflow job that can run at various time intervals or when data becomes available.

- **Bundle**: A higher-level Oozie abstraction that will batch a set of coordinator jobs.

Oozie is integrated with the rest of the Hadoop stack supporting several types of Hadoop jobs out of the box (such as Java MapReduce, Streaming MapReduce, Pig, Hive, Spark, and Sqoop) as well as system-specific jobs (such as Java programs and shell scripts). Oozie also provides a CLI and a Web UI for monitoring jobs. An example of a simple Oozie workflow is shown in Figure 4.7. In this example, Oozie runs a basic MapReduce operation. If the application was successful the job ends; if there was an error, the job is killed.

Oozie workflow definitions are written in Hadoop Process Definition Language (hPDL), which is an XML-based process definition language. Oozie workflows contain several types of nodes.

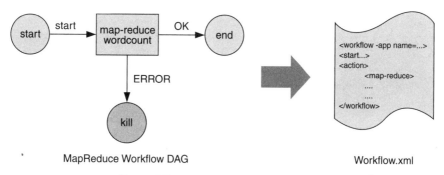

Figure 4.7   A simple Oozie DAG workflow.

- **Start/Stop control flow nodes** define the beginning and the end of a workflow. These include start, end, and optional fail nodes.

- **Action nodes** are where the actual processing tasks are defined. When an action node finishes, the remote systems notify Oozie and the next node in the workflow is executed. Action nodes can also include HDFS commands.

- **Fork/join nodes** allow parallel execution of tasks in the workflow. The fork node allows two or more tasks to run at the same time. A join node represents a rendezvous point that must wait until all forked tasks complete.

- **Control flow nodes** enable decisions to be made about the previous task. Control decisions are based on the results of the previous action (e.g. file size or file existence). Decision nodes are essentially switch-case statements that use JSP EL (Java Server Pages-Expression Language) that evaluates to either true or false.

A more complex workflow that uses all the above nodes is shown in the example workflow in Figure 4.8. More information on Oozie can be found at http://oozie.apache.org/docs/4.0.0/index.html.

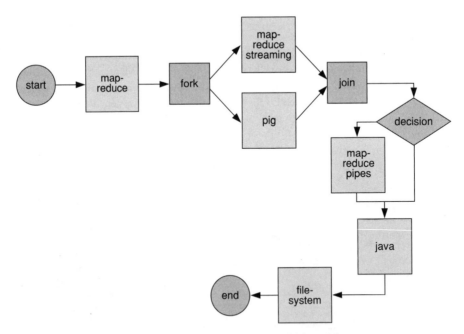

Figure 4.8   A more complex Oozie DAG workflow.

# Apache Falcon

Apache Falcon simplifies the configuration of data motion by providing replication, life cycle management, lineage, and traceability. These features provide data governance consistency across Hadoop components that is not possible using Oozie. For instance, Falcon allows Hadoop administrators to centrally define their **data pipelines**, and then Falcon uses those definitions to auto-generate workflows in Apache Oozie. In simple terms, proper use of Falcon helps keep your active Hadoop cluster from becoming a confusing mess.

For example, Oozie lets you define Hadoop processing through workflow and coordinator (a recurring workflow) jobs. The input datasets for data processing are often described as part of coordinator jobs that specify properties such as path, frequency, schedule runs, and so on. If there are two coordinator jobs that depend on the same data, these details have to be defined and managed twice. If you want to add shared data deletion or movement, a separate coordinator is required. Oozie will certainly work in these situations, but there is no easy way to define and track the entire data life cycle or manage multiple independent Oozie jobs.

Oozie is useful when initially setting up and testing workflows and can be used when the workflows are independent and not expected to change often. If there are multiple dependencies between workflows or there is a need to manage the entire data life cycle, then Falcon should be considered.

As mentioned, as Hadoop's high-level workflow scheduler, Oozie may be managing hundreds to thousands of coordinator jobs and files. This situation results in some common mistakes. Processes might use the wrong copies of datasets. Datasets and processes may be duplicated, and it becomes increasingly more difficult to track down where a particular dataset originated. At that level of complexity, it becomes difficult to manage so many dataset and process definitions.

To solve these problems, Falcon allows the creation of a pipeline that is defined by three key attributes:

- A **cluster** entity that defines where data, tools, and processes live on your Hadoop cluster. A cluster entity contains things like the namenode address, Oozie URL, etc., which it uses to execute the other two entities: feeds and processes.

- A **feed** entity defines where data live on your cluster (in HDFS). The feed is designed to designate to Falcon where your new data (that's either ingested, processed, or both) live so it can retain (through retention policies) and replicate (through replication policies) the data on or from your Cluster. A feed is typically (but doesn't have to be) the output of a process.

- A **process** entity defines what action or "process" will be taking place in a pipeline. Most typically, the process links to an Oozie workflow, which contains a series of actions to execute (such as shell scripts, Java Jars, Hive actions, Pig actions, Sqoop Actions, you name it) on your cluster. A process also, by definition, takes feeds as inputs or outputs and is where you define how often a workflow should run.

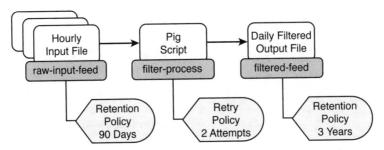

Figure 4.9    A simple Apache Falcon workflow.

The following example will help explain how Falcon is used. Assume there is raw input data that arrives every hour. These data are processed with a Pig script and the results saved for later processing. At a simple level an Oozie workflow could easily manage the task. However, high-level features, not available in Oozie, are needed to automate the process. First, the input data have a retention policy of 90 days, after which old data are discarded. Second, the processing step may have a certain number of retries should the process fail. And, finally, the output data have a retention policy of three years (and location). It is also possible to query data lineage with Falcon (i.e., Where did this data come from?). The simple job flow is shown in Figure 4.9.

## What's Next in Data Ingestion?

As the Hadoop platform continues to evolve, innovation in ingestion tools continues. Two important new tools are now available to ingestion teams that we would like to mention:

- **Apache Nifi** is a recent addition to the data ingestion toolset. Originally created at the NSA and recently open sourced and added to the Apache family, Nifi provides a scalable way to define data routing, transformation, and system mediation logic. An excellent UI makes building data flows in Nifi fast and easy. Nifi provides support for lineage tracking and the security and monitoring capability that make it a great tool for data ingestion, especially for sensor data.
- **Apache Atlas** provides a set of core data governance services that enables enterprises to effectively deal with compliance requirements on Hadoop.

## Summary

In this chapter

- The Hadoop data lake concept was presented as a new model for data processing.
- Various methods for making data available to several Hadoop tools were outlined. The examples included copying files directly to HDFS, importing CSV files to Apache Hive and Spark, and importing JSON files into HIVE with Spark.

- Apache Sqoop was presented as a tool for moving relational data into and out of HDFS.

- Apache Flume was presented as tool for capturing and transporting continuous data, such as web logs, into HDFS.

- The Apache Oozie workflow manager was described as a tool for creating and scheduling Hadoop workflows.

- The Apache Falcon tool enables a high-level framework for data governance (end-to-end management) by keeping Hadoop data and tasks organized and defined as pipelines.

- New tools like Apache Nifi and Atlas were mentioned as options for governance and data flow on a Hadoop cluster.

# 5

# Data Munging with Hadoop

*If you torture the data long enough, it will confess.*

Ronald Coase, Economist

## In This Chapter:

- What data quality is, the different types of data quality issues that arise in data, and how to address them with Hadoop
- The importance of feature generation, various types of features, and how to generate features for your model with Hadoop
- Feature selection and dimensionality reduction and its importance in addressing the curse of dimensionality

As every data scientist knows, about 70–80% of the time spent in data science projects is in what is commonly known as **data munging**—a popular term that refers to two main activities:

- Identifying and remediating data quality problems
- Transforming the raw data into what is known as a **feature matrix**, a task commonly referred to as **feature generation** or **feature engineering**

This chapter describes why Hadoop is essential for data munging of large datasets and provides some examples of data munging techniques with Hadoop.

A variety of examples are shown throughout the chapter. For consistency, these examples have been created from the same dataset, the CMS dataset, described below.

As part of the US government's efforts to make the healthcare system more transparent and accountable, the Centers for Medicare and Medicaid Services (CMS) released data surrounding payments rendered to and procedures provided by physicians to Medicare beneficiaries. The data contains information such as

- The NPI (National Provider Identifier) of the physician rendering services
- The physician's specialty

- The code of the procedure rendered
- The place of service
- Aggregate payment information for the rendering physician

The examples in this chapter are based on the CMS data from 2013.

# Why Hadoop for Data Munging?

Before the era of very large datasets, most data munging in data science was done with the same tools used for modeling: R, Python, SAS, SPSS, and others. The raw data was small enough to fit in memory on a desktop, a laptop, or, if needed, a back-end server.

Nowadays, in the era of big data, raw data size is typically measured in terabytes or petabytes, and thus processing such large datasets in memory becomes difficult, if not impossible.

Hadoop is an ideal platform for both storing such datasets and processing them at large scale. The most common tools for data munging at large scale are Pig, Hive, or Spark. In the rest of the chapter we show examples of various data munging tasks performed with these tools.

# Data Quality

In a typical enterprise environment, you find various datasets coming from various sources such as operational databases, social networks, or sensor data. It is almost always the case that these data sources have significant data quality issues that need to be addressed before any data mining activity is started.

## What Is Data Quality?

Data quality is not a new idea. In fact, it dates back to the early days of mainframe computing, when "data quality control" was sold as a service to many organizations and later on moved inside the corporate walls. One of the earliest use cases for data quality arose from maintaining customer names and addresses. Companies used expensive mainframe computers to maintain a list of their customers along with their mailing address, in order to send them all kinds of marketing materials. Keeping tabs on change of address and other related information became crucial for the success of such marketing efforts and resulted in large, expensive data quality projects. At some point, government agencies decided to make data in the National Change of Address (NCOA) registry available and thus saved companies millions in automating this process.

In the context of data science, data quality has a broad interpretation, and we classify it into five distinct areas: completeness, validity, consistency, timeliness, and accuracy.

**Completeness** refers to having all the parts of the data. For example, consider a dataset that includes customer records, where each record is composed of first name, last name, age, gender, street address, city, and zip code. It's possible (and unfortunately often the case) that one or more of these fields includes many missing values—for example, we may not know the age of some portion of this population.

Missing values are notoriously difficult to deal with in a data mining context, and so it is important to make every effort to avoid missing data, or at the very least minimize this phenomenon. In many cases, the missing data may be due to a problematic ingestion process, which is easily fixable once discovered.

**Validity** refers to whether data values are actual, legitimate attributes of the thing they represent. Continuing with our previous example, consider a case where zip code data sometimes contains values that are not authentic—the five numbers simply do not correspond to any actual zip code in use. This is clearly a very bad situation, even worse than missing data, since our modeling efforts will work very hard to model the wrong thing. Fixing these at the source is of utmost importance.

**Consistency** refers to having data items represented in the same manner. For example, we can decide that the gender field must have a value of "M," "F," or NULL (representing unknown gender), but then all datasets must consistently adhere to this agreement or be translated from their original representation to the new one. As another example, consider what might occur if the same customer record has an address in Florida and a zip code in California. Clearly here data across fields is inconsistent, and this needs to be addressed. This example becomes especially challenging in situations where multiple datasets, each individually consistent but with different conventions, are merged.

**Timeliness** usually refers to having values that are not stale. For example, if the address and zip code were correct at one time but are now incorrect because the customer has since moved to a different house, the data is not timely. This goal is especially difficult to achieve as it requires mature processes for re-evaluation and updating of data.

**Accuracy** can mean various things in the context of data quality, but we usually think of it in the numerical sense. For example, the age of a customer might be 75 whereas our data says 78.

## Dealing with Data Quality Issues

Detecting or identifying data quality issues is not as easy as it may appear. We now describe four high-level approaches that are common in practice:

- Cell-based rules
- Static "value distribution" rules
- Differential "value distribution" rules
- Outlier analysis

It is important to understand that some of these approaches are either fundamentally probabilistic or may not be sufficient by themselves, and that false positives can and will happen. Building techniques and infrastructure whereby data quality issues are corrected when there is a deterministic and repeatable error and an alert is raised when the indication is only suspected will save time and headaches in the future.

## Cell-Based Rules

The first and most common approach is to define a set of cell-based rules to identify, and where possible correct, data quality issues on each individual cell in the data. These rules can check for valid format, valid value, or various other properties to which the data must adhere.

To demonstrate what these rules might look like, let's continue our earlier example of the customer record. Here are some possible example rules for this data:

- **Rule 1**: First/last name must contain only alphabetical characters, and the first character must be capitalized.
- **Rule 2:** Zip code must contain five numerical digits and be a valid zip code (check against an external database of valid zip codes).
- **Rule 3:** Age must be a numerical integer value between 0 and 120 (or some other reasonable value at the higher end of the range).

For any of these rules, it is not always clear what to do if a data quality issue is discovered. For example, if you find a zip code that looks like "123456," do you convert it to "12345" or "23456," or do you just put NULL instead, representing an unknown value? The solution is often problem dependent and/or domain specific. An "easy" solution that is often applied is to use NULL instead of the invalid value, but that results in more missing values, which is problematic for later modeling steps.

A more robust approach to a solution might be possible in many cases. For example, if the address field is valid, we can look up the zip code using the address and not only get a valid zip code but also validate the consistency of the address with the zip code.

## Static "Value Distribution" Rules

Another common approach to data quality issue detection is to compare the distribution of a certain field to an "expected distribution" and raise an alert if the actual distribution is "too distant" from the expected distribution.

Going back to our customer record example, we might determine a certain expected distribution of the ages within our customer base. For example, we might know that 20% of our customers are under 18, 20% are between 18 and 25, 20% are between 25 and 50, and 40% are 50 or above. Measuring the actual distribution in our dataset and comparing it to these expected values, we can trigger an alert if the actual percentages are more than 2% off the expected percentage values.

An interesting and well-known example of comparing value distributions is the application of Benford's Law[1] to various real-world data. Also known as the First-Digit Law, this technique is named after physicist Frank Benford, who discovered a surprising pattern in the occurrence frequency of the digits 1 through 9 as the first number in

---

1. https://en.wikipedia.org/wiki/Benford%27s_law

naturally occurring numbers.[2] The law provides a distribution of the first digit that looks like the following:

| Leading digit | Frequency |
| --- | --- |
| 1 | 30.1% |
| 2 | 17.6% |
| 3 | 12.5% |
| 4 | 9.7% |
| 5 | 7.9% |
| 6 | 6.7% |
| 7 | 5.8% |
| 8 | 5.1% |
| 9 | 4.6% |

In fact, the distribution follows a simple mathematical formula. For every digit d = 1…9, the probability of it being the first digit in the number is approximately

$$P(d) = \log_{10}(1 + \frac{1}{d})$$

It's important to realize that this law applies only to naturally occurring numbers and would not be valid for data that is controlled or assigned by humans. So, for example, zip codes will not show this distribution, whereas payment data should.

Benford's Law is often applied to payment information to discover fraud, but it is also usable as a data quality check. If the distribution of data values that represent naturally occurring data in a field does not adhere to these frequencies, you may have a data quality issue on your hands.[3]

### Differential "Value Distribution" Rules

Many datasets are re-created regularly (e.g., on a weekly basis) to reflect the latest changes and updates in the source of the data.

Another common technique in data quality checking is to compare the distribution of certain data fields against their distribution a week or a month prior. The main idea here is that for some fields we may not know what the static distribution of the values needs to be, so instead we make sure that week over week this distribution does not change by much, or changes within a certain given amount of expected variation.

— ——— ———

2. A more comprehensive discussion of this technique applied to data quality is available here: www.aae.wisc.edu/lschechter/benford.pdf.

3. Although named after Benford for his 1938 paper on the topic, this technique was in fact discovered much earlier, in 1881, by mathematician Simon Newcomb.

As an example, consider the zip code. We might measure the percentage of customers who fall within a certain zip code or set of zip codes that represent a certain geographic location. We can then measure this on a weekly basis and trigger an alert if the week-over-week change is higher than some threshold.

This necessitates comparing the "distance" between the previous or historical distribution of values and the current distribution. Once a distance is defined, automated reporting can happen based on thresholds. There are a few approaches to this which range from the purely statistical chi-squared test to the information theoretic Kullback-Leibler divergence pseudo-metric.

The chi-squared test is a well-known statistical test that can be used to determine whether two random variables, which are represented by our two distributions, come from the same distribution or not. If the test determines that the distributions are different, you might have a data quality issue and should consider looking further into the data.

The Kullback-Leibler divergence is a pseudo-distance metric that gives an indication of the distance between two distributions. The farther the distance between the distributions, the more likely there is a data quality issue. Commonly, as in most situations where a distance function is used, a threshold is set that is used when deciding whether or not to raise an alert about a potential data quality issue.

## Outlier Analysis

Outlier analysis or detection is a broad set of techniques to find situations where the current data point(s) varies in some significant and detectable way from its historical context. An easy-to-understand example would be looking for spikes in heart rate. These spikes represent an abnormal scenario, where normality is defined by the context of previous results.

Outlier analysis can be performed on univariate data (single cells) or multivariate data (multiple cells). The only requirement is that the data have some history. Often, in the context of data mining, we look at things like historical counts broken down by category.

As an example, in clinical informatics with drug data, we might look for outliers in the trend of the number of pain medications prescribed month over month.

The trick to outlier analysis is forming some time series out of the data that makes some sense. After this, the individual techniques to find outliers vary from the very statistical and simplistic to much more complex. Probably the most common approach is looking at the current value and determining the percentage change between it and the previous value. This method is a very simplistic (and sometimes misleading) approach, but it is one that we have found is understood and is used naturally as a "gut-feel" indicator.

The more statistically sound version of the simplistic outlier technique just described is to use a variance statistic rather than a simple percentage. This generally takes the form of using a sliding window of data, taking the mean or median, and computing some variance statistic like standard deviation. Given the current point, the distance in terms of variance from the mean is computed, and if that distance is beyond a threshold, the point is considered an outlier (e.g., if the point is 3 standard deviations from the mean of the window, it is considered an outlier). This technique, or variants thereof, has been used in the manufacturing industry in the form of statistical process control. Furthermore, the technique is the basis for the control or Shewhart chart, where the variance computed is the standard deviation divided by the square root of the sample size.

One challenge to this technique is that it may not perform as well on a wide variety of distributions due to the dependence on variation statistics like standard deviation. Another, more robust technique that is used to great effect is median absolute deviation, or MAD. Similar to what was just discussed, we start with a window of data denoted as W, and then the median absolute deviation is defined as:

$$MAD(W) = median(|x_i - median(W)|)$$

Now, with the current data point x, we can compute a z-score normalized by the MAD:

$$x_z = \frac{0.6745(x - median(W))}{MAD(W)}$$

Armed with this modified z-score, we can use a threshold to determine whether $x$ is a potential outlier or not. The authors of a paper describing this technique's use, Iglewicz and Hoaglin,[4] indicate a threshold of 3.5 to mark potential outliers. We have found that the kind of threshold to actually use is very dependent upon the dataset, but the technique has worked to great effect on real-world data.

## Missing Value Imputation

If your data has a lot of missing values, it is often necessary to find a suitable technique for the imputation of those missing values.

The simplest way to impute a missing value X is by calculating the mean or median of this value from a certain representative population. The trick is to find a good representative population, and sometimes that might be impossible. Consider, for example, a dataset of houses, where each record contains the following fields: zip code, number of bedrooms, last price sold, size in square feet, and number of floors. If the missing values are in the price column, a reasonable first approximation might be the average price from a similar population, such as houses with the same number of bedrooms. On the other hand, if your missing value is for a variable such as the zip code, or any other discrete or categorical variable, calculating an average or taking the median (or even the mode) is nonsensical. More complex imputation of missing values is possible using machine learning techniques. Essentially, you can build a regression model for a given variable Y that has missing values, using some other variables $X_1...X_n$ that don't have missing values. R has an implementation of this principle in the missForest package, which uses the random forest machine learning algorithm for imputation of values. Although this is potentially more accurate, keep in mind that when dealing with large amounts of data, applying such a machine learning approach often comes with a large computational penalty.

---

4. Boris Iglewicz and David Hoaglin (1993), *How to Detect and Handle Outliers*, Vol. 16 in *ASQC Basic References in Quality Control: Statistical Techniques*, Edward F. Mykytka, Ph.D., editor.

## Using Hadoop for Data Quality

Although data quality is not a new topic, the adoption of Hadoop and the exponential growth in the collection and storage of new kinds of data has refocused many data scientists on data quality. Furthermore, the sheer size of the data makes manual data quality solutions impractical and requires more automated approaches.

When dealing with large raw datasets, a data quality engine is often integrated into the data ingest process. Any data import—be it with Sqoop, Flume, or a custom solution— is followed by data quality checks.

Depending on the data type, frequency of updates, and volume, in some cases we can keep both the original (raw) dataset as well as the "clean" dataset (after data quality rules have been applied). Since Hadoop storage is relatively inexpensive, the cost of retaining this extra copy is not high. Keeping this raw dataset enables any issues that may arise with data quality to be debugged more easily.

Furthermore, you may find advantageous the creation of merged datasets with data consistency issues addressed. For instance, if you need to merge data from multiple systems, each with different conventions for indicating gender, you may create a merged view with the gender conventions made consistent.

The implementation of data quality logic depends highly on the ingest pipeline architecture, but it is common to implement these quality checks with Pig or Hive, typically using user-defined functions (UDFs) for the rules.

### Example: Pig UDF for HCPCS Codes

Procedures rendered in the course of treating a patient are coded, often using a coding standard called Current Procedural Terminology (CPT). The CMS encodes procedures in a generalization of this scheme called HCPCS (Healthcare Common Procedure Coding System), which we use in our example.

Healthcare workers often enter these codes manually, so they are prone to errors, and data quality checks are required. A simple way to validate an HCPCS code is by using a regular expression. This method is a simple example of a cell-based data quality rule.

Our example dataset has listed the HCPCS code of the procedure rendered to a Medicare beneficiary by every provider who submitted for reimbursement from the government. The following implements, using Pig, a simple validity check for HCPCS codes and generates a report of the erroneous codes and the count per code:

```
ROWS = load 'medicare_part_b.medicare_part_b_2013_raw' using HCatLoader();
HCPCS_CODES = foreach ROWS generate hcpcs_code,
➥ REGEX_EXTRACT(hcpcs_code,'(^[A-Z0-9]\\d{3,3}[A-Z0-9]$)',1) as match;
INVALID_CODES = filter HCPCS_CODES by match is null;
INVALID_CODE_G = group INVALID_CODES by hcpcs_code;
INVALID_CODE_CNT = foreach INVALID_CODE_G generate group as hcpcs_code,
➥ COUNT(INVALID_CODES) as count;
rmf medicare_part_b/bad_codes;
STORE INVALID_CODE_CNT into 'medicare_part_b/bad_codes' using
➥ PigStorage(',');
```

We use a complex regular expression to identify valid HCPCS codes as follows:

- They start with either a capital letter or a number.
- The next sequence is three digits.
- The code ends in either a capital letter or a number.

Pig's REGEX_EXTRACT returns NULL if the regular expression match is not met, so our hcpcs_code field in relation ROWS would therefore be NULL if the HCPCS code in the original file is invalid.

The report generated can and should be used, ideally, to correct the syntactic mistakes or, at a minimum, to get a firm grasp on the expected set of bad data and types of mistakes that are most common. Our dataset, thankfully, is quite clean, though there are some empty fields.

# The Feature Matrix

The second big step in data science that involves data munging revolves around converting the raw data into what is known as a feature matrix, as previously mentioned. A feature matrix is the de-facto standard input representation for machine learning algorithms.

In most machine learning settings, we represent objects of interest (such as users, customers, machines, etc.) as points in some $N$-dimensional space, or a **feature vector**. Each cell in a vector can be a continuous value, or a discrete/categorical value, and all feature vectors have the same ordering of features. The set of all feature vectors is typically referred to as the feature matrix.

More formally, let A be a matrix of M rows and N columns, where $A_{i,j}$ represents the j-th feature of the i-th instance. In this example, instance i would be a customer data row in Table 5.1. $A_i$ is a row of this matrix, which represents a feature vector of length N with all the features of instance i.

Let's look at a simple example. We want to build a feature matrix for customers of our business, and we choose to represent each customer using five features:

- Age (continuous)
- Zip code (categorical)
- Last purchase price (continuous)
- Number of items in last purchase (continuous)
- Average purchase price (continuous)

Our feature matrix in this case will look something like what is in Table 5.1 (where $A_{1,1} = 25$, $A_{1,2} = 94301$, $A_{1,3} = 250$, etc.).

Table 5.1    **An Example Feature Matrix.**

|  | Age | Zip code | Last purchase price ($) | Number of items in last purchase | Average purchase price ($) |
|---|---|---|---|---|---|
| Customer 1 | 25 | 94301 | 250 | 5 | 200.5 |
| Customer 2 | 35 | 55423 | 20 | 2 | 50.0 |
| Customer 3 | 75 | 33423 | 78 | 3 | 52.6 |
| ... |  |  |  |  |  |
| Customer M | ... |  |  |  |  |

## Choosing the "Right" Features

Deciding which features to use for a given problem is where a lot of the magic of data science happens. There are no quick and fast rules that work in every circumstance, and common sense and experience play an important role here.

It is very common to experiment with various feature options, iterating and measuring the model's performance, until reaching the final set of features that provide the best outcome.

Although choosing the right modeling approach among the possible machine learning algorithms (such as linear regression, support vector machines, neural networks, random forest, etc.) is often important in a machine learning setting, it is often much more critical to choose or generate the correct set of features. In fact, experimenting with various features and refining the feature matrix is often where the data scientist spends most of his or her time.

## Sampling: Choosing Instances

Sampling techniques are often used in the generation of a feature matrix, whereby a subset of the overall population is identified and used for subsequent processing.

Sampling may be probabilistic (e.g., random sampling or stratified sampling) where each original instance has some specified likelihood to be chosen, or non-probabilistic where some instances may never be selected.

### Example: Sampling with Pig, Hive, and Spark

Consider our example Medicare dataset; it's often advantageous to take only a sample of the whole dataset for processing. Of course, there are many types of sampling and a variety of ways to accomplish this in the Hadoop ecosystem.

With Pig, there are a variety of options for sampling. The built-in SAMPLE operator provides simple probabilistic sampling:

```
DEFINE HCatLoader org.apache.hive.hcatalog.pig.HCatLoader();
ROWS = load 'medicare_part_b.medicare_part_b_2013_raw' using HCatLoader();
SAMPLE_ROWS = sample ROWS 0.2;
rmf medicare_part_b/ex2_simple_sample;
STORE SAMPLE_ROWS into 'medicare_part_b/ex2_simple_sample' using
➥ PigStorage(',');
```

The second parameter (in this case 0.2) defines the percentage of instances from the relation that are kept, in this case 20%.

For this dataset, you may want to obtain a random sample of providers. In other words, unlike the previous example of a random sample of all rows, we now want to have all the rows for a given sample of providers.

Apache DataFu,[5] an Apache project dedicated to providing Pig UDFs for common tasks that often show up in data science data munging, provides several Pig UDFs for sampling, such as sampling by key and weighted sampling.

SampleByKey can help us obtain the desired user-based sample:

```
DEFINE HCatLoader org.apache.hive.hcatalog.pig.HCatLoader();
DEFINE SampleByKey datafu.pig.sampling.SampleByKey('0.2');
ROWS = load 'medicare_part_b.medicare_part_b_2013_raw' using HCatLoader();
SAMPLE_BY_PROVIDERS = filter ROWS by SampleByKey(npi);
rmf medicare_part_b/ex2_by_npi_sample;
STORE SAMPLE_BY_PROVIDERS into 'medicare_part_b/ex2_by_npi_sample' using
➥ PigStorage(',');
```

This results in roughly 20% of the providers and all rows for each of those providers.

Hive provides random sampling functionality similar to Pig's using the TABLESAMPLE operator. With TABLESAMPLE you can ask to sample by percentage or a specific number of samples. For example,

```
SELECT * FROM medicare_part_b.medicare_part_b_2013_raw
➥ TABLESAMPLE(10000 ROWS)
```

results in 10,000 rows, randomly sampled from the medicare_part_b_2013_raw table, whereas

```
SELECT * FROM medicare_part_b.medicare_part_b_2013_raw
➥ TABLESAMPLE(20 percent)
```

results in roughly 20% of the rows from the original table.

Spark has a sampling feature in its RDD and DataFrame API. For example, the following code shows how to sample a Spark DataFrame using the PySpark API:

```
from pyspark import SparkContext
from pyspark.sql import HiveContext
hc = HiveContext(sc)
# load medicare dataset as a Spark dataframe
rows = hc.hql("select * from medicare_part_b.medicare_part_b_2013")
#Create a new Spark dataframe with 20% sample rows, without replacement
sample = rows.sample(False, 0.2)
```

---

5. https://engineering.linkedin.com/datafu/datafu-10.

## Generating Features

Generating features may involve various types of processing of raw datasets, including various kinds of aggregations or transformations. Let's take a look at the common categories of features.

### Simple Features

Simple features are features that are exactly the same as or very similar to the raw data in the source dataset. For example, the age or zip code of a customer is a simple feature. We don't have to perform any transformation of it, just use it directly.

In some cases, simple transformation may be needed such as discretization or normalization (see the section later in this chapter titled "Feature Manipulation"). For example, we may want to use an age group feature derived (discretized) from the age value, with age ranges of 0–18, 18–25, 25–35, 35–50, and 50+ and categorize each customer into one of these age groups.

### Aggregated Features

Aggregated features differ from simple features in that they require a more complex computation over a range of raw data.

For example, consider the "average purchase price for a customer." To compute this feature one needs to aggregate all purchases for a customer and compute the average price. Depending on the feature definition and the raw data layout, this task is typically a bit more complex and requires more compute resources than simple features.

The "last purchase price" also falls under the aggregated feature category. It requires looking at all transactions for a customer, extracting the latest one (by date), and taking the price from that purchase.

When using Pig or Hive, in most cases the simple features already exist in the data or are derived as simple transformations of existing features, whereas complex features are computed as an aggregation.

### Example: Feature Generation with Hive

For example, consider our Medicare dataset. We can consider as an aggregated feature for each provider the percentile of the number of times each procedure was performed:

```
SELECT d.NPI as provider, d.HCPCS_CODE as code,
CASE
    WHEN cast(LINE_SRVC_CNT as int) <= p.percentiles[0] THEN "10th"
    WHEN cast(LINE_SRVC_CNT as int) <= p.percentiles[1] THEN "20th"
    WHEN cast(LINE_SRVC_CNT as int) <= p.percentiles[2] THEN "30th"
    WHEN cast(LINE_SRVC_CNT as int) <= p.percentiles[3] THEN "40th"
    WHEN cast(LINE_SRVC_CNT as int) <= p.percentiles[4] THEN "50th"
    WHEN cast(LINE_SRVC_CNT as int) <= p.percentiles[5] THEN "60th"
    WHEN cast(LINE_SRVC_CNT as int) <= p.percentiles[6] THEN "70th"
    WHEN cast(LINE_SRVC_CNT as int) <= p.percentiles[7] THEN "80th"
    WHEN cast(LINE_SRVC_CNT as int) <= p.percentiles[8] THEN "90th"
    WHEN cast(LINE_SRVC_CNT as int) <= p.percentiles[9] THEN "95th"
    WHEN cast(LINE_SRVC_CNT as int) <= p.percentiles[10] THEN "99th"
    ELSE "99+th"
```

```
END as percentile
from medicare_part_b.medicare_part_b_2013 d
join
(
  select HCPCS_CODE,
    percentile(cast(LINE_SRVC_CNT as int),
      array( 0.1, 0.2, 0.3 , 0.4, 0.5, 0.6, 0.7, 0.8, 0.9, 0.95, 0.99)
    ) as percentiles
  from medicare_part_b.medicare_part_b_2013
  group by HCPCS_CODE
) p on d.HCPCS_CODE=p.HCPCS_CODE;
```

### Complex Features

There are features that require a rather complex computation that is not a simple aggregation, which we call **complex features**.

For example, let's assume that our previously defined customer record does not include the city field. If we want to add "city" to our feature list, we may look it up using the zip code. We consider this a complex feature since it requires a complex lookup in another data source.

It is difficult to provide a comprehensive overview of all the different types of complex features you may find in practice, so we will just cover a few examples here:

- Extracting features from text, including the application of natural language processing (NLP) techniques to the text input
- Extracting features from time-series data
- Extracting features from media data files such as audio, video, or image/PDF

## Text Features

We want to give special treatment to text features, which are increasingly more common in data science projects.

With text documents as your input data, it is common to use a bag-of-words model where each text (sentence or document) is represented as a bag (multiset) of its words, disregarding the order of the words. It is common to remove common words such as "the," "is," or "a" as they often don't carry any significant information for the task at hand and are considered noise words.

With our feature matrix representation, each word is now a feature represented by a column in the matrix A, and $A_{i,j}$ represents some value reflecting the appearance of word j in the document i. In the simple case, $A_{i,j}$ can be the number of times word j appears in document i, but other formulations exist, most notably that of TF-IDF (term frequency-inverse document frequency).

With TF-IDF, the value in $A_{i,j}$ is a multiplication of two quantities:

- TF: term frequency
- IDF: inverse document frequency

Let f(d,w) denote the raw frequency of the word w in document d. There are four common formulations for the TF term:

- Raw: $TF(d, w) = f(d, w)$

- Boolean: $TF(d,w) = \begin{cases} 1, & f(d,w) > 0 \\ 0, & \text{otherwise} \end{cases}$

- Logarithmic: $TF(d,w) = \begin{cases} 1 + \log\big(f(d,w)\big), & f(d,w) > 0 \\ 0, & \text{otherwise} \end{cases}$

- Augmented frequency: $TF(d,w) = 0.5 + \dfrac{0.5 \cdot f(d,w)}{\max\big\{f(d,w) : w\varepsilon d\big\}}$

Each of these formulations provides a different variation on the basic theme of raw count.

The IDF component is a measure of how much information the word provides and is computed for each word across the whole corpus of text:

$$IDF(D,w) = \log \frac{N}{\big|\{d\varepsilon D : w\varepsilon d\}\big|}$$

where $N$ is the size of the corpus $D$.

The IDF component is the logarithmically scaled fraction of the documents that contain the word out of the whole corpus. IDF serves the purpose of emphasizing rare words while minimizing the impact of more common words.

For example, the word *the* is a common word and thus may appear in many of the documents in the corpus $D$. If we assume *the* appears at least once in every document in $D$, then $\big|\{d\varepsilon D : w\varepsilon d\}\big|$ will equal $N$, and thus IDF = 0. This result essentially removes this word because it's "not important" as it is very common. On the other hand, if we have a word that is not as common, like *natural*, the denominator will be lower, and thus the IDF value will be higher than 0.

## Example: TF-IDF with Spark

Spark provides TF–IDF functionality as part of its MLlib machine learning library. Consider a corpus of documents stored in HDFS under the folder hdfs://corpus/ with multiple text files inside the folder:

```
from pyspark import SparkContext
from pyspark.mllib.feature import HashingTF
from pyspark.mllib.feature import IDF

sc = SparkContext()
documents = sc.wholeTextFiles("hdfs://corpus/").map(lambda (file,
➥ contents): contents.split(" "))
```

```
tf = HashingTF().transform(documents)
tf.cache()

idf = IDF().fit(tf)
tfidf = idf.transform(tf)
```

In this example, we first read all the files in the folder corpus into a Spark RDD called doc-uments (using the `wholeTextFiles` function), which contains for each file in that directory the list of words in that file. (Note that we implement the simplest possible word separation just by splitting on space.) We then use the `HashingTF` function to compute **term frequency** (`tf`) for each term in each document. Finally, we use the `IDF()` function to compute the IDF vectors and merge the two with `idf.transform(tf)` into the final TF-IDF score.

Note that Spark implements the **hashing trick** as part of its TF-IDF functionality; we discuss the hashing trick later in this chapter.

### NLP: Named Entity Extraction

Named entity recognition or extraction (NER) refers to the classification of elements in text into a set of predefined categories of interest such as person name, company name, and location but also includes categories like percent, money, weight, email address, and others.

Named entity extraction tools are often implemented using hand-crafted rules or machine learning models that are optimized to identify named entities in sentences.

For example, consider this text:

"England won the World Cup."

as opposed to

"The World Cup took place in England."

In the first example, "England" stands for an organization, whereas in the second it stands for a location. When analyzing text and creating features from text, making this type of distinction can be critically important for accuracy of the model.

For instance, if we have a file on HDFS called corpus with sentences in it, one sentence per line, we could use Spark's Python bindings along with the very powerful natural language processing library NLTK from Python to extract the named entities, line by line:

```
from pyspark import SparkContext
import nltk
def get_entities(text):
    tokens = nltk.tokenize.word_tokenize(text)
    pos = nltk.pos_tag(tokens)
    sentt = nltk.ne_chunk(pos, binary = True)
    ret = []
    for subtree in sentt.subtrees(filter=lambda t: t.label() == 'NE'):
        val = ' '.join(c[0] for c in subtree.leaves())
        ret.append(val)
    return ret
entities=sc.textFile("corpus").map(lambda sentence :
➡ get_entities(sentence)).collect()
```

### NLP: Sentence Negation

Another common problem with text is identifying positive or negative intent in a sentence. For example, consider a system to identify whether a patient has diabetes by looking at a doctor's text notes.

A simple implementation might just look for specific words that could identify a diabetes diagnosis such as *diabetes*, *diabetic*, or *glucose*.

However, consider the sentence "The patient has diabetes" versus "The patient does not have diabetes." It is critically important for such a system to identify the negative intent in the second sentence and not blindly look for the keyword *diabetes*.

### NLP: Word Vectorization

word2vec[6] is an algorithm originally developed by Google to compute a vector representation for words inside of a corpus (set of documents) such that "similar" words (based on usage) are close to one another, where closeness is defined in terms of cosine similarity. Furthermore, now that we have a vector space, arithmetic can be performed on the vector representations to combine words (addition) or remove connotations of one word from another. The latter can be used to represent analogy. For instance, vec(king) − vec(male) + vec(female) is close in this vector space to vec(queen).

Often this vectorized format is a useful way of looking at textual data and can facilitate doing things like including multiple similar words together or finding similar words to include as features. It has been used to great effect for feature generation and for creating many of the traditional NLP tools, like named entity recognizers or machine translators.

There is a very nice implementation of word2vec in Spark's MLlib:

```
from pyspark import SparkContext
from pyspark.mllib.feature import Word2Vec
sc = SparkContext(appName='Word2Vec')
tokenized_data = sc.textFile("corpus").map(lambda row: row.split("\\s"))
word2vec = Word2Vec()
w2v_model = word2vec.fit(tokenized_data)
synonyms = w2v_model.findSynonyms('king', 10)
```

## Time-Series Features

Many real-world datasets have a temporal aspect to them—they consist of a series of data points, typically successive measurements made of a time interval. Such datasets are often called "time-series data."

A very common example is measuring the stock price of a company over time. We get a value for that stock every day, or every hour, or even every minute. The values are successive, and there is significance to the order in which they occur. Other examples might be ocean tides, temperature measurements of a jet engine, and many other cases that represent an event sequence measured over time.

---

6. https://code.google.com/archive/p/word2vec/

In the context of feature generation, it is uncommon to see the individual measurements or events serve as features, but instead the features are formed via some aggregate or derivative of the time-series data.[7]

Methods for time-series analysis may be divided into two classes: frequency domain and time domain.

The full scope of time-series analysis techniques is beyond the scope of this book. We would like to mention only some common techniques that we find most useful with many types of datasets: autoregressive (AR), moving average (MA), autoregressive moving average (ARMA), autoregressive integrated moving average (ARIMA), hidden Markov models (HMMs), Fourier transform, wavelet transforms, and dynamic time warping.

## Features from Complex Data Types

Another common task in feature generation is the extraction of said features from complex data types including:

- Specialized text file formats such as XML or JSON
- Audio files such as MP3 or WAV
- Image files such as JPEG, GIF, or TIFF
- Video files such as MP4 or WMV
- PDF files

Let's look at a few common examples of how features are extracted from these complex data types.

### Extracting Text from PDF Files

A rather common use case is the extraction of text and subsequently of text-based features from PDF. The typical processing flow includes converting the PDF to text with optical character recognition (OCR) software and then subsequently creating features from the text.

One of the interesting characteristics of PDF is that it also includes some metadata such as page numbers, page titles, and other such data that can be beneficial for creating better features.

For example, imagine we have a PDF file composed of multiple pages from a car accident report in an insurance company. We may know that the first page, for example, contains meta information about the customer such as first name, last name, policy number, and so on. Instead of blindly extracting text and words from the PDF, we can use this knowledge to direct our system to recognize these "identifying features" (using "named entity extraction" techniques) from the first page and extract text normally from subsequent pages.

---

7. This is quite different from another, separate topic of forecasting, which is a very common goal in time-series analysis. We will not discuss forecasting here.

### Features from Audio Data

As more audio content is being stored and managed, several applications have emerged for mining audio data. Some practical applications include:

- Speech recognition—Translating audio to text
- Music analysis—Identifying genre, artist/singer, mood, and other characteristics
- Voice analysis—Identifying specific voice prints in phone recordings, such as for terrorist identification
- Medical analysis—Medical applications such as automated analysis of heart sounds

In all of these applications (and many others not mentioned here), one of the most critical steps, and a nontrivial one, is the preprocessing of raw audio data to generate features that are useful for achieving the learning goals.

Some typical techniques include frequency analysis through fast Fourier transform (FFT), filtering, noise removal, Linear Predictive Coding (LPC), and others. A thorough treatment of this topic is well beyond the scope of this book. However, we would just like to emphasize that this kind of preprocessing tends to be very task specific, so, for example, the features one would use for music may be very different from those used for heart-sound analysis.

### Features from Image or Video Data

Image and video content is now widely available. With smartphones, Snapchat, YouTube, surveillance cameras everywhere, and even a microscopic camera that can go into your body and help with medical procedures—pictures and video data are all around us.

Extracting useful features from images and video calls for some specialized techniques that have been perfected by the research community over decades, including:

- For images—edge detection, corner detection, face detection, etc.
- For video—scene segmentation, motion detection, etc.

As with audio data, detailed coverage of feature extraction for image and video is beyond the scope of this book.

## Feature Manipulation

After extracting the features that are most useful for modeling, it is sometimes necessary to manipulate the feature values in order to prepare them for the modeling, performing tasks such as discretization, feature scaling, and one-hot encoding.

### Feature Value Discretization

Often we have a feature whose value is continuous, but we want it to be discrete. For example, the "age" feature might be an integer and we would like to group people into age groups instead, for example: under 18, 18–25, 25–35, 35–50, and 50+.

In some cases, the specific discrete values, as well as the mapping function between original values and discrete values, are known or determined by the problem we are trying to solve. In our example of age groups, it is sometimes the case that certain age groupings are common in the business environment, and we would like to match that mapping.

In other cases, the discretization follows some pattern in the data and is important to achieving optimal model accuracy. For example, if our population consists of only children under 18, the previously discussed discretization is completely ineffective. It would result in a feature that has only a single value for all instances, making it redundant and superfluous.

A rather simplistic form of discretization that is popular is **thresholding**, where a binary feature (with two possible values: 0 or 1) is created by comparing the value of the continuous variable to a threshold value. The discretized feature receives a value of 1 if the original value is above the threshold and 0 otherwise.

### Scaling Feature Values

Some machine learning techniques (but not all) converge to a better result when the features are centered around zero and have variance in the same order of magnitude.

If this is not the case, a feature with a very high variance, for example, might dominate the objective function and prevent the algorithm from learning correctly.

In practice, most input datasets don't have this property, and thus we have to apply scaling, that is, transform the data to have a mean of zero and unit variance.

### One-Hot Encoding

Many machine learning techniques cannot handle categorical values. One-hot encoding is a practical technique used in such cases that transforms a categorical variable into a set of binary features.

As an example, consider the categorical variable color, which may contain one of these values: blue, red, green, or yellow. A one-hot encoding of this variable will result in four new binary variables, named after each of the values (blue, red, green, and yellow).

To represent each original value in the new scheme, you simply put a 1 in the appropriate new variable and 0 in the other three. For example, blue and green are represented as follows:

| Value | Blue | Red | Green | Yellow |
|-------|------|-----|-------|--------|
| Blue  | 1    | 0   | 0     | 0      |
| Green | 0    | 0   | 1     | 0      |

## Dimensionality Reduction

Dimensionality reduction is the mapping of data from the original feature space of N dimensions to a new feature space of lower dimension M where M<<N, such that uninformative variance in the data is discarded. Dimensionality reduction has a long history as a method for data visualization, but more importantly it often leads to better features for learning and inference.

**The Curse of Dimensionality**

To understand the importance of dimensionality reduction, we have to first explain a well-known phenomenon in data mining known as **the curse of dimensionality**. In fact, this term is often used to describe a few different phenomena in multiple domains, but we will focus on its importance in machine learning and data mining.

The curse of dimensionality is not a problem of high-dimensional data per se, but an issue that arises with high-dimensional data in the context of a specific algorithm, where the high-dimensional feature vectors cause the algorithm to not scale well, either computationally or in the sense that it cannot learn the target function correctly.

More concretely, there are a few specific problems that arise. From the point of view of learning theory, we have the following problems:

- As we use a large number of features, ultimately some of them are noisy, and the more features we have, the more noise exists that the learning system must overcome. Furthermore, it is more likely that some features are correlated.

- Every increase in the number of dimensions requires exponentially more training instances to cover the $N$-dimensional space of feature values and thus makes learning exponentially more difficult to deal with.

- The concept of distance becomes less precise as the number of dimensions increases, since the distance between any two points in any given dataset converges.

From a computation point of view, the computational effort to learn predictive models or run a clustering algorithm usually depends on the number of features and might grow exponentially in complexity with that number.

**Feature Selection**

One way to reduce dimensionality is to select a subset of the features. Feature selection techniques can be categorized as follows:

- Filter methods, where a scoring function (such as mutual information, chi-square, etc.) is used to score the relevance of each feature to the target variable. Based on the score, the top N features are selected and used for modeling.

- Wrapper methods, where subsets of features are selected, and with each subset a full model-infer-measure cycle is performed, where the subset that provides the best result is ultimately chosen. Wrapper methods tend to choose better features than filter methods but are prone to overfitting.

- Embedded methods perform feature selection as part of the model construction process. A good example of this is the Least Absolute Shrinkage and Selection Operator (LASSO ) for building linear models, which penalizes the regression coefficients, shrinking many of them to zero (which means they "disappear" or are deselected).

- Domain-specific methods where, in some cases, the domain provides natural ways to reduce dimensionality. For example, with text data it is common to remove all **stop words** (such as *to*, *the*, *a*, and other common words) or to use **stemming** (both *Daniel* and *Daniel's* reduce to *Daniel*).

## Feature Projection—PCA and Friends

Another methodology for dealing with high-dimensional datasets is of a more unsupervised nature, using feature projection. The main idea here is that instead of selecting a subset of the raw features, we create a whole new set of features by projecting the data into a lower dimension, in a way that minimizes the error of reconstructing the original features from the new features.

One of the most common of these projection methods is called principal component analysis, or PCA. In PCA, we take the original feature matrix A, normalize it to the mean, and create its covariance matrix $\Sigma_A$. The top P eigenvectors (with the highest eigenvalues) of $\Sigma_A$ form our principal components—our new features. In practical applications, it's typical to take enough eigenvectors to cover 80–90% of the variance.

Similar to PCA, some other variants of dimensionality reduction exist, such as independent component analysis (ICA), linear discriminant analysis (LDA), and latent semantic indexing (LSI).

### *Example: Dimensionality Reduction with Spark*

The following code example shows how to perform principal component analysis with Spark. In this example, we assume there is already a `RowMatrix` built that contains all of our features:

```
import org.apache.spark.mllib.linalg.Matrix
import org.apache.spark.mllib.linalg.distributed.RowMatrix

// Assume we've built a row matrix somehow before the PCA
val mat: RowMatrix = ...  // some RowMatrix as input to PCA

// Perform PCA to find top 20 principal components
// Principal components are stored in a local dense matrix 'pc'
val pc: Matrix = mat.computePrincipalComponents(20)

// Project rows to linear space spanned by top 20 principal components
val projected: RowMatrix = mat.multiply(pc)
```

## The Hashing Trick

In natural language text, a relatively small number of unique words are used very often, and very many words are quite rare. For example, the word *data* is much more frequent in this book than the word *semantic*.

This distribution of the words is also called **Zipf's Law**. If you choose a random word from the dictionary, chances are that word is rarely used in your data. Even if you choose a pair of words from the dictionary, the likelihood of both words appearing frequently in your text is very small.

The so-called hashing trick (mentioned earlier in the chapter) takes advantage of this fact to enable a powerful feature reduction for text data; it is especially powerful if the number of words (or n-grams) you have in your text is in the thousands or even millions. To apply the "hashing trick" we follow these steps:

- Identify a suitable hashing function with an output range of the size compatible with the (reduced) number of features you desire.
- Run every word or n-gram through your hashing function and the output of the function becomes your feature—a column index.

This seems odd at first, but it works because of the properties of the hash function (making collisions rare) and Zipf's Law, which guarantees *any* two words have a low chance of collision.

Practical experiments also confirm this. In practice, the normal (high-dimensional) bag-of-words has roughly the same performance as the (low-dimensional) post-hashing-trick data structure. Whenever a collision does occur, it is usually between two rare words, and in most cases rare words do not improve the accuracy of the model anyway.

## Summary

In this chapter

- You learned the different types of data quality issues that arise in data and how to address them with Hadoop.
- You learned about the importance of feature generation, and how to generate features from large datasets with Hadoop tools like Pig or Spark.
- We reviewed various types of features, including simple, complex, text, time-series, and others.
- You learned about various ways to manipulate feature values such as discretization, one-hot encoding, and the hashing trick.
- You learned about feature selection and dimensionality reduction and its importance in addressing the curse of dimensionality.

# 6

# Exploring and Visualizing Data

*A good sketch is better than a long speech.*

Napoléon Bonaparte

## In This Chapter:

- Visualizing data can provide guidance on and insights into otherwise difficult to understand tabular, text-based data. The advantages and some pitfalls of visualization are presented.

- Choosing the right method for visualization is an important first step. Common types of presentation charts are explored and explained in the context of data science.

- The menu of data visualization tools is large. A brief description of some popular data visualization tools is provided.

- The goal of data visualization with Hadoop and big data is the same is it is with any other data set. However, there are some important issues to keep in mind as the data set grows in size.

## Why Visualize Data?

Data visualization refers to a set of techniques often used to represent data in a graphical manner.

Since our brain is capable of processing images faster and more efficiently than reading textual information, visualization is an extremely efficient way to understand complex data and identify patterns within this data.

Visualization is used in many types of applications, including:

- Tracking business metrics such as customer growth, revenue, or profitability
- Monitoring system metrics such as latency, response time, or uptime
- Visualizing customer segments
- Scientific visualization in areas such as physics, biology, and chemistry

## Motivating Example: Visualizing Network Throughput

To show the value of visualization, let's look at a simple example. Consider a basic TCP network connection report indicating that this connection seems to perform poorly at times. Running a network test yields the time series results shown in Listing 6.1. The first thing to notice is the amount of data and the precision to which it is reported. Note that some data was removed to make the listing more readable. The data plots presented in Figures 6.1 and 6.2 use all of the raw data.

Listing 6.1 TCP Network Data for 10Gb Ethernet Connection

```
Time      Throughput
0.000009  0.832672
0.000009  2.484703
0.000009  4.962730
0.000009  6.642901
0.000009  10.732942
0.000009  15.646943
0.000009  20.307985
0.000009  22.754678
0.000010  25.143004
0.000010  27.476959
0.000010  36.783738
0.000010  38.995069
0.000010  48.616004
0.000010  50.924660
0.000010  72.220666
0.000010  76.769224
0.000010  93.381360
0.000010  98.102704
0.000010  100.107533
0.000010  146.455460
0.000010  147.317372
0.000010  188.794830
0.000010  186.953481
0.000010  188.841299
0.000011  270.672748
0.000011  272.481987
0.000011  274.394542
0.000011  351.795725
0.000012  504.789793
0.000012  505.600630
0.000012  642.967597
0.000012  644.940953
0.000013  876.241226
0.000013  879.311261
0.000014  1080.895784
0.000014  1081.299586
0.000017  1342.076785
0.000017  1356.069978
0.000024  989.478183
0.000031  994.553659
```

```
0.000031 993.382850
0.000031 1006.075902
0.000020 2341.426009
0.000020 2344.847975
0.000022 2880.498526
0.000025 3708.358544
0.000025 3712.915547
0.000030 4209.928688
0.000029 4334.698820
0.000036 5204.014528
0.000044 5717.610987
0.000044 5664.566118
0.000044 5656.346172
0.000058 6514.094510
0.000058 6477.378004
0.000058 6466.840155
0.000073 6859.199973
0.000100 7478.694485
0.000125 7968.246798
0.000125 8000.771409
0.000126 7956.891948
0.000179 8384.965176
```

Looking for a networking issue in two long columns of numbers is not easy. If you look hard enough and do some comparisons, you will probably see an artifact in Listing 6.1, but it is easier to visualize the data and look in there for features or artifacts that may be causing the problem. Figure 6.1 is a plot of the data in Listing 6.1 (the plot was created using R).

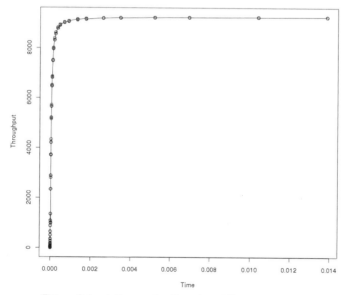

Figure 6.1    A time-series line plot of Throughput (Mb/s)
versus Time (seconds) for a network connection.

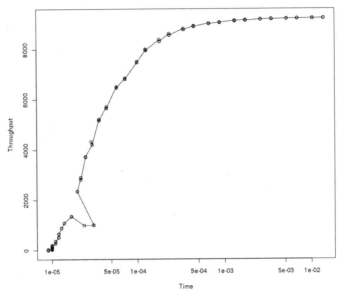

Figure 6.2    A time-series line plot of Throughput (Mb/s)
versus log Time (seconds) for a network connection.

Initial inspection of the graph does not indicate any unusual behavior; the data points seem to indicate smooth predictable performance. Closer inspection of Figure 6.1 indicates a problem with the plot, however. Most of the data points are in the 0.000 to 0.002 second range. One way to spread out the points in this type of plot is to use a logarithmic scale for the axes that seem "compressed." If the plot is redone with the X-axis (Time) on a log scale, Figure 6.2 results.

The plot now indicates some type of issue between the throughput range of 1000 and 2000 Mb/s. If the original data in Listing 6.1 is examined, the artifact is now easily found. The correct plot, however, makes the artifact leap out from the data.

The correct visualization can help make difficult to spot artifacts or features much clearer than tables of data. Tabulated data are useful, however, when exact values and/or numeric comparisons are needed. Visualization can show trends or the "shape" of the data.

## Visualizing the Breakthrough That Never Happened

Although extremely helpful, visualization can also be misused, leading the viewer to the wrong conclusions.

We have all read the headline touting the improved performance of a new or updated product. In many cases some performance metric is plotted on the y-axis using a bar chart similar to Figure 6.3. On first inspection, the chart seems to indicate break-through performance over the competition (Companies X, Y, and Z). Someone viewing Figure 6.3 might conclude that the new product represents a performance breakthrough.

Upon further examination, however, you notice that the y-axis seems to start at a somewhat arbitrary value of 5.7, and the difference between the highest and lowest

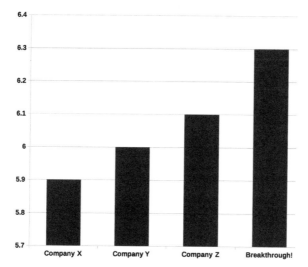

Figure 6.3    A bar graph used in a misleading manner to indicate improved performance.

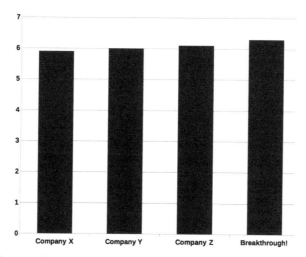

Figure 6.4    A bar graph used correctly to indicate the reality of performance improvements.

values is 0.4 units. If the chart in Figure 6.4 is created with a y-axis starting at zero, a different story emerges. Looking at the data in Figure 6.4, you can see that the breakthrough is better than the other products but only marginally so.

From a marketing perspective Figure 6.3 creates more excitement, but from a reality standpoint, Figure 6.4 is closer to the truth and should be used if considering purchase of the product. Of course, other factors should be considered as well, such as price-to-performance, power usage, reliability, etc.

One particular troubling aspect of Figure 6.3 is the spreadsheet/charting package used to create the chart has, by default, an auto-scaling function that decided the range of the y-axis. Obviously, the auto-scaling is there to help zoom in on the differences, but it can also make those same small differences seem significant when visualizing results. To avoid overzealous interpretations of data, the default graph should always include the full range of data or use some form of normalization to respect a proper scale (e.g., percentages or baselines).

# Creating Visualizations

Creating compelling visualization is somewhat of an art. It involves understanding the data to visualize, crafting a story around the data, choosing the right chart types to use, and rendering the final graphics.

Let's look at some of the basic types of visualization charts and what they are most suitable for. The types of visualization types we cover is in no way exhaustive, but does provide a basic methodology for visualizing data.

Importantly, the best chart or graph type to use is often determined by the question you are asking[1]; let's review four chart types and the types of questions they are often used to answer:

1. **Comparison Charts**—Used to answer questions about how two or more variables compare to each other. For example, comparing sales revenue between various states over time.

2. **Composition Charts**—Used to answer questions about the composition of various data items. For example, showing the breakdown of grocery product revenues by product category (e.g., produce, breads, frozen, etc.).

3. **Distribution Charts**—Used to answer questions about the underlying distribution of data. For example, showing the distribution of sales by month.

4. **Relationship Charts**—Used to answer questions about the relationships between datasets or variables. For example, showing the correlation between month of the year and predicted sales volume.

To illustrate several common chart types, we will use monthly sales data for three beverages (Iced_Coffee, Hot_Coffee, Hot_Tea). The data are presented in Table 6.1. The charts we present were generated using the R language. The data and the R scripts used for generating the charts can be found on the book web page (see Appendix A, "Book Web Page and Code Download").

---

1. A popular guide for choosing charts is available from Dr. Andrew Abela at
   http://extremepresentation.com

Table 6.1  **Example data used for charts.**

| Month | Iced_Coffee | Hot_Coffee | Hot_Tea |
|-------|-------------|------------|---------|
| Jan | 1 | 12 | 14 |
| Feb | 3 | 15 | 14 |
| Mar | 6 | 14 | 9 |
| Apr | 4 | 9 | 6 |
| May | 9 | 10 | 12 |
| Jun | 10 | 8 | 11 |
| Jul | 15 | 2 | 10 |
| Aug | 12 | 5 | 4 |
| Sep | 8 | 4 | 6 |
| Oct | 4 | 9 | 6 |
| Nov | 2 | 12 | 16 |
| Dec | 3 | 19 | 11 |

## Comparison Charts

A comparison chart is used to compare or relate variables over time. You may display a single variable or compare the values of different variables over a sorted index value (e.g., time).  An example from the retail industry is counting the number of transactions per day for a single store or multiple stores.

There are various types of comparison charts, including bar and column charts, line charts (time series), circular area charts, and bullet charts.

Two simple bar charts are shown in Figure 6.5.

Note that some will argue that the correct terms for the charts in Figure 6.5 are column chart, and bar chart. Charts showing the bars running horizontally from left to right are considered by some to be a canonical form of bar chart. In practice, the term bar chart is used for either orientation.

A line chart is often used to compare variables over a time. Figure 6.6 shows a single line chart and a multiple line chart. The lines in line charts should not be considered as indicating the values of variables between the data points (i.e., on the line). The lines are merely used to connect data points visually and help the viewer see possible shapes or trends.

If you compare Figure 6.5 to Figure 6.6, you might notice that the bar or column charts tend to focus the attention of the viewer on the differences between the columns, whereas viewers of the line charts tend to focus on the shape or trend aspect of the comparison.

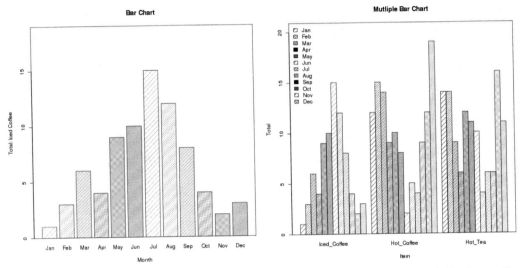

Figure 6.5   Two example bar charts. The chart on the left compares the values of Iced Coffee by month. The chart on the right compares each beverage over 12 months. The data could also be shown grouping all three beverages by month.

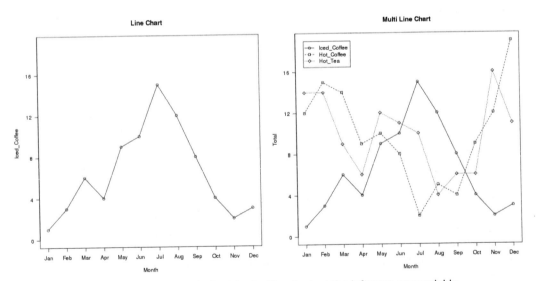

Figure 6.6   Two example line charts. The chart on the left uses one variable (Iced Coffee) and the chart on the right plots all three variables.

## Composition Charts

A composition chart displays and contrasts the internal distribution of data components or values, which typically means splitting out a total into constituent parts. For instance, total sales for the day may be a combination of three products—sales of product A, product B, and product C.

A composition chart can be used to see how much each value contributes to the whole. Typical examples of composition charts include pie charts, donut charts, stacked bar charts, and stacked area charts. The simplest (and perhaps most overused) composition chart is the pie chart, an example of which is shown in Figure 6.7. Pie charts provide a quick visual representation of a single metric.

Pie charts, however, are often used incorrectly and can make comparisons difficult. Consider Figure 6.7. What slice is bigger: April or October? In actuality they are both the same. The December slice looks similar, but is actually smaller. The geometry of circle slices (triangles) does not represent small differences in the data well. The same information from Figure 6.7 is plotted in Figure 6.5 (left). The differences between data are quite clear in Figure 6.5 (left) and the December data are distinctly different than the April or October results. To make pie charts easier to understand, percentages are often included in the chart. However, a simple table with the same information is often more clear.

Finally, pie charts can be useful for two or three values that are distinctly different in terms of frequency of occurrence. Basically, a pie chart is good at showing fractional composition of two or three possible results (e.g., Out of 1598 respondents, 487 said "yes," 1278 said "no," and the remaining 167 said "no opinion."). In many cases there is a better alternative to a pie chart.

Bar or column charts can also be used to show the composition of metrics. The two graphs in Figure 6.8 show the contribution of each variable by value (stacked bar chart) and by percent (100% stacked bar chart) to the total amount over the data index.

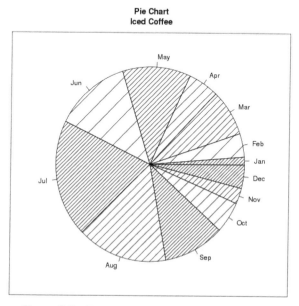

Figure 6.7    Example of a pie chart for Iced Coffee.

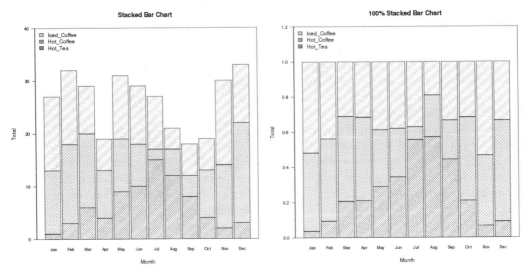

Figure 6.8    Two examples of stacked bar charts. The chart on the left shows
the contribution of each variable to the total value. The chart on the
right shows the percent contribution to the total.

An interesting variation of the 100% stacked bar chart is the stacked area chart shown in
Figure 6.9. Table 6.2 is an abbreviated listing of the data used to create the chart in Figure 6.9.

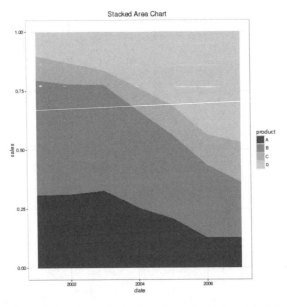

Figure 6.9    An example of a 100% stacked area chart.

Table 6.2  **Abbreviated example data used for stacked area chart.**

| Date | Product | Sales |
|------|---------|-------|
| 2001 | A | 12 |
| 2001 | B | 19 |
| 2001 | C | 4 |
| 2001 | D | 4 |
| 2002 | A | 14 |
| 2002 | B | 21 |
| 2002 | C | 4 |
| 2002 | D | 6 |
| ... | ... | ... |
| 2006 | A | 5 |
| 2006 | B | 12 |
| 2006 | C | 5 |
| 2006 | D | 17 |
| 2007 | A | 6 |
| 2007 | B | 11 |
| 2007 | C | 8 |
| 2007 | D | 22 |

The 100% stacked area chart shows the percentage each product contributed to total sales for the year. This type of chart is good for showing the composition of a total into its constituent components over time.

## Distribution Charts

A distribution chart displays data in a way that provides clues to the underlying statistical distribution of the variables plotted.

Common distribution charts are column/bar charts (single variable), histograms (single variable), scatter charts or plots (two variables), 3D area charts (three variables), or dot charts. Examples of scatter and bubble charts can be found in the "Relationship Charts" section. Figure 6.10 shows a histogram and dot chart for the example data. The histogram is for the Iced_Coffee sales values and a dot chart is for two variables (Iced_Coffee and Hot_Coffee) of the example data. In both cases, the chart can give an indication of how the data are grouped (or not grouped). In particular, the Histogram in Figure 6.10 (left) indicates the frequency of Iced Coffee sales amounts.

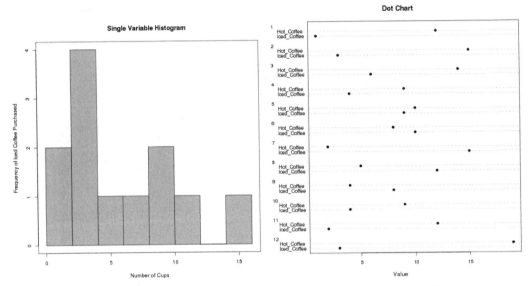

Figure 6.10   A histogram for the Iced Coffee data is on the left and
a dot chart for Iced Coffee versus Hot Coffee is on the right.

Another type of distribution chart is the box-and-whisker[2], an effective way to display a variable's minimum, median, and maximum values, as well as the lower quartile, upper quartile, and highlight anomalies. The box-and-whisker plot provides an easy way to represent some aspects of the distribution of a data set.

Figure 6.11 (left) shows the components of a box-and-whisker plot. The box region indicates the interquartile range (IQR) that represents the data from the 25th (Q1) to the 75th (Q3) percentile. The IQR is where 50% of the data points are located.

The whiskers add 1.5 times the IQR to the 75th percentile (Q3) and subtract the same from the 25th percentile (Q1). If the distribution is normal, the whiskers should include 99.3% of the data. Any data that are beyond the whiskers are considered outliers and are indicated as data points. Figure 6.11 (right) presents a box-and-whisker plot for the data in Table 6.2.

## Relationship Charts

When looking for relations between data, a relationship chart can be very helpful. Common relationship charts may indicate a connection or correlation between two or more variables. Example relationship charts include scatter plots (two variables), bubble plots (three variables), heat maps, circular network, and grouped bar charts.

---

2. Originally created by John W. Tukey.

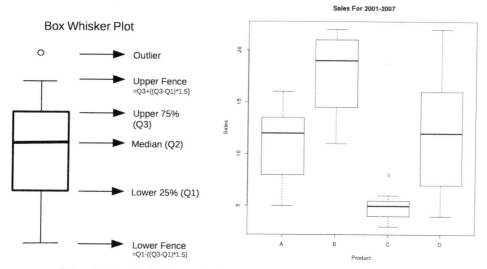

Figure 6.11    The features of a box-and-whisker plot are shown on the left.
The right image is a box-and-whisker plot of the data in Table 6.2.

As an example, consider the use case of comparing sales for iced coffee vs. hot coffee. Figure 6.12 shows both a scatter and a bubble chart used for such comparison. The scatter chart is a simple comparison of those two variables, whereas in the bubble chart the

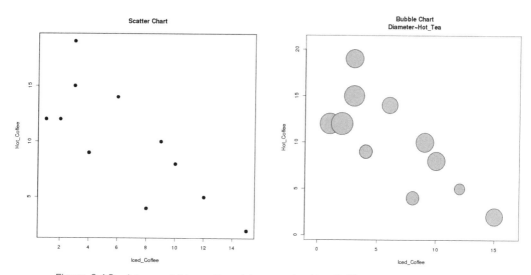

Figure 6.12    A two variable scatter plot comparing Hot_Coffee and Iced_Coffee sales
is on the left and a three variable scatter plot or bubble plot is on the right.
The value of Hot_Tea is used to size the circular points in the bubble plot.

Hot_Tea variable is used to set the size of the bubbles representing each Iced_Coffee, Hot_Coffee pair.

In this case, we can see from the visual chart that sales of iced coffee and hot coffee seem to have a weak negative correlation—when hot coffee sales are up, the sales for iced coffee are relatively low and vice-versa.

When searching for possible relationships between multiple variables, a **scatter plot matrix** as shown in Figure 6.13 is a useful tool.

In this example, any two-variable combination from our three variables of Iced_Coffee, Hot_Coffee, and Hot_Tea are plotted as part of the matrix. The diagonal represents plotting the variables against themselves and is labeled with the variable used in that particular row and column. Using a scatter matrix, it is possible to easily identify negative and positive correlations between variables through a visual diagram.

In Figure 6.13 a weak positive correlation can be noted between the Hot_Coffee and Hot_Tea (i.e., a positive correlation is where both variables increase or decrease in the same direction. A perfect correlation would be a diagonal line with a positive slope.). Conversely, Hot_Coffee and Iced_Coffee seem to indicate a week negative correlation (i.e., a negative correlation is where variables move in the opposite direction. As one variable increases, the other variable decreases. A perfect negative correlation would be a diagonal line with a negative slope.). There seems to be no correlation between Hot_Tea and Iced_Coffee because the data points appear to be more randomly dispersed.

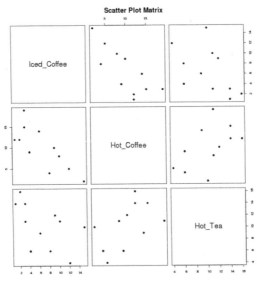

Figure 6.13   A scatter plot matrix for variables Iced_Coffee, Hot_Coffee, and Hot_Tea from the example data.

# Using Visualization for Data Science

Data scientists often make use of data visualization for various purposes, as part of the workflow of data exploration, model building, and monitoring of model performance. Those purposes include the following:

- Before any modeling commences, data quality assessment is often required to ensure the data is cleaned up properly as we have discussed in Chapter 5, "Data Munging with Hadoop." Visualization is a great tool for this purpose; for example, consider the age variable in a given dataset—it is useful to use a distribution chart like a histogram to understand how age is distributed and whether or not it is consistent with expectations.

- During exploratory data analysis and discovery, as we prepare the data for modeling and consider various possible features for modeling, visualization is often used to:
    - Understand correlation or other types of relationships between variables using scatter plots.
    - Identify potential data outliers in a variable using distribution charts.

- When evaluating performance of data science systems (either offline or based on real production monitoring metrics), data visualization is commonly used to display performance over time (comparison charts) or performance of one model against another. A good example of this is receiver operating characteristic (ROC) curves or precision-recall curves, which we cover in Chapter 8, "Predictive Modeling."

# Popular Visualization Tools

There are numerous visualization tools available for creating good-looking charts and plots of data. Because data often need to be "massaged" before plotting, some of the most used visualization tools are actually built on top of powerful languages that are often used for statistics and offer matrix or data frame abstractions.

The following list provides some of the more popular visualization environments used by data scientists. There are other tools available that are not present in the list (for example, all spreadsheets have graphing capabilities).

## R

R is a programming language and software environment for statistical computing and graphics. The R language is popular among scientists, statisticians, and data analysts. R is used for both data analysis and presentation (charts and graphs). R is a GNU project supported by the R Foundation for Statistical Computing. More information can be found on the R web page at https://www.r-project.org/.

R includes the *base* package in its core components. This is the basic package that provides visualization support in R and includes most of the chart types needed. Due to some issues with the base graphics package, primarily surrounding tedious customization, awkward workflow, and no built-in support for encoding additional information in the graph, other packages became available over the years, including the following:

- The *lattice* package, authored by Deepayan Sarkar, was the first alternative to base graphics, and it now comes with the base distribution of R. It supports multi-panels (e.g., multiple scatter plots on a single page), conveying additional information via color, and other useful features that simplify the user's workflow as compared to the base package.

- The *ggplot2* package, authored by Hadley Wickham, which quickly became the package of choice for most R users. It is based on the "grammar of graphics"[3] and supports a variety of features such as multi-panels, mapping of variables into facets, layers, and much more.

## Python: Matplotlib, Seaborn, and Others

Python is a very popular interactive programming language used in many fields. The Python matplotlib library (http://matplotlib.org/index.html) is a 2D plotting library that creates publication-quality figures in a variety of hardcopy formats and interactive environments across many different platforms.

Although matplotlib is versatile and can be used in Python scripts, it is considered the "grandfather" of visualization tools in Python. It is extremely powerful, but with that power comes complexity—you can do anything with matplotlib, but it is not always so easy to figure out how.

If you are using the Pandas data frame package, it also has some integrated graphics functionality via the plot function.

Seaborn is another visualization library, based on matplotlib, which seeks to make the default data visualizations more visually appealing as well as making complex graphics a simpler task.

For the R fans, the more recent ggplot Python package implements a ggplot2-like interface for creating visualizations in Python.

## SAS

SAS (Statistical Analysis System) is a commercial software suite developed by SAS Institute for advanced analytics, multivariate analyses, business intelligence, data management, and predictive analytics. SAS was initially developed at North Carolina State University from 1966 until 1976, when SAS Institute was incorporated. SAS has several components that can be used for creating charts. See http://www.sas.com for more information.

- Graph-N-Go is mainly for reporting. Graphs can be saved in various formats including standard graphic format and html format. It only supports a basic set of chart types, however.

---

3. http://vita.had.co.nz/papers/layered-grammar.pdf

- SAS/Insight is another package that can be used to explore variables and relationships among variables. It offers a lot of good, detailed information on variables, such as univariate statistics. Its interactive nature provides a good tool for exploring data both graphically and analytically.

- SAS/Analyst supports both exploring and reporting. There are many types of graphs, and it also creates the customizable SAS code that can be used for generating new plots and revised analysis.

- SAS/Procs provides options to create more complex charts (including text-based alpha-numeric plots).

## Matlab

Matlab (matrix laboratory) is a multi-paradigm numerical computing environment developed by MathWorks.

Matlab enables matrix manipulations, plotting of functions and data, implementation of algorithms, creation of user interfaces, and interfacing with programs written in other languages, including C, C++, Java, Fortran, and Python.

A large selection of plotting options is available. See http://www.mathworks.com/products/matlab for more information.

## Julia

The Julia language (http://julialang.org) is a popular new environment for technical computing. As an open source application, Julia can produce various types of plots with various rendering back ends, both to files and directly in a browser. The language is Matlab-like, easy to use, interactive, and fast. Interactive features can be added to graphs and plots. See https://en.wikibooks.org/wiki/Introducing_Julia/Plotting for more information. Currently the GadFly (http://gadflyjl.org/) package seems to be the most popular Julia plotting library.

## Other Visualization Tools

Some other popular commercial packages are Tableau and QlikView. Both offer top-end graphic manipulation and plotting tools in addition to some business intelligence (BI) capabilities.

These tools are attractive to novice users because they provide an easy-to-use and fast method to visualize data without modeling or programming.

# Visualizing Big Data with Hadoop

As we've seen so far, visualization tools and techniques are extremely useful for various data science activities including data exploration, variable selection, and others. The obvious next question is: does visualization change when performed on larger datasets as opposed to smaller ones?

The short answer is no, it's more or less the same, with two main use cases:

- Sampling—In cases where individual points are plotted on a graph, in most cases you can just plot a sub-sample of the points to achieve the same result.
- Aggregation—When your visualization displays information at an aggregate level, you simply perform the aggregation on the large dataset using Hadoop and plot the results as usual.

Let's look at an example of a scatter plot between pairs of variables, where our input dataset (residing in Hive) is very large. Since we have a large number of data points, drawing a scatter plot with all the points is likely unneeded and would only cause the output graphics to take too long to produce. Instead, we can just sample the data with Hive's TABLESAMPLE operator, resulting in a sufficiently reduced size sample of the original dataset, and just draw the scatter plot based on that smaller dataset.

Another interesting example is to draw a histogram from a large dataset. In this case, we can use Hive, Pig, or Spark to compute the counts within each histogram bin at scale and then use any plotting package to display the results.

## Summary

In this chapter

- We presented a rationale for data visualization. Visual diagrams can represent complexities and patterns that are not easily discerned from large amounts of textual or numeric data.
- We provided a brief overview of data charts using simple example data. The examples included comparison charts, composition charts, distribution charts, and relationship charts. The example data and R scripts used to create the charts are available on the book web page (see Appendix A).
- We learned how visualization is used in data science.
- We described some commonly used visualization tools. Both commercial and publicly available software (open source) tools were mentioned.
- We covered how visualization approaches can be applied to big data and Hadoop processing.

# III

# Applying Data Modeling with Hadoop

# 7

# Machine Learning with Hadoop

*Essentially, all models are wrong, but some are useful.*

George E.P. Box

### In This Chapter:

- Overview of machine learning
- Machine learning task types
- Why use big data for machine learning?
- Tools for machine learning
- The future of machine learning and AI

In this chapter we introduce some common terminology, provide an overview of machine learning techniques, and discuss how big data can positively impact their accuracy and effectiveness.

## Overview of Machine Learning

Machine learning is a result of successful research in fields such as statistics, computer science, and applied mathematics. It borrows from all of these fields.

Historically, machine learning developed as part of artificial intelligence (AI) in the late 1950s, with the goal of building machines that can mimic human minds. Thus, the early models were based on the biology of the brain (the so-called perceptron was an algorithm for supervised learning of binary linear classifiers that can decide whether an input belongs to one class or another).

After a period of relative non-progress and the proliferation of rules-based systems for decision making, the decision tree re-invigorated machine learning once more with a modeling technique that provides good accuracy and is interpretable by a human being. At the same time, multi-layer neural networks were created with a new promise to overcome the limitations of the perceptron.

Around 1995 support vector machines were proposed and quickly adopted, and in 2000, more research led to significant advances in linear models, making them more robust and capable of modeling over much larger datasets. Later on, ensembles became popular with the introduction of random forest and gradient boosted trees.

Most recently, a set of techniques known as **deep learning** has driven renewed interest in multi-layer neural networks that combine supervised and unsupervised learning[1] techniques into a single framework, with a promise to revolutionize machine learning. These techniques have been used to great effect practically in Internet companies such as Google, Facebook, and Baidu, but are growing popular outside of search engines. We look at deep learning in Chapter 12, "Data Science with Hadoop—The Next Frontier."

# Terminology

To set up our discussion of machine learning, we introduce the following common terminology:

- **Observation**—In machine learning we often deal with observations. Each observation is a representation, as data, of some object or entity such as an email message, a customer, a piece of equipment, etc.

- **Feature**—Each observation is represented as a vector of features (also called variables or attributes) of the observation. For example, for a spam filtering model, we may choose a set of words (our features) to represent email messages (our observations). In this case each feature counts the number of times a keyword appears in an email message, and 0 represents the case where the keyword does not appear at all in the message.

- **Target**—With some machine learning techniques (such as supervised learning), we have a certain feature or variable about observations that we mark as "target" or "label", representing our desire to predict that feature value.

Often we call such representation a feature matrix, as described in Table 7.1.

Table 7.1    **An example of a feature matrix.**

|         | Feature 1 | Feature 2 | Feature 3 | Feature 4 | ... | Feature P |
|---------|-----------|-----------|-----------|-----------|-----|-----------|
| **Observ 1** | 1 | 0 | 2.3 | 0 | | 2 |
| **Observ 2** | 0 | 0 | 3.5 | 0 | | –3 |
| ... | | | | | | |
| **Observ N** | 1 | 1 | 10.2 | 1 | | –6 |

---

1. We will describe supervised and unsupervised learning later in this chapter.

The rows in this feature matrix represent observations (one row per observation), and the columns represent the features. Each observation is thus represented as a vector of P features.

Features are often numerical (float values) but can also be categorical (like spam or not-spam) or ordinal (heavy, medium, light user of Twitter).

# Task Types in Machine Learning

The basic idea behind machine learning is to automatically identify or "learn" patterns in data. There are two common settings for machine learning: supervised learning and unsupervised learning.

With supervised learning, a set of example observations is provided as a training set. The goal is to learn an association between the inputs (features) and output (target variable) by using the examples provided.

With unsupervised learning, the input data is simply a feature matrix of observations without a target variable. Thus it is often used for exploratory analysis, to gain insight into the data or as a step before supervised learning.

Although the scope of machine learning is rather broad, machine learning practitioners often focus on the following five major types of tasks:

- **Predictive modeling**—Learn a function given a set of examples (often called the training set). If the target variable for the learning is categorical in nature, the problem is called "classification" (for example, given an email message, classify it into spam or non-spam), and if the target variable is numerical, then the problem is called "regression" (for example, predict a price of a house given features like number of rooms, square footage, etc.). We cover predictive modeling in more detail in Chapter 8.

- **Clustering**—Identify natural groupings or clusters of observations that are similar to each other (as represented by their features). See Chapter 9.

- **Anomaly detection**—Identify observations that are anomalous if compared to some notion of normality. See Chapter 10.

- **Recommender systems**—Predict user preference for a product or item given historical preference data from other users.

- **Market basket analysis**—Identify patterns of association between items or variables that co-occur in the same observation. This technique is often also called association rules.

In the next few chapters we will look at some of these task types (specifically predictive modeling, clustering, and anomaly detection) in detail, explain how they work, discuss how Hadoop and big data can improve the effectiveness of these tasks, and show a real-world example of code for each task type.

# Big Data and Machine Learning

The quality of machine learning models is strongly dependent on the quality and size of data given to them. We live in an era where massive datasets are available broadly and are continuing to grow at a rapid pace (faster than Moore's law). For example:

- Online activity is now captured from website visits, Facebook and Twitter activity, search queries, WhatsApp messaging, and much more.

- Human instrumentation (heartbeat, steps, etc.) from wearable devices such as Fitbit, Jawbone, and Apple Watch is also captured.

- Sensor data is available (for example, from jet engines, trains, cameras, etc.) and is stored into massive datasets.

- Scientific datasets such as the capture of high-energy physics experiments, astronomical observations, or genetic data continue to grow.

Regardless of your task type (classification, regression, clustering, or anomaly detection), having more raw data translates into better and more accurate models:

- **New features**—Often big data means new data sources are available, enabling data scientists to create completely new features for their models, resulting in better models. For example, consider a risk model for a car insurance company. The company starts collecting real-time driving information (a data stream collected from sensors in the cars) and using this new data to create various new modeling features such as average driving speed, number of driving hours per day, etc.

- **Accurate features**—Most features used for data modeling are estimated from the raw data. With more data these estimates are often more accurate and have a smaller variance, which ultimately results in better models. To continue our example of a risk model for car insurance, consider the feature "average number of accidents per year." If previously, the company only kept one year's worth of historical accident data, this average is estimated from only one data point. With big data, the history could be kept for 10 years, enabling a more accurate estimate of the value of average number of accidents per year, calculated from 10 data points instead of only one.

- **More instances**—In many cases having more instances may help achieve better results. Although this is not always the case (and typically depends on the amount of instances relative to the number of features in your model), it is often worth exploring. Furthermore, if your dataset is unbalanced and includes a very rare class that is of interest, more instances will most likely improve your learning algorithm's performance. Consider for example a healthcare fraud detection system, where the number of fraudulent claims is 1/1000-th of the overall number of claims. In this case, having 100,000 instances initially sounds like a lot, but it's only 100 fraud cases, which may not be enough to learn the characteristics of such cases. Having one million instances in this scenario would mean 1000 fraud cases, which is likely to have a significant positive impact on the detection accuracy.

The challenge in having more data is that building and applying the model requires more processing power. Fortunately, there are two trends that help:

- The continued technological innovation that drives down the pricing and drives up performance of CPU, memory, and storage.
- The maturation of distributed computing platforms such as Hadoop and its parallel processing frameworks such as Pig, Hive, and Spark.

# Tools for Machine Learning

We live in an era where machine learning has moved from a field of academic study to being broadly used for practical applications. This trend is evident in the large number of existing (and often freely available and open sourced) machine learning libraries and tools that are mature, well implemented, and well tested. See Appendix C, "Additional Background on Data Science and Apache Hadoop and Spark," for links to many of the packages mentioned in the following.

Most tools and libraries were designed to work in-memory on a single machine, including:

- Most R machine learning packages such as caret, e1071, rpart, C50, randomForest, gbm, clust, glmnet, neuralnet, arules, and many others
- Python's scikit-learn package, which implements various supervised and unsupervised machine learning algorithms
- Java libraries for machine learning such as WEKA and RapidMiner
- Vowpal Wabbit, a C++ based machine learning library that is known for its speed and scale

Most of these packages or libraries are designed to work in memory on a single machine (which might be a single client node on a Hadoop cluster), although they often support simple parallelization using multi-core machines.

With big data this may often be a challenge since scaling is limited beyond the size of a single machine; however, in many practical situations even though the raw data may be very large, after pre-processing the feature matrix that results is small enough to fit in memory.

As an example, consider building a supervised learning model for churn prediction. Let's assume our business has 20 million subscribers and our model represents each customer with 100 features; if each feature is a float (4 bytes) we end up with a matrix of the size 20M x 100 x 4, or a little less than 4GB. With 64GB or more of RAM in a single machine, such a feature matrix can easily fit into memory.

For the case where a single machine solution does not scale (either due to memory or speed constraints), there are some Hadoop-based machine learning solutions available. The most exciting such toolset is Spark MLlib, the machine learning library that is part of Apache Spark (although we note that the Apache Flink community is also hard-at-work on an equivalent machine learning capability that may be available soon as an alternative).

Spark MLlib is a distributed machine learning library that uses Spark as the underlying execution engine and supports various machine learning algorithms such as the following:

- **Supervised learning**—Linear and logistic regression, decision tree, random forest, gradient-boosted trees, naïve Bayes, and isotonic regression
- **Clustering**—$k$-means clustering, latent Dirichlet allocation, Gaussian mixture
- **Collaborative Filtering**—Alternating least squares
- **Association Rules**—FP-Growth

With Spark MLlib, the algorithm runs directly on the Hadoop cluster, and thus takes advantage of the processing power and parallelization capabilities of Hadoop, which may result in substantial increases in speed and enable much larger feature matrices to be used.

A few other projects in open source implement various aspects of distributed machine learning: Apache Mahout, Apache Flink ML, Conjecture, and ML-Ease (a LinkedIn Project). Some closed-source implementations include SAS, Microsoft ML, and others.

## The Future of Machine Learning and Artificial Intelligence

Since the inception of artificial intelligence as a research topic, it always fascinated academics and practitioners alike, with promises of autonomous robots and machines that can talk and learn, think and behave like humans or even better than humans.

The era of big data is a new and exciting step in that direction. For the first time, technology platforms enable the rapid and efficient collection and storage of massive datasets and their utilization to drive research and application of machine learning at scale, with Hadoop at the center of it.

## Summary

In this chapter

- We briefly reviewed the history of machine learning and described the five types of tasks most commonly used by its practitioners: predictive modeling, clustering, and anomaly detection.
- We discussed why big data is important for machine learning and how it helps improve its accuracy and effectiveness with new types of features, more accurate features, and more instances from which to learn.
- We reviewed various tools, libraries, and platforms for machine learning algorithms, on a single machine (in Python or R) or in a distributed environment such as Hadoop (Spark MLlib).

# Predictive Modeling

*It's difficult to make predictions, especially if it's about the future.*

Niels Bohr

## In This Chapter:

- Overview of predictive modeling
- Classification versus regression
- Evaluating predictive models and cross-validation
- Algorithms for predictive modeling
- How to build an end-to-end solution for predictive models
- Example: classification of tweets for sentiment analysis with Spark

Based on supervised learning methods, predictive modeling is an extremely effective set of techniques that are inspired by the human mind's incredible ability to learn from examples.

## Overview of Predictive Modeling

Predictive modeling is the most ubiquitous machine learning technique in practice, with use cases in every conceivable domain.

Some common examples include the following:

- Classifying an email message as spam or no-spam
- Classifying a tumor as cancerous or benign
- Predicting whether a customer will churn or not
- Classifying search engine visitors into clickers or non-clickers of online ads
- Predicting whether a truck driver is going to commit a violation or not
- Classifying a tweet's intent into positive or negative
- Predict the Lifetime Value (LTV) of a customer
- Predict the price of a house
- Predict the likelihood of a borrower to repay a loan

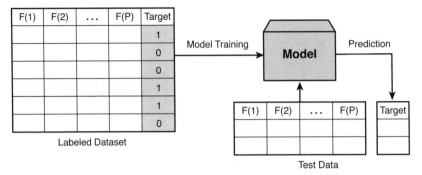

Figure 8.1    Diagram of predictive modeling flow.

In predictive modeling (or supervised learning), the goal is to learn a mapping of input observations x to outputs y given a set of N training examples (known as the "training set").

Each training example is represented as a vector of P features F(1)...F(P) (sometimes called "independent variables") alongside the target variable (sometimes called "dependent variable") y. This arrangement is depicted in Figure 8.1.

Using the training set, predictive modeling attempts to "learn" a function that will return the value of the target variable if given the corresponding feature vector of the observations in a way that is as accurate as possible under some definition of accuracy. The result of the training process is a model that can subsequently be used for prediction for new or unseen observations.

We next discuss the two forms of supervised learning known as classification and regression and see in more detail how supervised learning works in each case.

## Classification Versus Regression

When the target variable is categorical, then the supervised learning problem is called classification, whereas in the case of a continuous-valued numerical target variable the problem is called regression.

A target variable is considered categorical when there is a fixed number of categories that the variable can take. For instance, a model that predicts spam may have only two target categories: spam and ham. This kind of classification is considered a binary classification. Consider, however, the case when a model is predicting whether a patient has one of a host of illnesses. This situation would be a multi-class categorical classification.

To illustrate the classification case, consider the following use case: a cellular telephone provider is building a model to predict whether any of its customers is likely to churn (i.e., leave for another cellular provider) within the next 30 days. The model uses the following as features per customer: age, gender, days as a customer, number of minutes per day, number of minutes per month, and device type. This model is shown Figure 8.2.

In this case each customer maps to a single observation, represented by the various features (such as age, gender, etc.). The target variable denotes whether a customer has churned or not (in this case a binary Yes/No value), and because it is a binary variable this is

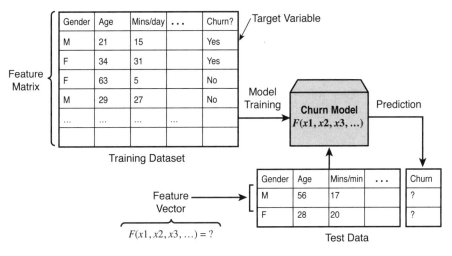

Figure 8.2    Classification example.

a classification problem. Using the complete training dataset of historical observations of both feature values and churn, the model is trained and can subsequently be used to predict churn.

To illustrate the regression problem setting, consider a healthcare insurance company that builds a model to predict the future healthcare costs for a given patient, based on historical costs, demographic data, existing medical conditions, and other similar features, as depicted in Figure 8.3.

In this example, the target variable is a continuous variable (future costs in dollars), thus this problem is categorized as regression.

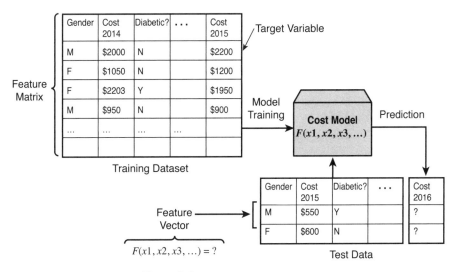

Figure 8.3    Regression example.

# Evaluating Predictive Models

Before deploying a model to production, it is common to evaluate its predictive performance to understand how it will perform in your production environment. Evaluating classifiers is different from evaluating regression models, and often the specific criteria used for evaluation depends on the problem context.

Furthermore, the data scientist often has various design choices when building predictive models, such as the following:

- *Which features to use.* Often there is a large space of possible features to choose from, and a wise choice of features often results in significantly better model outcomes.
- *Which algorithms to use.* For example, are we using decision tree, linear models, support vector machines (SVMs), or a random forest? (Various types of supervised learning algorithms will be discussed later in this chapter.)
- *Choosing values for various parameters of each model.* For example, with random forest the number of trees and the maximum depth of each tree needs to be specified.

Each such choice often results in a model that has different accuracy characteristics, and thus during the modeling cycle it is often necessary to evaluate various models and decide which one is the best performer.

A common practice is to randomly shuffle and then split the originally provided set of examples into three parts: a training set, a validation set, and a test set (a common split is 60% for training, 20% for validation, and 20% for testing). Following this split, we train various model choices using the training set and evaluate the performance of each model using the validation set. In splitting this dataset, it is important to try to make a good, even representation of the different types of target outcomes (i.e., equal number of each category for a classifier). If you present a biased number of one category, the classifier may predict poorly on real-world data that is not biased.

The algorithm type, feature set selected, and parameter values that provide the best performance on the validation set are then chosen and used for the final model; the performance of this final model is measured over the test set to get a final estimate of the overall model.

## Evaluating Classifiers

For classification, performance is measured using a variety of metrics derived from the so-called "confusion matrix" (also known as contingency table or error matrix). A confusion matrix is an NxN matrix (where N is the number of classes or predicted categories) where each row reflects instances in the actual class, and each column represents instances in the predicted class. Cells of the matrix count the number of instances that fall into each combination of actual versus predicted.

For example, in the common binary case the confusion matrix has only four cells as shown in Table 8.1.

Table 8.1    **Confusion matrix example.**

|  | | Predicted Class | |
|---|---|---|---|
|  | | Yes | No |
| **Actual Class** | Yes | TP = 82 | FN = 13 |
|  | No | FP = 7 | TN = 67 |

In this example, the data in the confusion matrix reflects the correct or incorrect classification decisions by the model:

- **True positives**—These are the cases where the model correctly predicted a "Yes" class. In Table 8.1 the corresponding value is TP = 82.

- **True Negatives**—These are the cases where the model correctly predicted a "No" class. In Table 8.1 the corresponding value is TN = 67.

- **False Negatives**—These are the cases where the model incorrectly predicted a "No", whereas the actual class was "Yes". In Table 8.1 the corresponding value is FN = 13.

- **False positives**—These are the cases where the model incorrectly predicted a "Yes", whereas the actual class was "No". In Table 8.1 the corresponding value is FP = 7.

After constructing the confusion matrix, it may be used to compute various metrics of accuracy that highlight different aspects of the classification task:

- **Accuracy** is defined as $(TP+TN)/(TP+TN+FP+FN)$, and reflects the percentage of correctly classified instances.

- **Precision** (or positive prediction value) is defined as $TP/(TP+FP)$. Focusing on the "Yes" class, precision reflects the percentage of instances classified as "Yes" (positives) that were actually of that category. Intuitively, high precision means our classifier makes very few mistakes on instances it identifies as positive.

- **Recall** (also known as sensitivity or True Positive Rate) is defined as $TP/(TP+FN)$, and reflects the percentage of instances that are in fact of class "Yes" that were correctly identified as "Yes" by our classifier. Intuitively, high recall means our classifier successfully identifies a majority of the positive instances as such.

- **Specificity** (or True Negative Rate) is defined as $TN/(FP+TN)$, and reflects the percentage of negative instances that were correctly classified by our model out of the overall negative instances. Intuitively, high specificity means our classifier correctly identifies most of the negative instances.

Which metrics are important really depends on the use case, and often the decision threshold can result in a trade-off between the metrics. For example, if you are developing a model for customer churn, you might look at the trade-off between precision and recall. You can certainly build a model with high precision and low recall (using a high threshold value) where very few customers will be predicted to churn but most

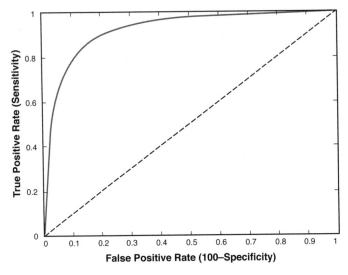

Figure 8.4    ROC curve.

of those would actually churn, or one with high recall and low precision (using a low threshold value); however, it is often difficult to maximize both precision and recall at the same time.

A common step in evaluating the performance of a classifier is to draw a receiver operating characteristic (ROC) curve (see Figure 8.4) or a precision–recall curve (see Figure 8.5).

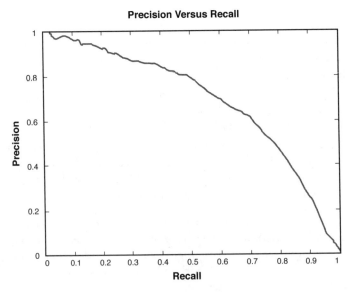

Figure 8.5    Precision/recall curve.

The ROC curve plots true positive rate (sensitivity) against false positive rate, and helps you visualize how the number of correctly classified positive examples varies with the number of incorrectly classified negative examples. Similarly, the precision-recall curve plots precision against recall, providing a different view of the classifier trade-offs.

When comparing classifiers, a useful metric is the area-under-the-curve (AUC) of the ROC curve. A random classifier would provide as many true positives as false positives, which translates into the dashed curve and an AUC of 0.5 A perfect classifier would have ROC-AUC of 1.0, and any practical classifier would have a score somewhere in the middle, with higher values corresponding to better classifiers.

The AUC for the precision-recall curve is also a useful metric, particularly when we are dealing with an unbalanced class distribution (fraud detection is a good example, where the number of examples in the dataset of fraud is much smaller than the number of examples for non-fraud), since it does not account for true negatives.

## Evaluating Regression Models

For regression, performance is measured as the error rate on the validation set. There are two popular error metrics:

- root mean squared error (RMSE)—root mean squared error is defined as

$$RMSE(\hat{y}) = \sqrt[2]{\frac{\sum_{i=1}^{n}\left(\hat{y}_i - y_i\right)^2}{n}}$$

- mean absolute error (MAE)—mean absolute error is defined as

$$MAE(\hat{y}) = \frac{\sum_{i=1}^{n}\left|\hat{y}_i - y_i\right|}{n}$$

In the preceding, $n$ is the number of instances, $y_i$ is the i-th actual target value and $\hat{y}_i$ is the i-th predicted value.

RMSE is the most common error metric for numerical regression. Compared to MAE, RMSE amplifies and more severely punishes larger errors.

## Cross Validation

When evaluating predictive models, it is common practice to use cross-validation to ensure your estimated accuracy metrics are robust and helps prevent over-fitting of the model.

A common form of cross-validation is called $k$-fold cross-validation, where the complete training set is randomly partitioned into $k$ partitions. We then repeat the following process $k$-times (i=1...$k$):

1. Train the model using all partitions except the i-th.
2. Compute the trained model's accuracy on the i-th partition (used for validation).

The overall performance metric is then computed as the average of the metrics over all iterations. If $k$ is taken as the size of the training set, then each partition is comprised of a single instance, and this is known as leave-one-out cross validation.

This technique is more popular than the more conventional validation approach (i.e., holding out training, test, and validation data) because it has been shown to be a more useful estimator of accuracy in situations where the training set is small or if there is not a good distribution or spread of the data to get a representative sample for testing.

## Supervised Learning Algorithms

When training a supervised learning model there are many types of algorithms to choose from, including: $k$-Nearest-Neighbors, neural nets, decision trees, support vector machines, generalized linear models, random forest, and gradient boosted trees.

Although the mathematical details, statistical assumptions, and mechanics behind each of these modeling techniques differ, they all work in a similar fashion: given a training set of features and target variables, they learn a function to estimate the target function given the feature variables.

Let's briefly describe a few of the most common algorithms:

- **$k$-Nearest neighbors**—These algorithms define a distance metric between observations and use this metric for classification or regression. Core to this technique is the capability to determine the $k$-nearest neighbors of any given observation. For classification, an unseen observation is then classified to the most popular class amongst its $k$-nearest neighbors. Similarly, in regression, the mean of the $k$-nearest neighbors is used.

- **Neural Networks**—the brain structure, a densely populated set of interconnected neurons is the inspiration behind **neural network** algorithms. Neural networks are an attempt to simulate the brain's structure and learning capabilities by learning from examples.

- **Generalized linear models**—GLMs such as **logistic regression** and **linear regression** are learning techniques that model the target variable as a linear function of the features. Linear models are widely used in practice, and recent extensions such as least absolute shrinkage and selection operator (LASSO) and elastic net make them very robust and effective.

- **Decision trees**—Decision trees are a very common non-linear learning technique that uses tree-like structure to describe optimal decisions, where each non-leaf node in the tree represents a decision.

- **Tree ensembles**—Another class of supervised learning algorithms is tree ensembles. One such powerful technique is random forest, whereby a set of decision trees is constructed, each using a random subset of the training examples and features. For both classification and regression, each tree is used to make a single decision, and a vote based on the outputs of all the trees is used to make the final decision.

It is beyond the scope of this book to cover each algorithm and its mathematical foundation in detail. However, the interested reader can find these details in many of the books about machine learning listed in Appendix C, "Additional Background on Data Science and Apache Hadoop and Spark." Instead we would like to highlight a few important considerations when experimenting with these techniques:

- Many of these techniques can be used for either classification or regression. For example, a decision tree can be used for both. Linear models are used for regression and the logistic regression variant is used for classification.

- In general, each algorithm makes some assumption about the data. Therefore, a specific algorithm may work better for a specific dataset whereas another may be more suitable for a different dataset. It is often difficult to determine the underlying distribution of the real-world dataset, and some experimentation is often necessary for and beneficial to determining the best algorithm to use.

- Some algorithms are faster to train or predict with than others. For example, with *k*-NN there is literally no training time, but prediction time may be longer than other algorithms. On the other hand, linear models may take longer to train, but prediction is rather fast since they essentially compute a dot product. Random forest training and testing time depends (amongst other things) on the number of trees in the forest.

- Some algorithms take more memory to train and to store the resulting model, while others take very little space. For example, with *k*-NN the whole training set is needed in memory for prediction, whereas linear models only require a single floating point number per feature of the model.

- Ensemble methods (such as random forest or gradient boosted trees) are meta-methods, where an ensemble of simple models is built and a voting mechanism determines the final result. In practice, these methods have shown to often be more robust to over-fitting and are often easier to tune.

# Building Big Data Predictive Model Solutions

Now that we understand the various flavors of predictive models and how to evaluate their performance, let's look at the end-to-end solution architecture.

From an architecture point of view, predictive models include two parts:

- Model training—Learning the target function from training examples.
- Prediction—Applying the model to unseen data.

## Model Training

The flow of creating a model or set of models typically looks like the process represented in Figure 8.6.

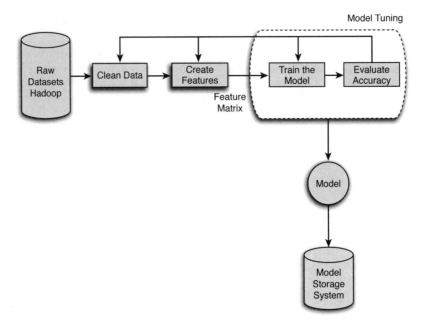

Figure 8.6    Model factory architecture.

The raw datasets that reside on Hadoop (either directly on HDFS or as tables in Hive) are processed (using Hive, Pig, or Spark) to perform data cleaning and normalization, followed by feature generation. The output of these steps is the feature matrix and labels that comprise the training set for the predictive model.

It is important to emphasize the importance of cleaning and normalization, as discussed further in Chapter 5, "Data Munging with Hadoop." A good set of predictive features is very important and can dramatically improve the value of the model being built. Specifically, with big data it is sometimes crucially important to carefully perform feature selection or use dimensionality reduction techniques (such as principal component analysis) to reduce the likelihood of over-fitting and enable the algorithm to perform optimally.

At this point model tuning is performed. This step is an iterative process that involves multiple cycles of training and evaluation, until the optimal settings of the model (the ones that provide the best accuracy) are achieved. Some common steps during model tuning are:

1. Trying out various algorithms (e.g., logistic regression, decision tree, neural network), to see which one performs best.

2. Optimizing the parameters of each modeling algorithm. For example, the number of trees in random forest or the regularization parameter $\lambda$ in linear regression.

3. Cross validation for model evaluation (described previously).

All of this work requires multiple executions of train -> evaluate, which thankfully are independent of each other and can be executed in parallel. Thus, Hadoop's parallel processing capabilities come-in handy, enabling the data scientist to run these models in parallel and finish the tuning faster.

Once the best model is chosen, it is often stored back into Hadoop for later use in the prediction flow. It is important to consider two aspects of model storage—format and versioning.

Most machine learning packages produce models as objects (in the object-oriented programming sense) in their native environment, and those can be stored to disk for use later in prediction. However, these native objects require that predictions occur on the same platform used for model generation.

An alternative is to use predictive modeling markup language (PMML), an XML-based standard that captures machine learning models. With PMML, the prediction workflow can use any PMML execution engine regardless of where the model was generated. Unfortunately, support for PMML is lacking in many popular data science packages, so practical use of PMML is sparse.

When many models are generated in a large complex system, model versioning becomes an important capability—allowing the system operator to control and audit which version of the model was used to predict which outcome. Model versioning is not widely supported by popular data science packages, and thus it is often implemented in a custom manner.

## Batch Prediction

A common prediction flow is that of batch prediction, where we make a prediction for a large set of objects periodically. For example, we might want to re-predict the likelihood to churn every day for each of our customers. This procedure is shown in Figure 8.7.

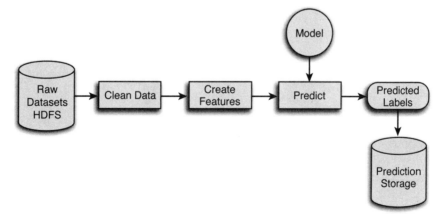

Figure 8.7    Batch prediction.

First we go through the same exact flow of data cleaning and feature generation that we used during training, but in this case we don't have labels (we want to predict the labels). Then we retrieve the model from the model storage facility and make the prediction for each instance in our dataset—resulting in labels (for classification) or values (for regression). We then store these outputs into a prediction storage location for future use.

Continuing our example of predicting churn, we might store the result (churn/ not-churn) for each customer and then kick off another application to look at this data and take some action, such as sending the customers likely to churn some special offer.

## Real-Time Prediction

With real-time prediction we typically want to predict for a single object (e.g., one customer) and do it in near-real-time (seconds), as shown in Figure 8.8.

An application usually kicks-off the flow by specifying the object (e.g., customer) for which prediction is needed. Kafka and Storm or Spark Streaming are often used to trigger the processing flow of data cleaning and feature generation, followed by prediction using the model from the learning phase. The result (predicted label or value) is then sent back to the application.

As an example, consider a real-time fraud detection application, where upon arrival of a credit-card transaction, the details of this transaction are used to generate features and then predict whether this transaction is likely to be fraudulent or not. If it is suspected as fraudulent, then the application might take action such as blocking the transaction from being processed.

The near-real-time flow offers some challenges due to a tight response time (often an answer is required within a second or less). This constraint requires not only choosing a machine learning algorithm that can predict within this time frame, but also puts constraints on the feature generation flow, which needs to complete within the same time frame.

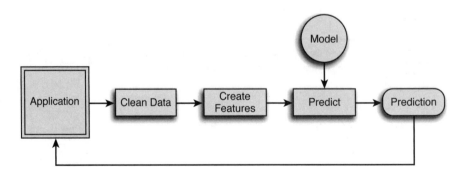

Figure 8.8    Near-real-time prediction.

# Example: Sentiment Analysis

Twitter and other micro-blogging websites have long been a source of information about consumer sentiment, especially since people tend to discuss various issues as well as post their feelings, complaints, or praise of various products and services on Twitter.

In this section we demonstrate how to build a sentiment classifier for tweets.

## Tweets Dataset

In this example, we use the sentiment140 corpus, comprised of about 1.6M tweets, each with the following information:

- The polarity of the tweet: 0 = negative, 2 = neutral, 4 = positive)
- ID of the tweet
- Date of the tweet
- The query (if available)
- The user of the tweet
- The text of the tweet

We also use the AFINN wordlist,[1] which provides a **sentiment score** for 2476 English words to help our classifier achieve better accuracy.

Each row of this dataset is simply

- Word
- Score

where score is an integer value between –5 (most negative) and 5 (most positive).

## Data Preparation

First, we load all the dataset into HIVE using shell scripting:

```
# ingest sentiment140 dataset
curl http://cs.stanford.edu/people/alecmgo/trainingandtestdata.zip >
➡ sentiment.zip
unzip sentiment.zip
hadoop fs -rm sentiment
hadoop fs -mkdir sentiment
hadoop fs -put testdata.manual.2009.06.14.csv
➡ training.1600000.processed.noemoticon.csv sentiment/

# ingest positive/negative word list
hadoop fs -rm wordlist
hadoop fs -mkdir wordlist
hadoop fs -put data/AFINN-111.txt wordlist/
```

---

1. http://www2.imm.dtu.dk/pubdb/views/publication_details.php?id=6010

We then use HIVE to create two tables:

- tweets—The main table with tweet data
- sentiment_words—The table with word sentiment scores

```
DROP TABLE tweets_raw;
CREATE EXTERNAL TABLE tweets_raw (
  `polarity` int,
  `id` string,
  `date` string,
  `query` string,
  `user` string,
  `text`  string)
ROW FORMAT SERDE 'org.apache.hadoop.hive.serde2.OpenCSVSerde'
STORED AS TEXTFILE
LOCATION '/user/jupyter/sentiment'
tblproperties("skip.header.line.count"="0");

DROP TABLE tweets;
CREATE TABLE tweets STORED AS ORC AS SELECT * FROM tweets_raw;

DROP TABLE sentiment_words;
CREATE EXTERNAL TABLE sentiment_words (
  `word` string,
  `score` int)
ROW FORMAT DELIMITED
FIELDS TERMINATED BY '\t'
STORED AS TEXTFILE
LOCATION '/user/jupyter/wordlist/';
```

Note that the we import the tweets as an external Hive table first, then recast it into an ORC table to improve performance. For the sentiment_words table, we don't bother generating it as ORC since it's very small.

## Feature Generation

Now that we have our datasets conveniently stored as Hive tables, let's use Spark's DataFrames API to generate a feature matrix for our model.

We represent each tweet as follows:

- A TF-IDF-based vector of words from the text of the tweet
- A positive and negative sentiment score, based on the sentiment wordlist
- Temporal features including month, day-of-week, and hour-of-day

We use Spark for the feature generation, although we can equally use Hive or Pig for this type of processing.

First, we create a SparkContext, and a HiveContext:

```
# Set up Spark Context
from pyspark import SparkContext, SparkConf
```

```
SparkContext.setSystemProperty('spark.executor.memory', '8g')
conf = SparkConf()
conf.set('spark.executor.instances', 8)
# 400MB for broadcast join
conf.set('spark.sql.autoBroadcastJoinThreshold', 400*1024*1024)
sc = SparkContext('yarn-client', 'ch8-demo', conf=conf)
# Setup HiveContext
from pyspark.sql import HiveContext
hc = HiveContext(sc)
```

Now we create some PySpark UDFs to use in our feature generation query. The first one, `tokenize()`, performs all the heavy lifting on the text.

- Replaces all whitespace with a single-space character
- Splits the text into words and makes everything lowercase
- Removes any words with less than two characters, or words that start with "@" (those are typically user names in Twitter)
- Replaces every URL (starts with "http") with the word "URL". We assume here that the text in the URL itself is not indicative of sentiment, and thus we can remove many unnecessary features.
- Removes any punctuation from the words
- Generates the final list of all words, as well as any two-word combinations (2-grams)

As an example, let's see how tokenization works for some example text:

```
tokenize("my name is Inigo Montoya; you killed my father; prepare to
➥ die.")

[u'my', u'name', u'is', u'inigo', u'montoya', u'you', u'killed', u'my', u'father',
u'prepare', u'to', u'die', u'my name', u'name is', u'is inigo', u'inigo montoya',
u'montoya you', u'you killed', u'killed my', u'my father', u'father prepare',
u'prepare to', u'to die']
```

The code for `tokenize()` is:

```
import re, string
import pyspark.sql.functions as F
from pyspark.sql.types import StringType, ArrayType, FloatType
# Define PySpark UDF to tokenize text into words with various
# other specialized procesing
punct = re.compile('[%s]' % re.escape(string.punctuation))
def tok_str(text, ngrams=1, minChars=2):
    # change any whitespace to regular space
    text = re.sub(r'\s+', ' ', text)
    # split into tokens and change to lower case
    tokens = map(unicode, text.lower().split(' '))
    # remove short words and usernames
    tokens = filter(lambda x: len(x)>=minChars and x[0]!='@', tokens)
```

```
    # repalce any url by the constant word "URL"
    tokens = ["URL" if t[:4]=="http" else t for t in tokens]
    # remove punctuation from tokens
    tokens = [punct.sub('', t) for t in tokens]
    if ngrams==1:
        return tokens
    else:
        return tokens + [' '.join(tokens[i:i+ngrams]) for i in
➥ xrange(len(tokens)-ngrams+1)]
tokenize = F.udf(lambda s: tok_str(unicode(s),ngrams=2), ArrayType(StringType()))
```

We also define two other UDFs: pos_score and neg_score. Given a set of words, these functions compute a sentiment score (positive and negative, respectively) reflected in the list of words, using the sentiment scores in the sentiment_words table.

```
# load sentiment dictionary
wv = hc.table('sentiment_words').collect()
wordlist = dict([(r.word,r.score) for r in wv])
# Define PySpark UDF to get sentiment score using word-list
def pscore(words):
    scores = filter(lambda x: x>0, [wordlist[t] for t in words if t in
➥ wordlist])
    return 0.0 if len(scores)==0 else (float(sum(scores))/len(scores))
pos_score = F.udf(lambda w: pscore(w), FloatType())
def nscore(words):
    scores = filter(lambda x: x<0, [wordlist[t] for t in words if t in
➥ wordlist])
    return 0.0 if len(scores)==0 else (float(sum(scores))/len(scores))
neg_score = F.udf(lambda w: nscore(w), FloatType())
```

Now that we have the UDFs ready, let's look at the Spark SQL code to generate our feature matrix:

```
tw1 = hc.sql("""
SELECT text, query, polarity, date,
  regexp_extract(date, '([0-9]{2}):([0-9]{2}):([0-9]{2})', 1) as hour,
  regexp_extract(date, '(Sun|Mon|Tue|Wed|Thu|Fri|Sat)', 1) as dayofweek,
  regexp_extract(date,
  '(Jan|Feb|Mar|Apr|May|Jun|Jul|Aug|Sep|Oct|Nov|Dec)', 1) as month
FROM tweets
""")
tw2 = tw1.filter("polarity != 2").withColumn('words', tokenize(tw1['text']))
tw3 = (tw2.select("user", "hour", "dayofweek", "month", "words",
  F.when(tw2.polarity == 4, "Pos").otherwise("Neg").alias("sentiment"),
  pos_score(tw2["words"]).alias("pscore"),
  neg_score(tw2["words"]).alias("nscore")))
tw3.registerTempTable("fm")
```

We store the resulting feature matrix in a Spark SQL temporary table called "fm".

As can be seen from the code, we first use a SQL query to extract the fields we need, while creating new fields for hour, dayofweek, and month using regular expressions.

We then filter out any tweets with a neutral sentiment (there are only 39 of those in the dataset, so to simplify we do not deal with them in this example) and use the `tokenize()` UDF to transform the text into words.

Finally, we create the final feature matrix including all the features: hour, month, day-of-week, words, pscore, and nscore. We convert the "polarity" field to a textual replacement with two possible values: Pos or Neg.

## Building a Classifier

We now turn to training a classifier. We use Spark's ML pipeline API to build a pipeline of transformation:

```
from pyspark.ml.classification import RandomForestClassifier
from pyspark.ml.feature import StringIndexer, VectorAssembler, IDF,
➥ RegexTokenizer, HashingTF
from pyspark.ml import Pipeline

# paramaters for modeling
numFeatures = 5000
minDocFreq = 50
numTrees = 1000

# Build Machine Learning pipeline
inx1 = StringIndexer(inputCol="hour", outputCol="hour-inx")
inx2 = StringIndexer(inputCol="month", outputCol="month-inx")
inx3 = StringIndexer(inputCol="dayofweek", outputCol="dow-inx")
inx4 = StringIndexer(inputCol="sentiment", outputCol="label")
hashingTF = HashingTF(numFeatures=numFeatures, inputCol="words",
➥ outputCol="hash-tf")
idf = IDF(minDocFreq=minDocFreq, inputCol="hash-tf",
➥ outputCol="hash-tfidf")
va = VectorAssembler(inputCols =["hour-inx", "month-inx", "dow-inx",
➥ "hash-tfidf", "pscore", "nscore"], outputCol="features")
rf = RandomForestClassifier(numTrees=numTrees, maxDepth=4, maxBins=32,
➥ labelCol="label", seed=42)
p = Pipeline(stages=[inx1, inx2, inx3, inx4, hashingTF, idf, va, rf])
```

The `StringIndexer` instances transform string variables to categorical variables. `HashingTF` and `IDF` compute TF-IDF on the words list for each tweet. `VectorAssembler` combines all the features into a single feature vector. `RandomForestClassifier` is the final training phase using a random forest algorithm.

We use a 70/30 split between training and testing, then train our model:

```
(trainSet, testSet) = hc.table("fm").randomSplit([0.7, 0.3])
trainData = trainSet.cache()
testData = testSet.cache()
model = p.fit(trainData)                    # Train the model on training data
```

Finally, we define a function to evaluate precision, recall and accuracy:

```
def eval_metrics(lap):
    tp = float(len(lap[(lap['label']==1) & (lap['prediction']==1)]))
    tn = float(len(lap[(lap['label']==0) & (lap['prediction']==0)]))
    fp = float(len(lap[(lap['label']==0) & (lap['prediction']==1)]))
    fn = float(len(lap[(lap['label']==1) & (lap['prediction']==0)]))
    precision = tp / (tp+fp)
    recall = tp / (tp+fn)
    accuracy = (tp+tn) / (tp+tn+fp+fn)
    return {'precision': precision, 'recall': recall, 'accuracy': accuracy}
```

We then measure the performance of our algorithm on the testset:

```
# Predict using test data
results = model.transform(testData)
lap = results.select("label", "prediction").toPandas()
m = eval_metrics(lap)
print m

{'recall': 0.6895734004601074, 'precision': 0.7560832948724393,
➥ 'accuracy': 0.733644830610336}
```

Even though this was a relatively simple example, the results are quite encouraging, with precision of 68%, recall of 75%, and overall accuracy of 73.3%.

The capability to parallelize the computation over multiple machines, along with Spark's effective in-memory distributed implementation of random forest, enables us to run this at large scale using a large number of $n$-grams without significant limitation.

# Summary

In this chapter

- You learned what classification is and how to measure its performance using metrics like precision and recall, as well as area under the ROC curve.

- You learned what regression is and how to measure its performance with mean absolute error (MAE) and root mean squared error (RMSE).

- You learned about the importance of cross-validation, model tuning, and how Hadoop's parallel processing capabilities can help in this process.

- You were introduced to the various algorithms available for supervised learning such as decision trees, neural networks, generalized linear models, and random forest.

- You learned how to build big data architectures for supervised learning supporting model training and batch or real-time prediction.

- You learned how to build a distributed classification model for sentiment analysis of tweets using Hadoop and Spark.

# Clustering

*In all chaos there is a cosmos, in all disorder a secret order.*

Carl Jung

**In This Chapter:**

- Overview of clustering
- Uses of clustering
- Similarity measures
- Clustering algorithms
- Evaluating clusters
- Clustering with big data
- Example: topic modeling of news

We have mentioned clustering several times in the previous chapters. In this chapter we provide a more detailed exposition of clustering. We start with an overview of clustering and describe the various ways clustering is used in data science. We then describe the importance of similarity metrics for clustering, some common clustering algorithms, and how clustering outputs are evaluated. We finish by describing how to apply clustering algorithms to big data using an extended example.

## Overview of Clustering

In clustering (also known as "cluster analysis"), the most common type of unsupervised algorithm, we are presented with an input dataset of observations. Unlike classification or regression, clustering does not require a label or target variable; instead it attempts to uncover natural groupings of these observations into clusters (sets of observations that are similar to one another).

Given an input dataset of observations, each represented by a feature vector, we define a similarity function f(A,B) between any two observations A and B. A clustering algorithm then takes the input feature matrix, a similarity function f, and the number of clusters desired (often denoted by K) and produces a segmentation of observations into clusters.

Table 9.1    **Example feature matrix for customer segmentation.**

| CustID | Apples | Pears | Cheese | Meat | Chicken | Yogurt | Chips |
|--------|--------|-------|--------|------|---------|--------|-------|
| 0 | 2 | 5 | 0 | 0 | 0 | 0 | 0 |
| 1 | 0 | 1 | 3 | 0 | 2 | 4 | 5 |
| 2 | 0 | 1 | 12 | 3 | 5 | 12 | 9 |
| 3 | 5 | 7 | 8 | 1 | 3 | 7 | 3 |
| 4 | ... | ... | ... | ... | ... | ... | ... |

Consider for example a grocery retailer who wants to identify natural behavioral clusters in their customer base. A simple model may represent each customer by a vector of features, such that each feature corresponds to the number of times they have purchased a given item, as shown in Table 9.1.

Given a certain desired value K, the algorithm then attempts to group customers together into K clusters such that the behavior of each pair of customers in the same cluster is similar as represented by their purchasing behavior (the number of items they have purchased from each type of item).

## Uses of Clustering

There are three main uses for clustering in data science: exploratory analysis, pre-processing for feature reduction, and anomaly detection.[1]

The most common use of clustering is for exploratory analysis. Here the goal is to uncover some new or previously unknown insight from the data. For example, you might use clustering to uncover previously unknown categories of certain diseases, to segment customers into certain groups that behave in a similar manner, or to cluster documents into topics.

Clustering is often used as an automated pre-processing step in an end-to-end data processing chain. For example, we might want to cluster individual products into product families before building a recommender system. In such situations, the purpose of clustering is to improve the overall performance of the system, which can usually be quantified by the overall performance of the system (for example, the overall improvement in sales associated with the recommender system).

For use with anomaly or outlier detection, we first cluster observations, and then use those clusters to calculate an anomaly score for each observation, based on its distance from the cluster center. The further away from the cluster center, the more anomalous the observation is deemed to be.

---

1. Anomaly detection is discussed in further detail in Chapter 10, "Anomaly Detection with Hadoop."

# Designing a Similarity Measure

The design of a good similarity measure is at the base of any clustering analysis, and in most cases is of great importance to its success. There is usually not a clear answer to "Which similarity measure is best for my problem?", and that is why clustering is often considered part science and part art.

In most cases, the similarity measure is computed between pairs of N-dimensional points, and with large datasets that computation may take a long time on a single compute node. Fortunately, computing the similarity measure for each pair of points is completely independent from other pairs, and thus this computation can easily be parallelized using Hadoop with Pig, Hive, or Spark.

Let's review a few commonly used approaches to similarity.

## Distance Functions

One common way to measure similarity is with a distance metric. In this case, the similarity is in some sense the inverse of the distance metric.

If your feature vectors are numerical, a common choice is the Minkowski distance between two numerical vectors, defined as:

$$d(A,B) = \sqrt[g]{\sum_{i=1}^{n} |A_i - B_i|^g}$$

Two well-known versions of the Minkowski distance are: Euclidean distance ($g=2$) and Manhattan (or Taxicab) distance ($g=1$). This distance metric has been extensively studied and is well suited to numerical attributes. Since with Minkowski distance the measurement unit of individual features can significantly impact the similarity output, normalizing the data (i.e., making the vector's length one) is recommended.

For binary feature vectors, distance measures are often calculated using a contingency table. Let's define the following variables:

$R$ = number of features where A=1 and B=0

$S$ = number of features where A=0 and B=1

$Q$ = number of features where A=0 and B=0

$T$ = number of features where A=1 and B=1

Then the distance is computed as follows:

$$d(A,B) = \frac{R+S}{R+S+Q+T}$$

This really measures the percent of features that are different (1/0 or 0/1) and is also known as Hamming distance.

In the case where the positive outcome (A=1 or B=1) is more important then the negative outcome, a preferred variant of this metric is

$$d(A,B) = \frac{R+S}{R+S+Q}$$

also known as the Jaccard coefficient. For categorical (also known as nomimal) features, a common choice for a distance metric is

$$d(A,B) = \frac{n-m}{n}$$

where $n$ is the size of the vector (number of features) and $m$ is the number of places where the value of $A$ matches the value of $B$.

For ordinal features, it is common to use Minkowski distances after mapping the values into the [0-1] range.

If our feature values are of mixed type (numerical, binary, categorical, etc.) then one may simply calculate the distance by combining all the methods mentioned above, each applied to the appropriate section in the feature vector.

## Similarity Functions

Instead of a reverse distance metric, there are various metrics that directly measure similarity. These functions have a large value when $A$ is similar to $B$, and have the largest value when the two vectors are identical. In some cases the similarity is only in the range [0...1], but that is not mandatory.

When the angle between two vectors is a meaningful measure of their similarity, then the cosine similarity is a useful metric, defined as:

$$s\_cos(A,B) = \frac{\sum_{i=1}^{n} A_i B_i}{\sum_{i=1}^{n} A_i^2 \cdot \sum_{i=1}^{n} B_i^2}$$

This essentially corresponds to a normalized dot product between the vectors. A related similarity metric is the normalized Pearson correlation defined as:

$$s\_pearson(A,B) = \frac{\sum_{i=1}^{n} (A_i - \mu_i)(B_i - \mu_i)}{\sum_{i=1}^{n} (A_i - \mu_i) \cdot \sum_{i=1}^{n} (B_i - \mu_i)}$$

where $\mu$ represent the average value of all vectors.

## Clustering Algorithms

There are a lot of clustering algorithms available. It is beyond the scope of this book to cover all of those algorithms in detail. Instead we wanted to highlight the various high-level approaches to clustering and mention a few of the leading approaches in each such category:

- **Partitioning-based**—divide the objects into K clusters and evaluate the quality of these clusters with some heuristic metric. *k*-means and PAM are partitioning-based clustering algorithms.

- **Hierarchical**—Clusters are constructed by starting with a cluster per object and recursively combining the two closest clusters at each step. Similarly a top-down approach would start with a single cluster and recursively divide, at each step, one of the clusters into two clusters. CURE is a hierarchical clustering algorithm.

- **Density-based**—Clusters are constructed by looking at point density within a certain neighborhood area. DBSCAN, OPTICS, and CLIQUE are density-based clustering algorithms.

- **Grid-based**—Using a single uniform grid-mesh, the entire data space is divided into cells and data objects are associated with cells. Clustering is then performed using the cells instead of the original data points, resulting in faster performance for large datasets. CLIQUE is a grid-based clustering algorithm.

- **Model-based**—Assuming data is generated from K probability distributions, clusters are constructed by estimating the likelihood of a point being generated from each such distribution, using an EM (estimate-maximize) approach.

- **Graph-based**—Using some similarity function, we represent each data point as a node in the graph, and draw an (undirected) edge between each pair of nodes if their similarity is higher than a certain threshold. Then we apply graph algorithms for clustering on the similarity graph. Spectral clustering is a graph-based algorithm.

An additional consideration for clustering algorithms is hard versus soft clustering. With hard clustering any observation may only belong to a single cluster, whereas soft clustering allows an object to belong to more than one cluster. For example, in classifying documents to topics it is often useful to allow a given document to be associated with more than a single topic.

# Example: Clustering Algorithms

*k*-means clustering and latent Dirichlet allocation (LDA) are the two most common clustering algorithms in practical use. We now describe these algorithms in more detail.

## *k*-means Clustering

Originating from the field of signal processing (where it is used for vector quantization), *k*-means clustering aims to minimize the within-cluster sum of squares error (SSE)

$$\underset{S}{argmin} \sum_{i=1}^{K} \sum_{x \in S_i} ||x - \mu_i||^{\wedge 2}$$

where $x = \{x_1, x_2, \ldots, x_n\}$ is the set of input vectors representing the n objects, $S = \{S_1, S_2, \ldots, S_K\}$ represents the resulting clusters, and $\mu_i$ represents the mean (or centroid) of observations in the i-th cluster.

*k*-means clustering uses Euclidean distance as its similarity metric. It starts with an initial set of centroids for each of the clusters, and iterates as follows until convergence is reached:

1. For each cluster, associate each point with the cluster whose centroid is closest to this point.
2. Re-compute cluster centroids as the mean of all points associated with this cluster in step 1.

*k*-means is relatively easy to implement in a Hadoop environment, as the two steps above tend to parallelize well. In step 1, the association of one point to its cluster centroids is completely independent from the same association for another point, thus this parallelizes easily. For step 2, you need to compute the new centroid over a large set of points, but that is also relatively easy to compute in a distributed environment using existing abstractions such as groupBy and aggregate.

In two dimensions, a clustering result may look like Figure 9.1.

The simplest version of *k*-means uses random initialization of cluster centroids. Even though it works well in many practical situations, it is not guaranteed to converge to the optimum.

A more recent approach called "*k*-means++" uses a smarter initialization procedure to ensure faster convergence as well as improves the likelihood to converge on a better solution (closer to the global minima).

Other important variants of *k*-means include the following:

- *k*-medians, which is a variant of *k*-means that minimizes the Manhattan distance instead of the Euclidean distance between points and cluster centroids
- *k*-Medoids (also known as PAM: partition around medoids), which is a variant that enables generic distance metrics

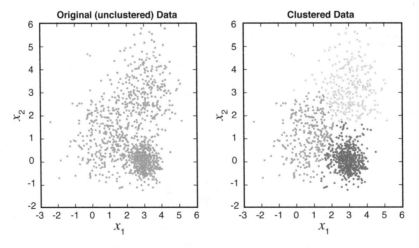

Figure 9.1   Example clustering output.

## Latent Dirichlet Allocation

Latent Dirichlet allocation[2] (LDA) is arguably the most popular topic modeling technique in use. LDA analyzes a corpus of documents and automatically organizes the documents into topics (clusters of documents). Thus it is a form of clustering for text documents.

From a statistical point of view, LDA assumes each document is represented as a mixture of (unknown) topics. Specifically, LDA assumes that every document in the collection is generated as follows:

1. Decide on the number of words N in the document.
2. Choose a topic mixture for the document (e.g., 20% topic A, 50% topic B, 30% topic C), using a Dirichlet Distribution.
3. Generate each word as follows:
   a. Probabilistically pick a topic T using the topic mixture distribution.
   b. Pick a word based on the distribution of words in the topic T you have chosen.

This generative model emphasizes that documents contain multiple topics, which is often true. For example, a document on foreign policy might have words drawn from the "politics" topic and words drawn from the "foreign" topic.

The goal of LDA is to automatically discover the topics from the document collection. Therefore it needs to uncover the topic distribution of each document and the word distribution within each topic.

In practice, LDA works extremely well and is one of the most common techniques for topic modeling. It is implemented in many common ML libraries.

In a distributed environment, Spark MLlib has a strong implementation of LDA that works well on large datasets in a Hadoop environment. We will look at an example of using Spark MLlib's implementation of LDA later in this chapter.

# Evaluating the Clusters and Choosing the Number of Clusters

Evaluating whether a given clustering result is good or not is problematic at best. In fact, many argue there is no principled way to achieve this, and the evaluation remains mostly a matter of perspective.

A common criterion is sum of squared error (SSE, the same metric that $k$-means minimizes), which measures the average intra-cluster similarities over all clusters and is most suitable for situations where the clusters are spherical and well-separated from each other.

Another way to evaluate a clustering scheme is to have a pre-determined classification set and measure how much the clustering algorithm matches this dataset. More specifically, metrics like mutual information or precision–recall F1 metric are often used.

---

2. https://www.cs.princeton.edu/~blei/papers/BleiNgJordan2003.pdf

In practice, subject matter experts (SME) can often provide further insight into cluster quality and evaluate the results in the context of their expertise. Using SME opinion is, of course, not automated, but is often useful in the early stages of performing clustering analysis.

Another challenge with most clustering algorithms is how to choose K, the desired number of clusters.

A simple strategy for choosing K is to run the clustering algorithm over a range of possible K values, in each case evaluate the clustering result using SSE, and then choose the K that provided the lowest value of SSE. Quite often business context provides a good guideline for possible values for K as well.

For example, consider a marketing department that would like to perform a segmentation of customers, and use the resulting segments to decide which version of an email communication to send out. The marketing experts often have some preconceived notion of reasonable clusters and how many they should have, which can be effectively used to limit the range of K we should try. The same marketing experts can also help evaluate the actual clusters produced by the algorithm and their quality.

# Building Big Data Clustering Solutions

Now that we understand clustering algorithms, let's look at the end-to-end solution architecture.

The flow of a clustering system typically looks like what is shown in Figure 9.2.

In implementing this, you have some latitude in the choices for the various components of this diagram. You will note, however, that the dominant theme is that you have two separate streams of data: batch and real-time streaming.

The streaming component is intended to cluster data points as they arrive across the wire. This data is generally kept in a distributed queue such as Apache Kafka which can provide some back-pressure support. This scoring should use a model that is initially trained and periodically retrained in batch. Examples of reasonable choices for a streaming component are Apache Storm or Apache Spark streaming.

The batch component must be capable of creating a model, so the choice can be somewhat limited. It generally falls between two possibilities:

1. Use a Pig script, Hive query, MapReduce job, or Spark job to sample the input data and do the data preparation and feature extraction. Then use a small data analytics utility such as scikit-learn or R on this sampled data to create the model and persist it to HDFS. Depending on the clustering model, this could be as simple as the centroids for each of the clusters, as in the case of k-means clustering, or a far more complex model containing distributional statistics of the underlying data in the case of LDA.

2. Use Apache Spark's MLlib or Apache Mahout to do both the data selection, feature extraction, and model creation in a single environment.

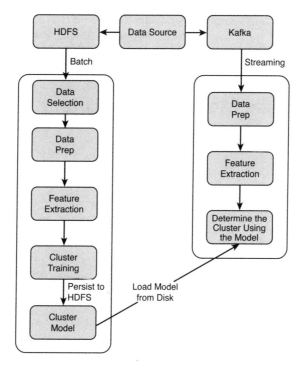

Figure 9.2    Big data architecture for clustering algorithms.

As the big data libraries such as MLlib and Mahout get more robust and gain more features, the second option becomes more viable and practical. This has a lot of benefits, chief among them being that you can use all of the data and construct the model at scale. That being said, you still see the first option chosen from time to time due to lack of support or buggy support for techniques that tend to work better for the data.

The data selection phase may seem odd in the situation where we are using all of the data, but for seasonal models, you will want to limit the training data used to create your clustering model.

You can see, however, that the feature extraction and data preparation is uniform for both pipelines. In fact, if this changes, then care must be taken to not cluster using a model trained assuming a different type of data preparation or feature vector representation. The kind of preparation here is data dependent, but an example for LDA would be stemming words and getting rid of the most popular words.

Hadoop is orchestrating both of these components within the boundaries of the cluster. This has the benefit of being able to fully utilize the cluster and use the scale-out capabilities of Hadoop. Furthermore, the tooling inside of Hadoop has gotten much more robust and intelligent as of late. In particular, Spark's MLlib library has been gaining a lot of traction in this regard. It has a very robust implementation of $k$-means with modern optimizations for efficiently initializing the potential centers to a near optimal solution called kmeans||. Also, as you'll see in the next example, the NLP-oriented topic modeling via latent Dirichlet allocation is supported with a well-thought-out and mature implementation.

# Example: Topic Modeling with Latent Dirichlet Allocation

The OHSUMED dataset is a set of 348,566 references from MEDLINE, the online medical information database, consisting of titles and/or abstracts from 270 medical journals over a five-year period (1987-1991).

For this example, we are using a subset of this dataset with 56,984 documents, and applying latent Dirichlet allocation to it for the purpose of topic modeling.

## Data Ingestion

We download the OHSUMED dataset from one of the mirrors and ingest it into HDFS:

```
$ wget http://disi.unitn.it/moschitti/corpora/ohsumed-all-docs.tar.gz
$ tar -zxvf ohsumed-all-docs.tar.gz
$ hdfs dfs -mkdir ohsumed
$ hdfs dfs -put ohsumed-all/* ohsumed/
$ rm -rf ohsumed-all
$ rm ohsumed-all-docs.tar.gz
```

## Feature Generation

First we read each document in the corpus from HDFS and tokenize it.

We use Apache OpenNLP to do the tokenization (separate sentences into words) and stemming (reducing each word to its base form; for example "pens" -> "pen"). Because OpenNLP is a separate package we have to add it to Spark with the sc.addJar command.

```
import org.apache.spark.rdd._
import collection.JavaConversions._
import opennlp.tools.tokenize.SimpleTokenizer
import opennlp.tools.stemmer.PorterStemmer

sc.addJar("/home/jupyter/notebooks/jars/opennlp-tools-1.6.0.jar")

// Load documents from text files, 1 element (text string) per file
val corpus = sc.wholeTextFiles("/user/jupyter/ohsumed/C*", 20).map(x =>
➥ x._2)

// read stop words from file
val stopwordFile = "/user/jupyter/stop-words.txt"
val st_words = sc.textFile(stopwordFile).collect()
➥.flatMap(_.stripMargin.split("\\s+")).map(_.toLowerCase).toSet
val stopwords = sc.broadcast(st_words)
```

```
val minWordLength = 3
val tokenized: RDD[(Long, Array[String])] = corpus.zipWithIndex().map { case
(text,id) =>
    val tokenizer = SimpleTokenizer.INSTANCE
    val stemmer = new PorterStemmer()
    val tokens = tokenizer.tokenize(text)
    val words = tokens.filter(w => (w.length >= minWordLength) &&
    (!stopwords.value.contains(w))).map(w => stemmer.stem(w))
    id -> words
}.filter(_._2.length > 0)

tokenized.cache()
val numDocs = tokenized.count()
```

After reading all the corpus of documents and the stop-word list (stored as a Spark broadcast variable), we use Spark to tokenize each sentence and return a list of words. We filter out words that are:

- Less than three characters long
- Included in our stop-words list

Finally, we filter out any empty text fields with no words and cache the resulting tokenized RDD.

With a large set of documents, it is often useful to limit the vocabulary of words and keep only the most common words. We do that next:

```
val wordCounts: RDD[(String,Long)] = tokenized.flatMap {
  case (_,tokens) => tokens.map(_ -> 1L)
}.reduceByKey(_ + _)
wordCounts.cache()
val fullVocabSize = wordCounts.count()
val vSize = 10000
val (vocab: Map[String, Int], selectedTokenCount: Long) = {
    val sortedWC: Array[(String,Long)] = {wordCounts.sortBy(_._2,
➡ ascending=false) .take(vSize)}
    (sortedWC.map(_._1).zipWithIndex.toMap, sortedWC.map(_._2).sum)
}
```

Now that we limited the vocabulary, we continue to represent each document as a vector of features (each feature corresponding to a word in the vocabulary) with TF-IDF encoding:

```
import org.apache.spark.mllib.linalg.{Vector, SparseVector, Vectors}
import org.apache.spark.mllib.feature.IDF
val documents = tokenized.map { case (id, tokens) =>
// Filter tokens by vocabulary, and
// create word count vector representation of document.
    val wc = new mutable.HashMap[Int, Int]()
    tokens.foreach { term =>
        if (vocab.contains(term)) {
          val termIndex = vocab(term)
```

```
            wc(termIndex) = wc.getOrElse(termIndex, 0) + 1
        }
    }
    val indices = wc.keys.toArray.sorted
    val values = indices.map(i => wc(i).toDouble)
    val sb = Vectors.sparse(vocab.size, indices, values)
    (id, sb)
}

val vocabArray = new Array[String](vocab.size)
vocab.foreach { case (term, i) => vocabArray(i) = term }

val tf = documents.map { case (id, vec) => vec }.cache()
val idfVals = new IDF().fit(tf).idf.toArray
val tfidfDocs: RDD[(Long, Vector)] = documents.map { case (id, vec) =>
    val indices = vec.asInstanceOf[SparseVector].indices
    val counts = new mutable.HashMap[Int, Double]()
    for (idx <- indices) {
        counts(idx) = vec(idx) * idfVals(idx)
    }
    (id, Vectors.sparse(vocab.size, counts.toSeq))
}
```

The resulting RDD, tfidfDocs, is an RDD of (id,vec) pairs, where id is a unique ID of the document, and vec is a sparse vector representing the TFIDF features of the document.

## Running Latent Dirichlet Allocation

We are now ready to run LDA. We ask MLlib to run for 50 iterations and discover 5 topics in the dataset:

```
import scala.collection.mutable
import org.apache.spark.mllib.clustering.{OnlineLDAOptimizer,
➥ DistributedLDAModel, LDA}
import org.apache.spark.mllib.linalg.{Vector, Vectors}

val numTopics = 5
val numIterations = 50
val lda = new LDA().setK(numTopics).setMaxIterations(numIterations).
➥ setOptimizer("online")
val ldaModel = lda.run(tfidfDocs)
```

When LDA finishes, ldaModel includes the model that was uncovered by the LDA. We can use the following code to print the topics, each represented with the top five most important words (or bigrams):

```
val topicIndices = ldaModel.describeTopics(maxTermsPerTopic = 5)
topicIndices.foreach { case (terms, termWeights) =>
    println("TOPIC:")
    terms.zip(termWeights).foreach { case (term, weight) =>
        println(s"${vocabArray(term.toInt)}\t$weight")
    }
    println()
}
```

Table 9.2    **Top five most important words for ldaModel topics.**

|   | Term 1 | Term 2 | Term 3 | Term 4 | Term 5 |
|---|--------|--------|--------|--------|--------|
| 1 | infect | HIV | children | patient | risk |
| 2 | tumor | cell | carcinoma | cancer | lesion |
| 3 | cell | protein | activ | alpha | antibody |
| 4 | injuri | CSF | fractur | patient | laser |
| 5 | arteri | pressur | coronari | hypertens | ventricular |

The results are summarized in Table 9.2.

As we can see, the topics (one per row in Table 9.2) are described in terms of top-five keywords, which usually provide a good sense for the topic itself. In this, our topics seem to be:

1. HIV

2. Cancer

3. Immunology

4. Something about injuries related to CSF (cerebrospinal fluid)

5. Coronary disease

It is a common challenge with topic modeling to provide a single interpretation for topics, as we can see, for example, in topic 4, which seems to combine a few sub-topics.

# Summary

In this chapter

- You learned about clustering, an unsupervised learning technique that is used for pre-processing of data (dimensionality reduction) or for data exploration to gain insights into the implicit structure of the data.

- We covered how to build an appropriate similarity metric for our clustering analysis and, specifically, how to deal with continuous and categorical variables and mixed feature sets.

- We surveyed some of the various approaches to clustering, including $k$-means, latent Dirichlet allocation, and other common techniques.

- You learned how to evaluate the results of clustering and the difficulty of choosing the number of desired clusters K.

- We provided an example of how to build an end-to-end clustering solution for big data with Hadoop, including a batch and real-time component.

# Anomaly Detection with Hadoop

*It's in the anomalies that nature reveals its secrets.*

Johann Wolfgang von Goethe

## In This Chapter:

- Overview of anomaly detection
- Types of anomalies in data
- Approaches to anomaly detection
- Anomaly detection for time-series data
- How to build anomaly detection systems with Hadoop
- Example: anomaly detection with network traffic data

In this chapter we discuss anomaly detection (or outlier detection), a term referring to various techniques used to identify abnormal patterns within data.

## Overview

Anomaly detection techniques are designed to identify patterns in the data that do not conform to a well-defined notion of expected or normal behavior. Given a set of observations, anomaly detection techniques identify one or more observations that appears to deviate markedly from other instances of the sample in which it occurs.

The exact mathematical definition of *deviate markedly* varies and is often domain specific. In many cases, an anomaly score is generated that reflects the degree of anomaly for each instance in the set. With score-based algorithms a threshold is used to decide which observations are anomalous and which are not.

Recall from Chapter 5, "Data Munging with Hadoop," that statistical outlier detection is often useful as a feature pre-processing step for single variables—often called **extreme value analysis.** By removing outlier points from a certain variable in the data, subsequent data mining often becomes more accurate and successful. In this chapter we cover anomaly detection as a pure data-mining task.

## Uses of Anomaly Detection

Anomaly detection as a distinct data mining task has many practical use cases in various industry verticals. Uses include the following:

- Detecting fraudulent credit card transactions
- Detecting fraudulent healthcare claims
- Identifying hacker activities in network traffic
- Identifying faulty equipment (predictive maintenance)
- Detecting anomalous heartbeat patterns in an echocardiogram (ECG)

Anomalies in business systems often highlight some event that calls for critical action. For example, in fraud detection of credit card transactions the goal is to find some anomalous purchasing patterns that might indicate that a fraudster is using a lost or stolen credit card. Once identified, such suspect transactions can be suspended or cancelled. In network security, anomalous traffic patterns might indicate a computer system being hacked, resulting in further investigation and action to stop the hacking activity.

Very often, what constitutes an anomaly is context-dependent; for example, in fraud detection, a purchase of $100 might be considered anomalous for one person while for another it is completely normal. Similarly, certain network traffic patterns could be perfectly normal for a given network and anomalous for another.

## Types of Anomalies in Data

Data points in a dataset are often categorized into point anomalies and collective anomalies.

**Point anomalies** (also called **global anomalies**) are data points that can be considered anomalous with respect to the rest of the data. In Figure 10.1 the data points in the upper right-hand corner are probably anomalous data. If a point anomaly is only considered anomalous within a certain context, then it is often called a **contextual anomaly**

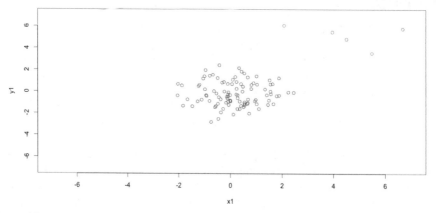

Figure 10.1   Point anomalies as indicated by the data points in the upper right-hand corner.

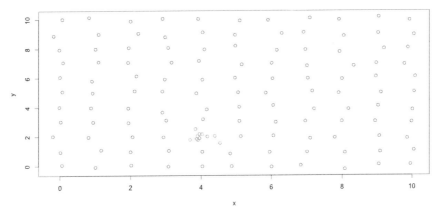

Figure 10.2    Collective anomaly around X=4,Y=2.

(also called **conditional anomalies**). For example, consider a set of temperature outputs from a jet engine, where most points are within a fixed range of normal temperature readings, whereas anomalous points are of extreme temperature values (either low or high).

A **collective anomaly** (often called a sequence anomaly) is a set of data points that individually might be normal but together are considered anomalies. As shown in Figure 10.2 the data points grouped around location X=4,Y=2 are a collective anomaly. For example, human electrocardiogram output may contain a collective anomaly because a low value may exist for an abnormally long time. The low value itself is not an outlier, but its successive occurrence for an extended time is an indication of anomalous behavior.

# Approaches to Anomaly Detection

There are many approaches to anomaly detection, most of which can be categorized into one of these categories: rules-based, unsupervised learning, supervised learning, or semi-supervised learning.

## Rules-based Methods

Some of the earliest and simplest techniques for anomaly detection use rules, whereby for each known type of anomaly we codify a rule to identify this anomaly.

Continuing our jet engine example, a rule might look like this:

*Rule: if temperature $> X$ or temperature $< Y$ then alert "anomalous temperature"*

Rule-based detection is often based on experts or domain expertise and specific experience with the data. Sometimes more automated techniques, such as decision trees or frequent item analysis, are used to guide the experts to the most complete and nuanced set of rules.

Although rules-based anomaly detection systems are relatively easy to understand and develop, they tend to be (like many other rules-based systems) difficult to maintain and improve over time due to their rigidity and static nature.

## Supervised Learning Methods

In cases where a labeled dataset of positive (normal) and negative (anomalous) examples is available, a classifier is often built with two classes: normal and anomalous (although multiple categories of normal and anomalous are also possible).

If our input is a time-series (e.g., temperature values over time), we often need to transform the data from a time-series into a form that is compatible with supervised learning—namely to a feature matrix. A common approach is to define a certain look-back window and define various features based on the subset of the time-series defined over that window from the event of interest. Sometimes better features can be generated in the frequency space, in which case techniques like FFT, DCT, or wavelet transforms are used.

Let's continue our example with the jet engine sensor data; consider building a supervised model for anomaly detection based on temperature values. We might look at all readings during the last 10 seconds, 30 seconds, and 60 seconds; from each such subsequence we can generate various aggregate values, such as:

- Average and median value
- Variance of value over time-window
- Minimum and maximum value
- Minimum and maximum of time-series derivative

With these features we can now construct a supervised learning model for anomaly detection.

If enough data from both classes is available, supervised learning can be quite effective for anomaly detection and often achieves better accuracy than unsupervised learning or static rules. It is also substantially more flexible than static rules, giving it the capability to adapt to rapidly changing environments and contexts.

In many practical situations, unfortunately, the lack of enough training examples (especially of the anomalous class) and an imbalanced class distribution (much more cases of normal than anomalous) presents significant hurdles that have to be overcome for this approach to be practical.

## Unsupervised Learning Methods

More often than not, a good training set for anomaly detection is either not available or too small. In these cases, unsupervised learning may achieve good results even without a training set.

### Statistical Identification of Point Anomalies

A simple and very common form of anomaly analysis, often performed on single-value (univariate) time-series data, works by computing the $Z$-score

$$Z_i = \frac{x_i - \tilde{x}}{sd}$$

where $x_i$ is the value of the variable, $\tilde{x}$ is the mean, and *sd* is the standard deviation. Typically, every data point with a *Z*-score of 3 or more (3 standard deviations from the mean) is considered an anomaly.

One challenge with this approach is that the presence of many outliers in the dataset might have a strong influence on the mean and standard deviation. An alternative approach that is more robust to outliers is called the median absolute deviation (MAD). With MAD you compute a modified *Z*-score replacing the mean with median, and the standard deviation with median absolute deviation, as follows. We first compute

$$MAD = 1.4826 * median(\lvert x_i - \check{x} \rvert)$$

where $\check{x}$ is the sample median. Then the modified *Z*-score is:

$$ZMAD_i = \frac{x_i - \check{x}}{MAD}$$

Typically, a data point with $\lvert ZMAD_i \rvert > 3.5$ is considered an anomaly.

Statistical outlier analysis is quite effective if the data being analyzed follows some known distribution or some distribution family. Even without these assumptions, often these techniques, especially robust ones like MAD, will perform admirably.

When your data is multidimensional as opposed to univariate, the approaches to point anomaly detection become more computationally intensive and more mathematically complex (e.g., using clustering algorithms as described next).

### Unsupervised Detection of Sequence Anomalies

Another category of unsupervised learning includes techniques, often referred to as prediction based, that model the time-series data as a random process, using well known time-series models such as moving average (MA), autoregressive (AR), or autoregressive integrated moving average (ARIMA).

This family of techniques is often used for forecasting of time-series datasets, such as sales volumes or revenue. Applied to anomaly detection, given a value $V_t$, you use such a model to predict the value $\widetilde{V_t}$ and assign to it an anomaly score based on the difference between its actual value ($V_t$) and the predicted value ($\widetilde{V_t}$).

### Anomaly Detection of Multivariate Datasets with Clustering

For some use cases, the data does not come in the form of a single variable time-series but rather an unordered set of (often multivariate) data points. A common approach in this case is clustering, whereby points are grouped into clusters, and points that are furthest away from the center of the cluster to which they belong (or to any cluster in the dataset) are considered anomalous. Furthermore, the distance from this center can be used as an anomaly score.

As with any clustering algorithm, a notion of similarity needs to be defined for anomaly detection, and we refer the reader to Chapter 9, "Clustering," for an in-depth treatment on similarity measures.

Although *k*-means clustering is very popular for clustering, it is known to be very sensitive to outliers, which is a problem in the anomaly detection setting.

A popular alternative often used in anomaly detection is **k-medoids** (also known as Partition Around Medoids or PAM), which is more robust to outliers and works well for anomaly detection. The $k$-medoids algorithm works in a similar way to $k$-means, with one significant difference: the center of each cluster is chosen as the medoid of that cluster (the medoid is a single data point with the minimum average distance to all other points in that cluster), instead of the mean.

Another unsupervised approach is **k-nearest neighbors**. Given an observation X, we count the number of points in a certain neighborhood of X (usually defined as a certain radius around that point). If that number of points in the neighborhood is below a certain threshold, then this point is considered anomalous.

**Local outlier factor** is another common algorithm for unsupervised anomaly detection, and is based on a concept of local density (similar to DBSCAN for clustering), where outliers are identified as points with relatively lower density as compared to their neighbors.

### Semi-Supervised Learning Methods

A semi-supervised learning approach to anomaly detection builds a model from a training set that includes only examples of what are termed normal points; it learns a boundary around the normal class and classifies anything else as an anomaly. Thus, it does not require anomalous examples in the training set.

One-class support vector machine (SVM) is a common algorithm in this category. It uses support vector machines to learn from the positive examples and classifies a data point as similar or different from the training set.

# Tuning Anomaly Detection Systems

An important consideration in most practical implementations of anomaly detection is tuning. Specifically, any anomaly detection system has to deal with two types of errors: false positive and false negatives.

False positives occur when our anomaly detection system identifies an anomaly that is not actually an anomaly, and a false negative is when a true anomaly goes undetected.

Every practical implementation has to consider the trade-off between these two types of errors. Consider, for example, a system to detect anomalous network traffic. When such anomalous activity is identified, often a network administrator is notified to further investigate and address the risk. If we have too many false positives, then the work load on the network administration team will be unbearable and costly (or they will just ignore all signals from the anomaly detection system). On the other hand, with many false negatives, the system's efficiency in detecting true anomalies drops. A good trade-off point needs to be identified to maximize true anomaly detection while making false positives consistent with capacity of the network administration team.

As with any system of this type, continued monitoring and evaluation of accuracy is necessary to understand when your model, be it supervised or unsupervised, is making assumptions about the data that are no longer valid.

# Building a Big Data Anomaly Detection Solution with Hadoop

Anomaly detection systems fit well within the Hadoop ecosystem. In particular, an anomaly detection system can be either batch (dealing with all the data at once) or real-time (dealing with the data as it streams in). Either one can be broken down into a few components, the choice of technologies depending on which type of system you want to construct:

- Event Store—For batch, this is likely HDFS. Whereas for real-time, it may be a distributed queue such as Apache Kafka.
- Distributed Processing System—For batch, this is likely either Spark or Pig or even MapReduce. For real-time data, it is most likely one of the streaming technologies, such as Spark Streaming, Storm, or Flink.

Within the boundaries of these streaming components, there are a few motivating characteristics that may affect the technology choice. For example, does the system operate on a single event or a small batch of events? (For instance, Spark Streaming uses micro-batching, whereas Storm and Flink operate on the individual events.) In general, whether micro-batching is acceptable or not is dependent upon the volume and velocity of your data and your latency requirements.

There is a distinct lack of projects specializing in constructing distributed outlier analysis systems for Hadoop. As such, you generally find yourself building your own implementation. The general layout of the system is as follows:

- Extract a key representing the outlier grouping and the value that you want to consider. For instance, if I'm looking at outliers in gifts for physicians of a specific specialty, the key is the physician specialty and the value is the amount that the physician was gifted.
- Group the events going over the system.
- Consider each event based on the data in some previous time window.

The choice of time windows is important, and seasonality should be considered. This step could be as simple as a machine learning model trained over the last month worth of data or it could be a running distributional sketch[1] of values over the last 15 minutes. In either case, there are a few things to consider when constructing such a system:

- Almost all outlier detection algorithms rely on some understanding of the trends of what happened historically; if you are storing a large amount of historical data in memory, you might run out of system memory. This situation is where

---

1. Sketch techniques use a sketch vector as a data structure to store the streaming data in a compact memory footprint. These techniques use hashing to map items in the streaming data onto a small sketch vector that can be easily updated and queried.

probabilistic sketching algorithms are used, such as distributional sketches or bloom filters.

- You must periodically monitor these systems for false positives and adjust things like lookback windows as your data changes in distribution or seasonality.

In short, the key to any good anomaly detection system system is to always be monitoring and adjusting the parameters of your system to the realities of the data. Building this in is an important phase for any successful system and should be baked into the architecture from the ground up.

# Example: Detecting Network Intrusions

In order to drive increased research in intrusion detection, in 1998 DARPA created a dataset that includes multiple weeks of simulated raw TCP data, along with some malicious packets simulating four types of attacks: denial of service (DoS), remote to local (R2L), user to root (U2R), and network probe.

In 1999, the original TCP dump files were pre-processed for utilization in the KDD intrusion detection benchmark and competition, resulting in what is known as the KDD-99 dataset.[2] The resulting dataset is comprised of a set of connection records, each including 41 features (see Table 10.1) describing the activity associated with that connection.

This dataset is often used to evaluate an anomaly detection system that classifies each network connection as normal or a potential intrusion. One of the challenges in this dataset, similar to many other anomaly detection datasets, is that some attack types are rare. For example, there are only 2 "spy", 3 "perl", and 2 "phf" attacks in the complete dataset, which often presents a difficulty for algorithms to learn the patterns associated with such attacks.

In this section we use supervised learning to build a simple network intrusion detection system using Spark MLlib and evaluate its performance on the KDD99 dataset.

## Data Ingestion

To ingest the dataset, we first download it from the KDD website and upload the data into a Hive table. The dataset is available as a flat file called kddcup.data, where each line represents a connection record and includes the comma-separated features shown in column one of Table 10.1.

---

2. http://kdd.ics.uci.edu/databases/kddcup99/kddcup99.html

Table 10.1  **kddcup.data connection record features.**

| Feature Name | Description | Feature Type |
|---|---|---|
| duration | Duration of the connection | Continuous |
| protocol type | Connection protocol (TCP, UDP, etc.) | Discrete |
| service | Destination service (Telnet, ftp, etc.) | Discrete |
| flag | Status flag of the connection | Discrete |
| source bytes | Bytes sent from source to dest | Continuous |
| destination bytes | Bytes sent from dest to source | Continuous |
| land | 1 if connection if from/to same host, 0 otherwise | Discrete |
| wrong fragment | Number of wrong fragments | Continuous |
| urgent | Number of urgent packets | Continuous |
| hot | Number of hot indicators | Continuous |
| failed logins | Number of failed log-ins | Continuous |
| logged in | 1 if successfully logged in, 0 otherwise | Discrete |
| # compromised | Number of compromised conditions | Continuous |
| Root shell | 1 if root shell obtained, 0 otherwise | Discrete |
| Su attempted | 1 if su attempted, 0 otherwise | Discrete |
| # root | Number of root accesses | Continuous |
| # File creations | Number of file creation operations | Continuous |
| # shells | Number of shell prompts | Continuous |
| # access files | Number of operations on access control files | Continuous |
| # outbound cmds | Number of outbound commands in an ftp session | Continuous |
| Is hot login | 1 if the log-in belongs to a hot list, 0 otherwise | Discrete |
| Is guest login | 1 if the log-in is a guest log-in, 0 otherwise | Discrete |
| Count | Number of connections to the same host as the current connection in the past 2 seconds | Continuous |
| Srv count | Number of connections to the same service as the current connection in the past two seconds | Continuous |
| serror rate | % of connections that have SYN errors in the count feature | Continuous |
| srv serror rate | % of connections that have SYN errors in the srv_count feature | Continuous |
| rerror rate | % of connections that have REJ errors in the count feature | Continuous |
| srv rerror rate | % of connections that have REJ' errors in the srv_count feature | Continuous |

*continues*

Table 10.1    **kddcup.data connection record features (*continued*).**

| Feature Name | Description | Feature Type |
| --- | --- | --- |
| same srv rate | % of connections to the same service | Continuous |
| diff srv rate | % of connections to different services | Continuous |
| srv diff host rate | % of connections to different hosts | Continuous |
| dst host count | Count of connections having the same destination host | Continuous |
| dst host srv count | Count of connections having the same destination host and using the same service | Continuous |
| dst host same srv rate | % of connections having the same destination host and using the same service | Continuous |
| dst host diff srv rate | % of different services on the current host | Continuous |
| dst host same src port rate | % of connections to the current host having the same src port | Continuous |
| dst host srv diff host rate | % of connections to the same service coming from different hosts | Continuous |
| dst host serror rate | % of connections to the current host that have an S0 error | Continuous |
| dst host srv serror rate | % of connections to the current host and specified service that have an S0 error | Continuous |
| dst host rerror rate | % of connections to the current host that have an RST error | Continuous |
| dst host srv rerror rate | % of connections to the current host and specified service that have an RST error | Continuous |
| is_anomaly | Normal or anomalous. Possible values are: normal or one of the possible attacks: back, guess_passwd, neptune, nmap, etc. | Discrete |

After downloading, we ingest the data into a Hive ORC table with the following Hive commands:

```
drop table kdd99_raw;
CREATE EXTERNAL TABLE kdd99_raw (
        `duration` int,
        `protocol` string,
        `service` string,
        `flag` string,
        `src_bytes` int,
        `dst_bytes` int,
        `land` string,
        `wrong_fragment` int,
```

```
        `urgent` int,
        `hot` int,
        `num_failed_logins` int,
        `logged_in` string,
        `num_compromised` int,
        `root_shell` int,
        `su_attempted` int,
        `num_root` int,
        `num_file_creations` int,
        `num_shells` int,
        `num_access_files` int,
        `num_outbound_cmds` int,
        `is_host_login` string,
        `is_guest_login` string,
        `count` int,
        `srv_count` int,
        `serror_rate` float,
        `srv_serror_rate` float,
        `rerror_rate` float,
        `srv_rerror_rate` float,
        `same_srv_rate` float,
        `diff_srv_rate` float,
        `srv_diff_host_rate` float,
        `dst_host_count` float,
        `dst_host_srv_count` float,
        `dst_host_same_srv_rate` float,
        `dst_host_diff_srv_rate` float,
        `dst_host_same_port_rate` float,
        `dst_host_srv_diff_host_rate` float,
        `dst_host_serror_rate` float,
        `dst_host_srv_serror_rate` float,
        `dst_host_rerror_rate` float,
        `dst_host_srv_rerror_rate` float,
        `is_anomaly` string)
ROW FORMAT SERDE 'org.apache.hadoop.hive.serde2.OpenCSVSerde'
STORED AS TEXTFILE
LOCATION '/user/hdfs/kdd';

DROP TABLE kdd99;
CREATE TABLE kdd99 STORED AS ORC tblproperties ("orc.compress" = "ZLIB")
AS SELECT
        protocol, service, flag, is_anomaly,
        CAST(land AS INT), CAST(logged_in AS INT),
        CAST(is_host_login AS INT), CAST(is_guest_login AS INT),
        CAST(duration AS INT), CAST(src_bytes AS INT),
        CAST(dst_bytes AS INT), CAST(wrong_fragment AS INT),
        CAST(urgent AS INT), CAST(hot AS INT),
        CAST(num_failed_logins AS INT), CAST(num_compromised AS INT),
        CAST(root_shell AS INT), CAST(su_attempted AS INT),
        CAST(num_root AS INT), CAST(num_file_creations AS INT),
        CAST(num_shells AS INT), CAST(num_access_files AS INT),
```

```
            CAST(num_outbound_cmds AS INT), CAST(count AS INT),
            CAST(srv_count AS INT), CAST(serror_rate AS FLOAT),
            CAST(srv_serror_rate AS FLOAT), CAST(rerror_rate AS FLOAT),
            CAST(srv_rerror_rate AS FLOAT), CAST(same_srv_rate AS FLOAT),
            CAST(diff_srv_rate AS FLOAT), CAST(dst_host_count AS FLOAT),
            CAST(dst_host_srv_count AS FLOAT),
            CAST(dst_host_same_srv_rate AS FLOAT),
            CAST(dst_host_diff_srv_rate AS FLOAT),
            CAST(dst_host_same_port_rate AS FLOAT),
            CAST(dst_host_srv_diff_host_rate AS FLOAT),
            CAST(dst_host_serror_rate AS FLOAT),
            CAST(dst_host_srv_serror_rate AS FLOAT),
            CAST(dst_host_rerror_rate AS FLOAT),
            CAST(dst_host_srv_rerror_rate AS FLOAT)
FROM kdd99_raw;
```

Note that since OpenCSV Serde reads all fields as strings, we have to cast all integer and floating point columns to the appropriate Hive type.

## Building a Classifier

Now that we have the data in a Hive table, we are going to build a feature matrix from the raw table attributes and train a random forest classifier using Spark MLlib on this dataset.

First we set up the SparkContext with 20 executors of 4G of RAM each, and then prepare the HiveContext to read the KDD dataset from Hive:

```
from pyspark import SparkContext, SparkConf
from pyspark.sql import HiveContext

SparkContext.setSystemProperty('spark.executor.memory', '4g')
conf = SparkConf()
conf.set('spark.executor.instances', 20)
sc = SparkContext('yarn-client', 'kdd99', conf=conf)
hc = HiveContext(sc)
kdd = hc.table("kdd99")
```

Next we prepare the training set and test set by splitting the original dataset randomly. Note that in the original KDD99 competition a specific and fixed training set was designated, but for the sake of simplicity, we use a 70/30 random split here:

```
(trainData, testData) = kdd.randomSplit([0.7, 0.3], seed=42)
trainData.cache()
services = trainData.withColumnRenamed('service','srv')
➥.select('srv').distinct()
# filter out any rows with a service not trained upon
testData = testData.join(services, testData.service==services.srv)
testData.cache()
```

First we use Spark's `randomSplit()` to create the training and testing datasets.

The service column is a very large categorical variable, and in order to ensure that the set of possible values is consistent between the training and testing datasets we list all the distinct values in the training set and then filter the test dataset to only include those values.

We further use `cache()` for both the training and testing datasets so they are kept in memory by Spark.

```
print "training set has " + str(trainData.count()) + " instances"
training set has 3429014 instances
print "test set has " + str(testData.count()) + " instances"
test set has 1469415 instances
```

Next we build a Spark ML pipeline for pre-processing of the features and running a Random Forest classifier on the training set. The pipeline uses four `StringIndexer` instances to convert the string fields protocol, service, flag, and is_anomaly to categorical variables, and due to the large amount of service categories, it further uses `OneHotEncoder` to convert that categorical variable into dummy 0/1 variables.

```
from pyspark.ml.feature import StringIndexer, VectorAssembler,
➥ OneHotEncoder
from pyspark.ml import Pipeline
from pyspark.ml.classification import RandomForestClassifier

inx1 = StringIndexer(inputCol="protocol", outputCol="protocol-cat")
inx2 = StringIndexer(inputCol="service", outputCol="service-cat")
inx3 = StringIndexer(inputCol="flag", outputCol="flag-cat")
inx4 = StringIndexer(inputCol="is_anomaly", outputCol="label")
ohe2 = OneHotEncoder(inputCol="service-cat", outputCol="service-ohe")
feat_cols = [c for c in kdd.columns +
        ['protocol-cat', 'service-ohe', 'flag-cat', 'label']
           if c not in ['protocol', 'service', 'flag', 'is_anomaly']]
vecAssembler = VectorAssembler(inputCols = feat_cols,
➥ OutputCol = "features")

rf = RandomForestClassifier(numTrees=500, maxDepth=6, maxBins=80, seed=42)
pipeline = Pipeline(stages=[inx1, inx2, inx3, inx4, ohe2,
➥ vecAssembler, rf])
model = pipeline.fit(trainData)
```

## Evaluating Performance

Now that our model is trained, let's use it to predict the category of attack for the test dataset

```
results = model.transform(testData).select("label", "prediction").cache()
```

and evaluate our performance. For evaluation we define a Python function called `eval_metrics()` that computes the per-category precision and recall as follows:

```
import pandas as pd
def eval_metrics(lap):
    labels = lap.select("label").distinct().toPandas()['label'].tolist()
```

```
    tpos = [lap.filter(lap.label == x).filter(lap.prediction == x).count()
➥    for x in labels]
    fpos = [lap.filter(lap.label == x).filter(lap.prediction != x).count()
➥    for x in labels]
    fneg = [lap.filter(lap.label != x).filter(lap.prediction == x).count()
➥    for x in labels]
    precision = zip(labels, [float(tp)/(tp+fp+1e-50) for (tp,fp) in
➥    zip(tpos,fpos)])
    recall = zip(labels, [float(tp)/(tp+fn+1e-50) for (tp,fn) in
➥    zip(tpos,fneg)])
    return (precision,recall)


(precision, recall) = eval_metrics(results)
ordered_labels = model.stages[3]._call_java("labels")
df = pd.DataFrame([(x, testData.filter(testData.is_anomaly == x).count(),
➥ y[1], z[1])
for x,y,z in zip(ordered_labels, sorted(precision, key=lambda x: x[0]),
➥ sorted(recall, key=lambda x: x[0]))],
➥ columns = ['type', 'count', 'precision', 'recall'])
print df
```

|    | type | count | precision | recall |
|----|------|-------|-----------|--------|
| 0  | smurf. | 842086 | 1.000000 | 1.000000 |
| 1  | neptune. | 321393 | 1.000000 | 0.999966 |
| 2  | normal. | 292343 | 1.000000 | 0.995658 |
| 3  | satan. | 4695 | 0.930990 | 0.999314 |
| 4  | ipsweep. | 3717 | 0.973635 | 0.921334 |
| 5  | portsweep. | 3102 | 0.987105 | 0.985517 |
| 6  | nmap. | 690 | 0.440580 | 1.000000 |
| 7  | back. | 678 | 0.855457 | 1.000000 |
| 8  | warezclient. | 284 | 0.000000 | 0.000000 |
| 9  | teardrop. | 292 | 0.047945 | 1.000000 |
| 10 | pod. | 78 | 0.000000 | 0.000000 |
| 11 | guess_passwd. | 11 | 0.000000 | 0.000000 |
| 12 | buffer_overflow. | 10 | 0.000000 | 0.000000 |
| 13 | warezmaster. | 6 | 0.000000 | 0.000000 |
| 14 | land. | 9 | 0.000000 | 0.000000 |
| 15 | rootkit. | 2 | 0.000000 | 0.000000 |
| 16 | imap. | 6 | 0.000000 | 0.000000 |
| 17 | multihop. | 2 | 0.000000 | 0.000000 |
| 18 | loadmodule. | 5 | 0.000000 | 0.000000 |
| 19 | ftp_write. | 4 | 0.000000 | 0.000000 |
| 20 | phf. | 0 | 0.000000 | 0.000000 |

As you can see, the precision and recall values for normal connections, as well as the most common categories like smurf, Neptune, satan, ipsweep, and portsweep, are very high. For rarer categories, the classifier does not work as well, and further work may be required to handle those cases.

# Summary

In this chapter

- You learned what anomaly detection is and its common use cases.
- You learned the common approaches to anomaly detection with machine learning including rules-based as well as supervised, unsupervised, and semi-supervised learning.
- You learned how to apply anomaly detection to time-series data.
- You learned how to build an anomaly detection system for big data with Hadoop.

11

# Natural Language Processing

*The voice that navigated was definitely that of a machine, and yet you could tell that the machine was a woman, which hurt my mind a little. How can machines have genders? The machine also had an American accent. How can machines have nationalities? This can't be a good idea, making machines talk like real people, can it? Giving machines humanoid identities?*

Matthew Quick<br>The Good Luck of Right Now

## In This Chapter:

- Overview of natural language processing, its history, and main use cases
- Tools for natural language processing with Hadoop
- Sentiment Analysis Example

## Natural Language Processing

Natural language processing (NLP) is the crossroads of three fields:

- Linguistics
- Computer Science
- Statistics

In a nutshell, it is the cross-disciplinary attempt to make computers extract meaning or structure from text written in human language. We'll beg the reader's forgiveness as the term meaning is loaded and vague, but we actually like its usage here. The kind of meaning that we try to extract with NLP expands as the techniques become better, more robust, more accurate, and computationally feasible.

This topic is an exceedingly natural fit to data science as it combines Computer Science, Math and an external domain (Linguistics). The intersection of these disciplines gives us a fascinatingly fertile set of problems to be solved. Some of these problems have solutions that are remarkably straightforward, while some are so difficult that even humans have significant error rates.

In this chapter, we briefly cover a few problems that make up the NLP domain and then focus on an example of Sentiment Analysis for the rest of the chapter.

## Historical Approaches

The desire for a computer to communicate in a way that reflects some attributes of human nature dates back to the earliest days of computing. In the 1950s we saw military motivations pushing the boundaries of machine translation in a historically important experiment[1] jointly conducted by Georgetown University and IBM to translate Russian sentences into English. The Georgetown-IBM experiment was an archetypal example of the earliest approach to natural language processing. Specifically, the experiment utilized a set of hard-coded rules and a dictionary to perform the translation. Despite the relative simplicity and rigidity of such approaches, they were surprisingly successful in a broad set of use cases and held prominence all the way through to the 1980s. The dominant group driving this forward were computational linguists, such as Noam Chomsky, who were searching for better and better models from which to construct rules of natural language.

With more complex rules and more powerful computers, these approaches had some successes. Take, for instance, ELIZA[2]—one of the most well-known examples of a program interacting with humans in a very human-like way. ELIZA was a chat-bot created in the 1960s by Joseph Weizenbaum designed to mimic a therapist. Despite having a fixed vocabulary and simple rules, it could use generic responses when drawn out of its depths by its human respondent to redirect the conversation. In the late 1980s we saw a shift in approach from the complex linguistic rules to a machine learning and statistical approach. This change was driven by the desire for a more adaptable system, as well as having the computational power available to drive such a system. Better algorithms and better computers have steadily brought us into the modern era where casual computers routinely interact with complex natural language processing every time they interact with search engines or automated telephone systems.

## NLP Use Cases

Basically, natural language processing exists to manipulate data in the format most comfortable for human interaction. High-level use cases involve things like the following:

- Translation from one language into another
- Automatic summarization of text
- Question answering

---

1. https://en.wikipedia.org/wiki/Georgetown%E2%80%93IBM_experiment
2. https://en.wikipedia.org/wiki/ELIZA

Each of these high level use cases requires multiple independent tasks that could be considered natural language processing by themselves. This approach follows the normal pattern that you may have noticed in previous chapters—data science begetting data science.

The main types of tasks common in NLP use cases include text segmentation, part of speech tagging, named entity recognition, sentiment analysis, and topic modeling.

## Text Segmentation

As humans, we organize text in a way that is helpful and meaningful to aid us in processing. Examples of these organizational constructs are sentences, paragraphs, words, or topics. Often, when we extract text to process, the extraction process fails to capture these organizational constructs for a variety of reasons. Furthermore, humans are remarkably resilient to missing punctuation or misspellings. There are, however, some cases where punctuation can change the entire meaning of a sentence or, at a minimum, make possible an ambiguous interpretation (e.g. "Let's eat grandpa." versus "Let's eat, grandpa.").

The task of instructing a computer in how to take raw, possibly noisy, text and organize it into meaningful units is called **text segmentation**.

Sentence segmentation is one of the simplest forms of text segmentation and is often easily approximated by looking for period characters as separators. But even in English this is just an approximation due to the use of periods in abbreviations, which may cause a false detection of sentence ending, as can be seen in the following example: "I have explained to Mr. Johnson that this is not acceptable."

## Part-of-Speech Tagging

Many of us learned in our early education about a helpful set of categories, called "parts of speech," which are associated with words. In English, the main parts of speech are noun, pronoun, adjective, verb, adverb, preposition, and so on. We also learned the plethora of exceptions, nuances, and inconsistencies related to associating a part of speech with a word.

The same problems that confuse an elementary school student can be impassible when it comes to constructing an automated approach to identifying parts of speech that works within acceptable error bounds.

At its heart, you can see where this would fit well within a machine learning/data science context. It's basically a very gnarly classification problem, and many approaches have been devised over the years to solve the problem. These techniques range from rules attempting to define the complex linguistic rules associated with grammar to traditional machine learning approaches to classification.

As an example, consider the following sentence "I want to get the new iPad." A simple part-of-speech tagger would classify each part as follows:

```
I|PRP  want|VBP  to|TO  get|VB  the|DT  new|JJ  iPad|NN
```

where a common standardized structure for parts of speech called the Penn treebank[3] tags are used (PRP=pronoun, VB=Verb, NN=noun, etc.).

---

3. https://www.ling.upenn.edu/courses/Fall_2003/ling001/penn_treebank_pos.html

## Named Entity Recognition

Named entity recognition is the task of tagging a word or a sequence of words with a given category, such as a person or a place. The categories are intended to be an interpretation and assignment of some meaning to the word or words being tagged.

Tagging a word with a part of speech is one type of challenge, but it's altogether a different challenge to tag multiple words with a category that may not follow rules that are as straightforward as grammar.

For example, named entity recognition will be able to determine that in the sentence "Bill Gates has money.", the words "Bill Gates" refers to a person. As you might imagine, this is a particularly useful task and imbues something much closer to meaning to words.

## Sentiment Analysis

Sentiment analysis is the process of predicting a sentiment for either a sentence or a document. The range of possible sentiments may vary in detail from simple positive/neutral/negative to varying degrees of positivity or negativity. This task is perhaps one of the most difficult things in natural language processing. While grammars may be ambiguous, sentiment analysis has to cope with the very human and very fuzzy concepts of irony and sarcasm.

As an example, consider "I want pizza so bad" versus "This pizza was so bad," where in the word "bad" has a positive sentiment in the first and a negative in the other.

## Topic Modeling

Topic modeling is a common NLP task where the goal is to extract the most salient or important topics that occur in a corpus of documents.

Often, when a document is about a specific topic or set of topics, we expect certain words to appear more often. Using this insight, topic modeling techniques use statistical and probabilistic approaches to identify the latent semantic structure of a corpus of documents and from that identify the key topics.

# Tooling for NLP in Hadoop

There are many ways to approach natural language processing problems within the Hadoop environment. Generally, you have two options:

- Use NLP libraries intended for a single node in UDFs in Hadoop. We will call this *small-model NLP* at scale.
- Use NLP libraries built into the Hadoop Data Science-oriented projects. We will call this *big-model NLP* at scale.

## Small-Model NLP

Most of the products inside of Hadoop that are intended to process data (such as Hive, Pig, Storm, Spark, and MapReduce) have extension points where users can define their own functions to operate on the data.

With the small model NLP approach, you implement a certain NLP task as a user-defined function for one of these Hadoop products, utilizing underneath the hood an existing NLP library such as OpenNLP, Stanford CoreNLP, NLTK, or Spacy.

There are a few pros and cons to this approach. The obvious con is that the language models within these libraries are created on a small subset of either your data, if you create the model, or 3rd party data if you use a public model. This can result in the machine learning algorithms underneath the hood of the NLP libraries not being exposed to as broad a set of situations as they might be if the models were run at scale.

This approach can also be computationally intensive per sentence, so you must be careful to spread the processing across many tasks. Since the normal approach to automatically computing the number of tasks takes into account mostly the data size, the predictions will result in far fewer tasks, creating a far more computationally intensive workload.

The most obvious benefit of this approach is that many of the cutting-edge techniques show up in these common NLP libraries, since they are a result of advanced academic research. The other benefit is that you have a broad range of competing projects from which to choose, and you can pick the one that best suits your needs, both from a functionality perspective and the programming language used (e.g., Java or Python).

Table 11.1 provides a quick guide to various capabilities in the most common NLP libraries: OpenNLP,[4] Stanford CoreNLP,[5] Spacy,[6] and NLTK.[7]

Table 11.2 lists a few libraries that specifically contain a topic modeling implementation.

Table 11.1    **Overview of NLP Library Capabilities.**

| Library Name | OpenNLP | Stanford CoreNLP | NLTK | Spacy |
|---|---|---|---|---|
| *License* | Apache V2 | GPL | Apache V2 | MIT |
| *Programming Language* | Java | Java | Python | Python |
| *Text Segmentation* | Yes<br>Pig Integration via Apache DataFu | No | Yes | Yes |
| *POS tagging* | Yes<br>Pig Integration via Apache DataFu | Yes | Yes | Yes |
| *Named Entity Recognition* | Yes<br>Pig Integration via Apache DataFu | Yes | Yes | Yes |
| *Sentiment Analysis* | No | Yes | Yes | No |

4. https://opennlp.apache.org/

5. http://nlp.stanford.edu/software/corenlp.shtml

6. https://spacy.io/

7. http://www.nltk.org

Table 11.2  **Libraries for Topic Modeling.**

| Library Name | Mallet | Gensim |
| --- | --- | --- |
| *License* | Apache V2 | LGPLv2 |
| *Programming Language* | Java | Python |

In some cases, Hadoop projects may wrap some of these libraries inside of their user-defined functions, making them readily accessible to programmers. Apache DataFu is a project that aims to provide tooling to aid the data scientist in the form of Pig user-defined functions. As such, it provides user-defined functions wrapping sentence segmentation and part of speech tagging using OpenNLP.

## Big-Model NLP

Two main open source data science Hadoop projects, Apache Mahout and Apache Spark (MLlib), have some support for natural language processing using Hadoop. Universally, both projects aim to support a wide breadth of algorithms across the domain of data science. Since they are not fully focused on natural language processing, there are substantial holes in the breadth of their natural language processing capabilities. Neither project has many options for specific implementations of NLP algorithms, but they do have tooling to extract a feature representation of documents or sentences that is the precursor to the NLP algorithms. For instance, if you can represent a sentence or document as a set of features, sentiment analysis becomes a multi-class classification problem.

### Apache Mahout

Apache Mahout was the first data science-oriented project for Hadoop, so it has a fair range of functionality. In addition to actual natural language processing algorithms, it has a nice set of tooling for text preparation. A common model for natural language processing is the bag-of-words model, in which documents are represented as a bag of word counts weighted by an importance score ignoring word order and generally considering only a subset of important words. This model creates a vector representation of each document, which is a useful representation for use inside of other machine learning algorithms, such as classifiers. Mahout has tooling to build this representation.

Additionally, Mahout provides topic modeling capabilities, which is an unsupervised algorithm that determines the important 'topics' from a set of documents as well as providing a topic distribution for unseen documents. For example, given a set of newspapers, the set of topics might be representative keywords from the different sections of the newspaper. Furthermore, it would, given an unseen, new article, indicate the proportion of each topic that would describe the article.

### Apache Spark MLlib

Apache Spark's MLLib sub-project is aimed at providing data science algorithms at scale. As part of this project, there is support for constructing bag-of-words representation specifically weighted with a term frequency–inverse document frequency (TF-IDF) importance score.

As mentioned in Chapter 5, "Data Munging with Hadoop," TF-IDF is a common relevancy measure for words inside of a document that are part of a corpus (i.e., collection) of documents. There are numerous formulations, but the general approach is for a document to take word (or term) frequency in that document and weight this by inverse document frequency (one over the number of documents the word appears in across the entire set of documents). This score roughly corresponds to how "important" that a word is to a document by discounting the impact of words that are used in the majority of documents.

Additionally, MLlib has support for a newer vectorization technique called word2vec. This method is a distributed vector representation for words that encodes the notion of word similarity as well as word analogy. This word representation is advantageous for those designing implementation of other NLP algorithms such as sentiment analysis or named entity recognition.

# Textual Representations

A common approach to handling natural language processing is actually to transform the natural language problem into another machine learning problem that we know how to solve. Take for instance the problem of classifying whether an email message is "spam or ham" (i.e., something we don't want to read versus something we do). In order to make that decision, conversion to a format suitable for another machine learning or data mining process is required. This process is called vectorization, which is the process of converting the document into a vector.

There are numerous approaches to this problem, as mentioned in Chapter 5. Let's take another look at two that are quite common: bag-of-words and word2vec.

## Bag-of-Words

The bag-of-words model is a simple yet surprisingly effective model used to convert documents into feature vectors. Initially you construct an ordered vocabulary for the corpus of documents to use, often with very common words (also called stop-words) pruned out. From that ordered vocabulary you have a mapping between words and dimensions.

With this word-to-dimension mapping, it is easy to take a document and create a vector where each dimension is associated with the number of times a word occurs in the document.

Take for instance an ordered vocabulary of:

1. cherry
2. dog
3. pie
4. market

If I were to vectorize the sentence "I took the dog to the market to get a cherry pie and everyone loved my dog!" I would create the following vector: <1,2,1,1> because cherry, pie, and market appear once, while dog appears twice.

As you can see, the model is quite simple. The order of the sentence is not even taken into account in this model. In order to encode more information in this quite simple model, there are some common modifications. Rather than the simple counts that we have used here, sometimes other quantities are used:

- **term frequencies**—The simple frequency of the word (or term) across all documents.

- **term frequency scaled by inverse document frequency (TF-IDF)**—As mentioned previously, this metric gives some notion of "unique" importance. It diminishes the importance of terms that are very common and heightens the importance of a relatively rare term that appears quite often in one document.

Other adaptations of the bag-of-words model include using pairs or triples of words instead of individual words (often called bi-grams or tri-grams, respectively). This feature allows for some word ordering to be included in the model.

Despite its simplicity, the bag-of-words model has been a staple of statistical and machine learning-based natural language processing for a decade.

## Word2vec

In 2013, a group of researchers from Google released a paper titled "Efficient Estimation of Word Representations in Vector Space"[8] in which they described an effective system that used a shallow, two-layer neural network to learn a mapping between words and vectors. Specifically, because they are learning and embedding into a vector space, the word vectors can be manipulated via vector arithmetic, and that manipulation has semantic meaning.

Take for instance a word2vec model trained on a large representative corpus of English documents. The angle between the computed vector (vector('king') − vector('male') + vector('female')) and vector('queen') is very small. This result is evidence that word2vec is learning a vector space embedding based on the angles between vectors that represent similar words. As such, you can find synonyms by looking for nearby vectors.

The group at Google found that this representation alone boosted accuracy when used to construct document vectors or as a drop-in replacement for bag-of-words in sentiment analysis.

However, as nice as this representation is, it is not entirely clear how to take word vectors and construct document vectors or sentence vectors. As such, there have been numerous adaptations to this technique using deep learning to construct higher level compositions like paragraph vectors and document vectors. In general, as a technique, it appears that a neural network model seems to have captured the attention of both practical and research NLP specialists as the vectorization technique of choice.

---

8. https://arxiv.org/abs/1301.3781

# Sentiment Analysis Example

An important task in natural language processing is determining sentiment of input text. People have studied using sentiment analysis to do everything from predict stock movements from twitter data to better understand product reviews from message board data.

Using supervised learning techniques, we have seen a simple example of sentiment analysis using Spark in Chapter 8, "Predictive Modeling." To illustrate how you might go about integrating more advanced NLP techniques for sentiment analysis into the Hadoop ecosystem, we will demonstrate how to implement sentiment analysis with Spark using the Stanford CoreNLP library, applied at scale.

## Stanford CoreNLP

One of the more interesting things in the NLP space in the past few years is the movement to use more complex model representations of documents. We discussed the bag-of-words model earlier, but there are other representations that take into account the structure of text. One of these representations was described in a 2013 paper entitled "Recursive Deep Models for Semantic Compositionality Over a Sentiment Treebank."[9]

That work was subsequently incorporated into Stanford CoreNLP, a natural language processing library from Stanford University. The resulting code is intended to predict sentence-level sentiment. The default set of training documentation was movie review data. As such, we'll incorporate this library into a custom Spark function that will take a document, extract the sentences, and generate the sentiment for each sentence.

## Using Spark for Sentiment Analysis

In this example, we can study how to use Spark with CoreNLP's very good sentiment analysis library to evaluate sentiment for a corpus of documents in a scalable way. As with every Spark application, we need to understand how the data flows through the application to understand the performance characteristics. In this situation, Stanford CoreNLP's sentiment analysis is quite computationally intensive, so we want to maximize parallelism by breaking our problem down into the following steps:

1. Split the documents into sentences using CoreNLP.
2. For each sentence, compute the sentiment using CoreNLP.
3. Group the sentences by document.
4. Aggregate a sentiment score for the document given the scores for the sentences.

Strictly speaking, the aggregation of sentence level results into document-level results is not really sensible. In fact, we should instead retrain on document level data, but for

---

9. Richard Socher, Alex Perelygin, Jean Wu, Jason Chuang, Christopher Manning, Andrew Ng and Christopher Potts, see http://www-nlp.stanford.edu/sentiment

our purposes and for simplicity, we will get a rough estimate of sentiment by deciding that a document is positive if more than half the non-neutral sentences are positive.

The following are a few key excerpts of methods from the complete Scala implementation (see Appendix A, "Book Web Page and Code Download,"—the full code is available from the book repository) using Spark to illustrate some of these activities. Take, for instance, splitting the document into its constituent sentences. This step can be done quite straightforwardly in CoreNLP:

```
/**
 * Split a document into sentences using CoreNLP
 * @param document
 * @return the sentences within the document
 */
def splitIntoSentences(document:String) : Iterable[String] = {
  val err = System.err;
  // now make all writes to the System.err stream silent
  System.setErr(new PrintStream(new OutputStream() {
    def write(b : Int ) {
    }
  }));
  val reader = new StringReader(document);
  val dp = new DocumentPreprocessor(reader);
  val sentences = dp.map(sentence => Sentence.listToString(sentence))
  System.setErr(err);
  sentences
}
```

Note the usage of DocumentPreprocessor, a CoreNLP class that is used to break down documents into sentences.

For a given sentence, we create a CoreNLP pipeline to do the full tokenization, parsing, and sentiment extraction with a few helper functions:

```
/*
 * Set up a sentiment pipeline using CoreNLP to tokenize, apply
 *part-of-speech tagging and generate sentiment estimates.
 */
object SentimentPipeline {
  val props = new Properties
  props.setProperty("annotators", "tokenize, ssplit, pos, parse,
➡ sentiment")
  val pipeline = new StanfordCoreNLP(props)
}
/*
 * Analyze an individual sentence using CoreNLP by extracting
 * the sentiment
 *
 * @param sentence
 * @return POSITIVE or NEGATIVE
 */
```

```scala
def analyzeSentence(sentence: String) : String = {
  val err = System.err;
  System.setErr(new PrintStream(new OutputStream() {
    def write(b : Int ) {
    }
  }));

  val pipeline = SentimentPipeline.pipeline
  val annotation = pipeline.process(sentence)
  val sentiment = analyzeSentence(annotation.get((new CoreAnnotations.
➥SentencesAnnotation).getClass).get(0))
  System.setErr(err);
  sentiment
}

 /*
  * Analyze an individual sentence using CoreNLP by extracting
  * the sentiment
  *
  * @param sentence the probabilities for the sentiments
  * @return POSITIVE or NEGATIVE
  */
def analyzeSentence(sentence: CoreMap) : String = {
  /* for each sentence, we get the sentiment that CoreNLP thinks
   * this sentence indicates.
   */
  val sentimentTree = sentence.get((new
➥ SentimentCoreAnnotations.AnnotatedTree).getClass)
    val mat = RNNCoreAnnotations.getPredictions(sentimentTree)
/*
 * The probabilities are very negative, negative, neutral, positive or
 * very positive.  We want the probability that the sentence is positive,
 * so we choose to collapse categories as neutral, positive
 * and very positive.
  */
  if(mat.get(2) > .5) {
    return "NEUTRAL"
  }
  else if(mat.get(2) + mat.get(3) + mat.get(4) >   .5) {
    return "POSITIVE"
  }
  else {
    return "NEGATIVE"
  }
}
/**
  * Aggregate the sentiments of a collection of sentences into a
  * total sentiment of a document.  Assume a rough estimate using
  * majority rules.
  * @param sentencePositivityProbabilities
  * @return POSITIVE or NEGATIVE
  */
```

```
def rollup(sentencePositivityProbabilities : Iterable[String]) : String = {
  var n = 0
  var numPositive = 0
  for( sentiment <- sentencePositivityProbabilities) {
    if(sentiment.equals("POSITIVE")) {
      numPositive = numPositive + 1
    }
    if(!sentiment.equals("NEUTRAL")) {
      n = n + 1
    }
  }
  if(numPositive == 0) {
    "NEUTRAL"
  }
  val score = (1.0*numPositive) / n
  if(score > .5) {
    "POSITIVE"
  }
  else {
    "NEGATIVE"
  }
}
```

Using these helper functions, we construct a method in Scala to parallelize first by document and then by sentence, compute sentiment, and aggregate the results using the rollup method.

```
/**
Calculate the sentiments per-document for a corpus of documents
  * @param inputPath A corpus of documents
  * @return A RDD containing the original document and the
  * associated sentiment
  */
def getSentiment( inputPath:RDD[String]): RDD[Tuple2[String, String]] =
{
 inputPath.flatMap( doc => SentimentAnalyzer.splitIntoSentences(doc).
➥ map( sentence => (doc, sentence))).map( doc2sentence =>
➥ (doc2sentence._1, SentimentAnalyzer.analyzeSentence(doc2sentence._2))).
➥ groupBy( x => x._1).map( doc2sentences =>
➥ (doc2sentences._1, SentimentAnalyzer.rollup(doc2sentences._2.
➥ map(x => x._2))))
}
```

We can consider this function to largely describe the steps above in code:

1. Split the documents into sentences using the function passed to the flatMap.

2. For each sentence, compute the sentiment using the function passed to the map.

3. Group the sentences by document in the groupBy.

4. Aggregate a sentiment score for the document given the scores for the sentences in the final map. The only complications are that `groupBy` returns a collection of document to sentence sentiment pairs and `rollup` requires a collection of sentence sentiments.

As the full code for this example is available from the book code repository (see Appendix A), we encourage the reader to download and study the application in full detail.

# Summary

In this chapter

- We discussed why natural language processing is important and how it provides a great amount of value to modern applications such as search, machine translation, or sentiment analysis. The world is inundated with unstructured or semi-structured data, and much of that is in the form of text. Having a good grasp of techniques capable of understanding and extracting insights and information from that data is extremely important.

- We briefly discussed the main types of tasks in NLP such as text segmentation, part of speech tagging, named entity recognition, and sentiment analysis.

- We reviewed the two main approaches for applying NLP at scale with Hadoop, which we called small-model NLP and big-model NLP, as well as the most common open-source tools for NLP such as OpenNLP, CoreNLP, and NLTK.

- We showed you an example of using Spark and Stanford CoreNLP for sentiment analysis at scale.

# Data Science with Hadoop—The Next Frontier

*We don't have better algorithms, we just have more data.*

Peter Norvig

**In This Chapter:**

- Automating data discovery
- Deep learning

Throughout this book we have seen how Hadoop provides a platform that enables a broad set of applications of data science for large datasets. With Hadoop, and utilizing its eco-system of tools such as Spark, Pig, and Hive, it is possible to run typical data science flows in an efficient and scalable manner on much larger datasets than ever before.

But, the availability of large amounts of data and the relatively low cost of its acquisition and storage enables new applications and techniques to emerge that were not possible before. Such techniques pave the way to the future of data science with big data and Hadoop.

In this chapter we discuss two examples of such techniques: automated data discovery and deep learning.

## Automated Data Discovery

Data is growing at a phenomenal rate, and in order to take full advantage of this new data there is a growing need for automated techniques to discover patterns in large datasets.

For example, consider a dataset of diabetes patients; an important goal might be to understand the intrinsic structure of this dataset, for example which patients have Type 1 diabetes versus Type 2 diabetes. Many existing unsupervised learning techniques, if applied to this problem, would rely on some hypotheses being formulated by an expert.

Consider *k*-means clustering where we assume data is organized into spherical shapes, and often the analyst must determine the number of clusters required and the similarity metric between points in the data.

To overcome this manual, and often difficult, task of identifying the right model formulation, a new set of techniques called topological data analysis[1] (TDA) extracts information embedded in large, high-dimensional datasets with minimal need for specific model specification.

Based on an extension of topology, a classical branch of mathematics, computational topology has seen recent advances and shown great promise in unstructured data understanding and organization. TDA utilizes the advances in computational topology theory to automatically identify "shapes" in high-dimensional data as patterns of interest. As shown in Figure 12.1, various geometric shapes (patterns) in the data such as loops (continuous circular segments), flares (long linear segments), or graph structures represent inherently interesting patterns in the data that TDA can automatically identify. This approach enables further investigation of these sub-groups of the dataset with standard statistical, machine learning techniques as well as visualization. A critical characteristic of TDA is that the shapes identified with these techniques are coordinate-free and invariant to small deformations—thus they really identify salient features of the underlying data.

Prior to this decade, this area of research was almost infeasible from a computational perspective. The computation resources required to make TDA practical were not available, and thus TDA remained a theoretical field of research. With the recent advances in computational resources, and especially the availability of distributed computing software like Hadoop or Spark, topological data analysis becomes not only feasible but necessary to tackle automatic detection of structure in large datasets.

TDA has the potential to enlighten data scientists concerning the underlying structure of dataset in various scientific research areas such as genomics, astronomy, geophysics, and others. In one example, TDA was used to help cancer researchers identify a unique subgroup of breast cancer patients who were more likely to survive.[2] Another use of the unsupervised clustering and data organization capabilities of TDA was exemplified by Ayasdi, a topological data analytics company. Ayasdi used its product to find 13 new, unique basketball positions based on the topological clustering of players by their statistics.[3]

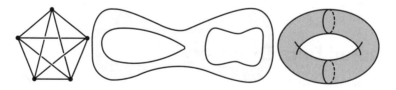

Figure 12.1    Examples of shapes identified by TDA: graph, figure-8 shape, torus.

---

1. https://en.wikipedia.org/wiki/Topological_data_analysis

2. http://www.ncbi.nlm.nih.gov/pmc/articles/PMC3084136/

3. http://www.wired.com/2012/04/analytics-basketball/

As advances in this area progress in line with Moore's law, there is no doubt that this will become a tool of choice in the working data scientist's toolbox.

To learn more about TDA, here are a few useful resources:

- The Ohio State University TDA research page: http://web.cse.ohio-state.edu/~tamaldey/course/CTDA/CTDA.html
- CMU TDA research group: http://www.stat.cmu.edu/topstat/
- TDA at the Institute for Advanced Study: https://www.ias.edu/ideas/2013/lesnick-topological-data-analysis
- Ayasdi: https://www.ayasdi.com/technology/

# Deep Learning

Over the many years of research in artificial intelligence and machine learning, it was always assumed that learning algorithms operate on top of representations of the underlying data objects, which is provided by a process often called feature generation or feature engineering.

As discussed at length in Chapter 5, "Data Munging in Hadoop," feature engineering is often a complex process involving deep expertise in the problem domain and one that requires significant investment of time and effort.

**Representation learning**[4] (also known as "feature learning") is a set of methods that utilize machine learning to automatically learn, without supervision or with semi-supervision, the optimal representation for a given problem.

Auto-encoding is one such well-known method of representation learning. Often the output, or representation, of a deep auto-encoder is used as input to another classifier, but an example of it being used on its own is in the area of semantic hashing. In this approach, unique vector representations for documents are created such that the closer they are according to a distance function, the more likely they are semantically similar (i.e., they are about the same topic). The auto-encoder automatically learned this representation just by being exposed to the data.

A good example can be found in a 2007 paper "Semantic Hashing" by Hinton and Salakhutdinov[5] where documents taken from 20 distinct news groups were grouped based on the learned vector representations.

Going beyond just representation learning, **deep learning** (also known as hierarchical learning) has recently emerged as a popular field in machine learning research. Deep learning combines supervised learning with representation learning. Using multi-layer neural networks (also known as "deep nets"), it enables the network to learn complex representation automatically as well as learn more complex non-linear models for the problem at hand.

---

4. https://en.wikipedia.org/wiki/Feature_learning

5. http://www.cs.toronto.edu/~fritz/absps/sh.pdf

Fundamental to this set of techniques is the idea that concepts in a certain level of abstraction are learned using concepts from a lower-level representation, which in turn learn using concepts from another level down and so on. As illustrated in Figure 12.2, this approach is in contrast to most "traditional" machine learning algorithms (such as general linear models (GLM), decision trees, or support vector machines (SVM), etc.) where a "shallow" architecture equivalent to one or two layers is involved.

Deep learning is extremely useful, for example, in applications of image processing, where the raw input consists of image pixels. With traditional learning methods, the modeler would have to apply various image processing algorithms to pre-process the pixels into more abstract features (such as edges, lines, shapes, etc.) before proceeding with the learning itself. With deep learning, the raw input of pixels is used as input into the first layer of the deep network and those intermediate features are automatically learned by the network. A good example of this type of learning can be found in the paper "Unsupervised Learning of Hierarchical Representations with Convolutional Deep Belief Networks" by Honglak Lee, Roger Grosse, Rajesh Ranganath, and Andrew Y. Ng.[6]

Deep learning's first real success at an industry scale was with acoustic modeling or speech recognition, followed quickly with applications in image and video processing, as well as language modeling and natural language processing.

Although deep learning is an extremely exciting and popular field of research, and is poised to transform how we use machine learning, it is still in its early phases of development.

**Deep Neural Network**

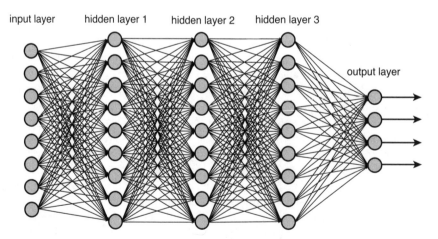

Figure 12.2    Deep network architecture with multiple layers.

6. http://www.cs.toronto.edu/%7Ergrosse/cacm2011-cdbn.pdf

There are two major challenges at the moment with implementing deep learning in practice:

- Deep learning requires significantly more data for training than other (more traditional) machine learning techniques. This challenge is where the Hadoop ecosystem comes in. Enabling the collection and storage of large amounts of data inexpensively makes deep learning practical for researchers as well as practitioners.

- Training a deep neural network requires significant computational resources, and training time on a single machine can be very long—sometimes days or even weeks. Hadoop can be helpful here as a grid compute platform providing a nice solution that enables the implementation of deep learning algorithms at scale. Graphical processing units (GPUs) are very popular for deep learning, given their ability to provide very fast floating point operations, and we expect to see GPU integration into the Hadoop scheduler (YARN) so that deep learning can be better integrated into the platform.

Although deep learning is still emerging as a technology, the momentum from both academia and industry has resulted in a variety of open source packages and libraries for deep learning that are already available: Theanos, Caffe, Torch, deepnet, deeplearning4j, and, recently, TensorFlow from Google.

Only a few libraries currently support distributed deep learning with Hadoop, most notably deeplearning4j, $H_2O$, and some beginning support in Spark's MLlib.

We expect to see a lot more innovation in deep learning, as tools and libraries that implement various deep learning algorithms become more robust, scalable, and easy to use.

To learn more about deep learning, here are some useful resources:

- Online book: http://www.deeplearningbook.org/ or http://research.microsoft.com/pubs/209355/DeepLearning-NowPublishing-Vol7-SIG-039.pdf

- Tutorial: http://deeplearning.net/tutorial/deeplearning.pdf

- Deep learning class at NYU: http://cilvr.cs.nyu.edu/doku.php?id=deeplearning:slides:start

- YouTube lectures from the University of Waterloo: https://www.youtube.com/playlist?list=PLehuLRPyt1Hyi78UOkMPWCGRxGcA9NVOE

# Summary

In this chapter we covered some of the new types of algorithms that previously were more academic in nature, and that recently, thanks to the capability to collect and store large amounts of data, have received more attention from researchers and practitioners alike.

In this chapter

- You learned about topological data analysis, a family of techniques used to identify patterns (shapes) in data based on geometric shapes that provides great insight into the inherent structure of data.
- We discussed deep learning as a family of algorithms that use multi-layer neural networks to combine representation learning with supervised learning, removing the need for domain-specific feature engineering.

# A

# Book Web Page and Code Download

A webpage with a question and answer forum, resource links, and updated information is available from the following link:

http://www.clustermonkey.net/practical-data-science-with-hadoop-and-spark

All example code can be found on the book's GitHub page:

https://github.com/ofermend/practical-data-science-with-hadoop-and-spark

# B

# HDFS Quick Start

This appendix is intended for those that have little or no experience with the Hadoop Distributed File System (HDFS). The following is intended to provide minimal background on a few commands that will help get you started with Apache Hadoop. It is not a full description of HDFS and is missing many of the important commands and features. In addition to this quick start, you are strongly advised to consult these two resources:

> http://hadoop.apache.org/docs/stable1/hdfs_design.html
>
> http://developer.yahoo.com/hadoop/tutorial/module2.html

The following section is a quick command reference that may help you get started with HDFS. Be aware that there are alternative options for each command, and the examples below are simple use cases.

The need for the hdfs command is because the HDFS file system is not local to the user. HDFS operates on a Hadoop cluster and consists of a NameNode (file system metadata node) and a number of DataNodes (where the data are actually stored). This arrangement is shown in Figure B.1.

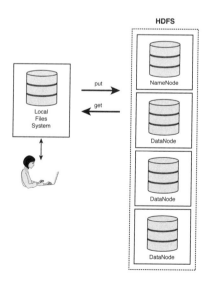

Figure B.1   User interaction with HDFS file system.

# Quick Command Dereference

To interact with HDFS, the `hdfs` command must be used. The following options are
available. All the general user commands use the `dfs` option. Only a few of these will
be demonstrated below.

```
Usage: hdfs [--config confdir] COMMAND
        where COMMAND is one of:
  dfs                  run a filesystem command on the file systems supported in
Hadoop.
  namenode -format     format the DFS filesystem
  secondarynamenode    run the DFS secondary namenode
  namenode             run the DFS namenode
  journalnode          run the DFS journalnode
  zkfc                 run the ZK Failover Controller daemon
  datanode             run a DFS datanode
  dfsadmin             run a DFS admin client
  haadmin              run a DFS HA admin client
  fsck                 run a DFS filesystem checking utility
  balancer             run a cluster balancing utility
  jmxget               get JMX exported values from NameNode or DataNode.
  oiv                  apply the offline fsimage viewer to an fsimage
  oev                  apply the offline edits viewer to an edits file
  fetchdt              fetch a delegation token from the NameNode
  getconf              get config values from configuration
  groups               get the groups which users belong to
  snapshotDiff         diff two snapshots of a directory or diff the
                       current directory contents with a snapshot
  lsSnapshottableDir   list all snapshottable dirs owned by the current user
                       Use -help to see options
  portmap              run a portmap service
  nfs3                 run an NFS version 3 gateway

Most commands print help when invoked w/o parameters.
```

## General User HDFS Commands

HDFS provides a series of commands similar to those found in a standard POSIX file
system. A list of those commands can be found by issuing the following command. A
few of these commands will be highlighted in the following sections.

**$ hdfs dfs**

```
Usage: hadoop fs [generic options]
        [-appendToFile <localsrc> ... <dst>]
        [-cat [-ignoreCrc] <src> ...]
        [-checksum <src> ...]
        [-chgrp [-R] GROUP PATH...]
        [-chmod [-R] <MODE[,MODE]... | OCTALMODE> PATH...]
        [-chown [-R] [OWNER][:[GROUP]] PATH...]
        [-copyFromLocal [-f] [-p] <localsrc> ... <dst>]
```

```
            [-copyToLocal [-p] [-ignoreCrc] [-crc] <src> ... <localdst>]
            [-count [-q] <path> ...]
            [-cp [-f] [-p] <src> ... <dst>]
            [-createSnapshot <snapshotDir> [<snapshotName>]]
            [-deleteSnapshot <snapshotDir> <snapshotName>]
            [-df [-h] [<path> ...]]
            [-du [-s] [-h] <path> ...]
            [-expunge]
            [-get [-p] [-ignoreCrc] [-crc] <src> ... <localdst>]
            [-getmerge [-nl] <src> <localdst>]
            [-help [cmd ...]]
            [-ls [-d] [-h] [-R] [<path> ...]]
            [-mkdir [-p] <path> ...]
            [-moveFromLocal <localsrc> ... <dst>]
            [-moveToLocal <src> <localdst>]
            [-mv <src> ... <dst>]
            [-put [-f] [-p] <localsrc> ... <dst>]
            [-renameSnapshot <snapshotDir> <oldName> <newName>]
            [-rm [-f] [-r|-R] [-skipTrash] <src> ...]
            [-rmdir [--ignore-fail-on-non-empty] <dir> ...]
            [-setrep [-R] [-w] <rep> <path> ...]
            [-stat [format] <path> ...]
            [-tail [-f] <file>]
            [-test -[defsz] <path>]
            [-text [-ignoreCrc] <src> ...]
            [-touchz <path> ...]
            [-usage [cmd ...]]

Generic options supported are
-conf <configuration file>     specify an application configuration file
-D <property=value>            use value for given property
-fs <local|namenode:port>      specify a namenode
-jt <local|jobtracker:port>    specify a job tracker
-files <comma separated list of files>    specify comma separated files to be
copied to the map reduce cluster
-libjars <comma separated list of jars>    specify comma separated jar files to
include in the classpath.
-archives <comma separated list of archives>    specify comma separated archives
to be unarchived on the compute machines.

The general command line syntax is
bin/hadoop command [genericOptions] [commandOptions]
```

## List Files in HDFS

To list the files in the root HDFS directory enter the following:

**$ hdfs dfs -ls /**

```
Found 8 items
drwxr-xr-x   - hdfs   hdfs          0 2013-02-06 21:17 /apps
drwxr-xr-x   - hdfs   hadoop        0 2014-01-01 14:17 /benchmarks
drwx------   - mapred hdfs          0 2013-04-25 16:20 /mapred
```

```
drwxr-xr-x    - hdfs   hdfs          0 2013-12-17 12:57 /system
drwxrwxr--    - hdfs   hadoop        0 2013-11-21 14:07 /tmp
drwxrwxr-x    - hdfs   hadoop        0 2013-10-31 11:13 /user
drwxr-xr-x    - doug   hdfs          0 2013-10-11 16:24 /usr
drwxr-xr-x    - hdfs   hdfs          0 2013-10-31 21:25 /yarn
```

To list files in your home directory enter the following:

**$ hdfs dfs -ls**

```
Found 16 items
drwx------    - doug hadoop          0 2013-04-26 02:00 .Trash
drwxr-xr-x    - doug hadoop          0 2013-10-16 20:25 DistributedShell
-rw-------    3 doug hadoop        488 2013-04-24 16:01 NOTES.txt
drwxr-xr-x    - doug hadoop          0 2013-11-21 14:34
QuasiMonteCarlo_1385061734722_747204430
drwxr-xr-x    - doug hadoop          0 2014-01-02 12:48 TeraGen
drwxr-xr-x    - doug hadoop          0 2014-01-01 16:31 TeraGen-output
-rw-------    3 doug hadoop 1083049567 2013-02-07 01:10 acces_log
drwx------    - doug hadoop          0 2013-04-25 15:01 bin
-rw-r--r--    3 doug hadoop         31 2013-10-16 17:09 ds-test.sh
drwxr-xr-x    - doug hadoop          0 2013-04-25 15:44 id.out
-rw-------    3 doug hadoop       2246 2013-04-25 15:43 passwd
drwxr-xr-x    - doug hadoop          0 2013-05-14 17:07 test
drwxr-xr-x    - doug hadoop          0 2013-05-14 17:23 test-output
drwx------    - doug hadoop          0 2013-05-15 11:21 war-and-peace
drwxr-xr-x    - doug hadoop          0 2013-02-06 15:14 wikipedia
drwxr-xr-x    - doug hadoop          0 2013-08-27 15:54 wikipedia-output
```

The same result can be obtained by issuing this command:

**$ hdfs dfs -ls /user/doug**

## Make a Directory in HDFS

To make a directory in HDFS use the following command. As with the -ls command, when no path is supplied the users home directory is used (i.e., /users/doug).

**$ hdfs dfs -mkdir stuff**

## Copy Files to HDFS

To copy a file from your current local directory into HDFS use the following. Note again that the absence a full path assumes your home directory. In this case, the file test is placed in the directory stuff, which was created previously.

**$ hdfs dfs -put test stuff**

The file transfer can be confirmed by using the -ls command:

**$ hdfs dfs -ls stuff**

```
Found 1 items
-rw-r--r--    3 doug hadoop          0 2014-01-03 17:03 stuff/test
```

## Copy Files from HDFS

Files can be copied back to your local file system using the following. In this case, the file we copied into HDFS, test, will be copied back to the current local directory with the name test-local.

```
$ hdfs dfs -get stuff/test test-local
```

## Copy Files within HDFS

The following will copy a file in HDFS.

```
$ hdfs dfs -cp stuff/test test.hdfs
```

## Delete a File within HDFS

The following will delete the HDFS file test.dhfs that was created in the preceding.

```
$ hdfs dfs -rm test.hdfs
```

```
Deleted test.hdfs
```

## Delete a Directory in HDFS

The following will delete the HDFS directory stuff and all its contents.

```
$ hdfs dfs -rm -r stuff
```

```
Deleted stuff
```

## Get an HDFS Status Report (Administrators)

A status report, similar to what is summarized on the web GUI, can be obtained by entering the following command (output is truncated).

```
$ hdfs dfsadmin -report
```

```
14/01/03 16:24:17 WARN util.NativeCodeLoader: Unable to load native-hadoop library
for your platform... using builtin-java classes where applicable
Configured Capacity: 747576360960 (696.23 GB)
Present Capacity: 675846991872 (629.43 GB)
DFS Remaining: 302179352576 (281.43 GB)
DFS Used: 373667639296 (348.01 GB)
DFS Used%: 55.29%
Under replicated blocks: 13
Blocks with corrupt replicas: 0
Missing blocks: 0
```

```
-------------------------------------------------
Datanodes available: 4 (4 total, 0 dead)

Live datanodes:
 .
 .
 .
```

## Perform an FSCK on HDFS (Administrators)

The health of HDFS can be checked by using the fsck (filesystem check) option.

**$ hdfs fsck /**

```
Connecting to namenode via http://headnode:50070
FSCK started by hdfs (auth:SIMPLE) from /10.0.0.1 for path / at Fri Jan 03
16:32:16 EST 2014
Status: HEALTHY
 Total size:     110594648065 B
 Total dirs:     311
 Total files:    528
 Total symlinks:             0
 Total blocks (validated):   1341 (avg. block size 82471773 B)
 Minimally replicated blocks: 1341 (100.0 %)
 Over-replicated blocks:     0 (0.0 %)
 Under-replicated blocks:    13 (0.9694258 %)
 Mis-replicated blocks:      0 (0.0 %)
 Default replication factor: 3
 Average block replication:  2.9888144
 Corrupt blocks:             0
 Missing replicas:           78 (1.9089574 %)
 Number of data-nodes:       4
 Number of racks:            1
FSCK ended at Fri Jan 03 16:32:16 EST 2014 in 74 milliseconds
```

# Additional Background on Data Science and Apache Hadoop and Spark

The following is a brief list of additional resources on various topics mentioned in the book.

## General Hadoop/Spark Information

- Main Apache Hadoop website: http://hadoop.apache.org
- Main Apache Spark website: http://spark.apache.org/
- Apache Hadoop documentation website: http://hadoop.apache.org/docs/current/index.html
- Wikipedia: http://en.wikipedia.org/wiki/Apache_Hadoop
- Eadline, Douglas. *Hadoop 2 Quick-Start Guide: Learn The Essentials of Big Data Computation in the Apache Hadoop2 Ecosystem*. Boston, MA: Addison-Wesley, 2015. http://www.informit.com/store/hadoop-2-quick-start-guide-learn-the-essentials-of-9780134049946.
- Gates, Alan. *Programming Pig*. Sebastopol, CA: O'Reilly & Associates, 2012. https://www.amazon.com/Programming-Pig-Alan-Gates/dp/1449302645.
- Capriolo, Edward, Wampler, Dean, and Rutherglen, Jason. *Programming Hive*. Sebastopol, CA: O'Reilly & Associates, 2012. https://www.amazon.com/Programming-Hive-Edward-Capriolo/dp/1449319335/ref=pd_sbs_14_t_1?ie=UTF8&psc=1&refRID=7B5KSFHC3NJ114N8N6W2.
- Karau, Konwinski, Wendell and Zaharia. *Learning Spark: Lightning-Fast Big Data Analysis*. Sebastopol, CA: O'Reilly & Associates, 2015.
- Eadline, Douglas. *Hadoop Fundamentals LiveLessons, 2nd Edition*. Boston, MA: Addison-Wesley, 2014. http://www.informit.com/store/hadoop-fundamentals-livelessons-video-training-9780134052403.

# Hadoop/Spark Installation Recipes

Additional information and background on the installation methods can be found from the following resources:

- **Apache Hadoop XML configuration files description**
  - https://hadoop.apache.org/docs/stable/ (scroll down to the lower left-hand corner under Configuration)
- **Officially Hadoop sources and supported Java versions**
  - http://www.apache.org/dyn/closer.cgi/hadoop/common/
  - http://wiki.apache.org/hadoop/HadoopJavaVersions
- **Oracle VirtualBox**
  - https://www.virtualbox.org
- **Hortonworks Hadoop Sandbox (Hadoop on a virtual machine)**
  - http://hortonworks.com/hdp/downloads
- **Ambari project page**
  - https://ambari.apache.org/
- **Ambari installation guide**
  - http://docs.hortonworks.com/HDPDocuments/Ambari-1.7.0.0/Ambari_Install_v170/Ambari_Install_v170.pdf
- **Ambari troubleshooting guide**
  - http://docs.hortonworks.com/HDPDocuments/Ambari-1.7.0.0/Ambari_Trblshooting_v170/Ambari_Trblshooting_v170.pdf
- **Apache Whirr cloud tools**
  - https://whirr.apache.org
- **Apache Spark installation guide**
  - http://spark.apache.org/docs/latest

# HDFS

- **HDFS background**
  - http://hadoop.apache.org/docs/stable1/hdfs_design.html
  - http://developer.yahoo.com/hadoop/tutorial/module2.html
  - http://hadoop.apache.org/docs/stable/hdfs_user_guide.html
- **HDFS user commands**
  - http://hadoop.apache.org/docs/stable/hadoop-project-dist/hadoop-hdfs/HDFSCommands.html

- **HDFS Java programming**
  - http://wiki.apache.org/hadoop/HadoopDfsReadWriteExample
- **HDFS libhdfs programming in C**
  - http://hadoop.apache.org/docs/stable/hadoop-project-dist/hadoop-hdfs/LibHdfs.html

# MapReduce

- https://developer.yahoo.com/hadoop/tutorial/module4.html (based on Hadoop version 1, but still a good MapReduce background)
- http://en.wikipedia.org/wiki/MapReduce
- http://research.google.com/pubs/pub36249.html

# Spark

- **Apache Spark quick start**
  - http://spark.apache.org/docs/latest/quick-start.html

# Essential Tools

- **Apache Pig scripting language**
  - http://pig.apache.org/
  - http://pig.apache.org/docs/r0.14.0/start.html
- **Apache Hive SQL-like query language**
  - https://hive.apache.org/
  - https://cwiki.apache.org/confluence/display/Hive/GettingStarted
  - http://grouplens.org/datasets/movielens (data for example)
- **Apache Sqoop RDBMS import/export**
  - http://sqoop.apache.org
  - http://dev.mysql.com/doc/world-setup/en/index.html (data for example)
- **Apache Flume steaming data and transport utility**
  - https://flume.apache.org
  - https://flume.apache.org/FlumeUserGuide.html
- **Apache Oozie workflow manager**
  - http://oozie.apache.org
  - http://oozie.apache.org/docs/4.0.0/index.html

# Machine Learning

- Hastie, Trevor, Tibshirani, Robert, and Friedman, Jerome. *Elements of Statistical Learning*. http://statweb.stanford.edu/~tibs/ElemStatLearn/.
- Leskovic, Jure, Rajaraman, Anand, and Ullman, Jeffrey. *Mining Massive Datasets*. http://infolab.stanford.edu/~ullman/mmds/book.pdf.
- Goodfellow, Ian, Bengio, Yoshua, and Courville, Aaron. (In press) *Introduction to Deep Learning*. Cambridge, MA: MIT Press, 2017. http://www.deeplearningbook.org/.
- Smola, Alex and Vishwanathan, S.V.N. *Introduction to Machine Learning*. New York: Cambridge University Press, 2008. http://alex.smola.org/drafts/thebook.pdf.
- Murphy, Kevin. *Machine Learning: A Probabilistic Perspective*. Cambridge, MA: MIT Press, 2012. https://www.amazon.com/Machine-Learning-Probabilistic-Perspective-Computation/dp/0262018020/ref=zg_bs_3894_4Book: Data-Intensive Text Processing with MapReduce. Jimmy Lin and Chris Dyer. University of Maryland, College Park. Manuscript prepared April 11, 2010. https://lintool.github.io/MapReduceAlgorithms/.
- Online course on machine learning: http://ciml.info/
- MOOC on machine learning by Andrew Ng: https://www.coursera.org/learn/machine-learning
- Online course on NLP: http://www.cs.columbia.edu/~mcollins/notes-spring2013.html

# Index